The Ethical University

Transforming Higher Education

The Ethical University

Transforming Higher Education

Edited by Wanda Teays
and Alison Dundes Renteln

ROWMAN & LITTLEFIELD
Lanham • Boulder • New York • London

Published by Rowman & Littlefield
An imprint of The Rowman & Littlefield Publishing Group, Inc.
4501 Forbes Boulevard, Suite 200, Lanham, Maryland 20706
www.rowman.com

86-90 Paul Street, London EC2A 4NE

British Library Cataloguing in Publication Information Available

Library of Congress Cataloging-in-Publication Data

Names: Teays, Wanda, editor. | Renteln, Alison Dundes, editor.
Title: The ethical university : transforming higher education / Edited by
Wanda Teays and Alison Renteln.
Description: Lanham : Rowman & Littlefield, [2022] | Includes index.
Identifiers: LCCN 2022021947 (print) | LCCN 2022021948 (ebook) | ISBN
    9781538154380 (cloth) | ISBN 9781538154397 (paperback) | ISBN
    9781538154403 (ebook)
Subjects: LCSH: Education, Higher—Moral and ethical aspects. |
    Universities and colleges—Corrupt practices. | Educational change. |
    Educational accountability.
Classification: LCC LB2324 .T44 2022 (print) | LCC LB2324 (ebook) | DDC
    378.001—dc23/eng/20220701
LC record available at https://lccn.loc.gov/2022021947
LC ebook record available at https://lccn.loc.gov/2022021948

♾™ The paper used in this publication meets the minimum requirements of
American National Standard for Information Sciences—Permanence of Paper
for Printed Library Materials, ANSI/NISO Z39.48-1992.

In memory of Bernadette Gonzaque Robert, who knew the path to transforming higher education, and Alan Dundes, who showed how an academic career could be ethical and rewarding.

Contents

Acknowledgments

Thanks to our contributors for their insightful chapters on ethical issues facing higher education and the path to transformation. We appreciate all of you: Michael Boylan, Cher Weixia Chen, Zenon Culverhouse, Darin Dockstader, Cora Drozd, Robert V. Labaree, Jonathan Liljeblad, Matthew Mahrt, Rita Manning, Glen Miller, Melissa L. Miller, Charles Milne, Laura Nader, Paul Renteln, Steve Sanders, and Rosemarie Tong.

Our gratitude also goes to Natalie Mandziuk, our editor at Rowman & Littlefield. We so appreciate your guidance and support.

Finally, thank you to the students, faculty, administrators, and staff who help create an ethical foundation for higher education.

Preface

Wanda Teays

Universities used to be called ivory towers. Many aren't so ivory anymore. One scandal after the next has weakened the foundation, leaving instability and calling out for retrofitting. In whatever direction we turn, we see institutions in disrepair: administrators failing to respond quickly when issues arise, staff succumbing to bribes, faculty in tenure disputes, coaches playing favorites, fraternities hazing new members, adjuncts and teaching assistants being exploited, parents trying to buy admission for their children, students committing one moral breach after another, and so on. The reality is that there are cracks in the ivory tower.

We expect a lot of our universities and colleges. They are commonly viewed as a source of knowledge and wisdom. The classes they offer and degrees they award, along with the faculty who serve a vital role in education, are—or should be—viewed with respect. When our expectations fall short due to ethical shortcomings, it is time to do some moral soul searching.

We should not fool ourselves about what we've achieved and how much more is required to reach our goals. And yet the journey is vital. We cannot move forward without examining where we are and acknowledging the territory we have left behind.

There are important concerns to be dealt with. The chapters in this book provide key insights into what it takes to transform a university by highlighting the challenges as well as the responsibilities and obligations we face. We are called to reflect on our values and traditions and what sort of institution we want to build and sustain. Our decisions, policies, and actions shape the collective identity and the reputation of the university.

Fortunately, we need not abandon hope. There are many members of the academic community taking stock of the ethical lapses and shortcomings. Yes, the moral fiber is full of holes. Yes, the scandals keep bubbling up to the surface. The problems are numerous, but so are the numbers of people working for change. The contributors to this text are testimony to that. They have taken the issues to heart and are paving the way to a stronger ethical base.

We take three avenues to examining the issues: the ethical framework, the university community, and the key challenges that need to be addressed. What holds the institution together over time are the values, principles, and traditions that contribute to moral character and lay a foundation for decision-making. From the board of directors and trustees to the faculty senate, from the various departments to individual faculty, from student affairs and staff to the full- and part-time students—the ethical framework supports the ontological core of the university.

Just as our values guide our actions, so do values help define the university. We examine this in part 1. We began with an overview of recent scandals and injustices challenging the integrity of the institution. We then look at the major ethical theories and see how they can provide a basis for institutional integrity. This is borne out by several ways universities respond to the challenges, such as setting clear guidelines for academic integrity and preserving the right to privacy in the face of increasing digitalization of the university.

Part 1 tackles these ethical concerns. This calls for policies set in place by honor codes, academic integrity committees, and student integrity boards to spotlight and enforce guidelines around honesty. Academic integrity should never be taken for granted; we ought not assume students necessarily grasp or honor the importance of integrity in their education and in professional development. That university presidents, political leaders, and faculty have plagiarized speeches and public lectures only shows the extent of moral decay—it doesn't justify it. In addition, the evolution of technology has made surveillance much easier to accomplish and the accumulation of data much simpler. Both warrant concerns around what rights can be protected and by whom and with what mechanism.

Moving on to the university community in part 2, we see three main types of constituents—namely, the administration and staff, the faculty, and the students. The ethical university requires moral leadership, which puts the administration in a key role. The members of the administration—university presidents, vice presidents, provosts, deans, directors, and department chairs—provide guidance and a structure for generating ideas and putting defensible policies in place. Because the decisions of administrators are often in the public eye, as with fundraising and responding to troublesome news coverage, they may find themselves accountable to a broader audience. That brings up an external role that the administration has to consider.

Much of their attention, however, is focused on internal affairs. Ideally, members of the administration provide support for faculty-driven initiatives and have policies and procedures in place to protect the interests of their students—for example, by providing a safe campus and access to health care. With forward thinking and planning, they help preserve high standards and a quality education for their students.

Some universities regard the student body as a collection of consumers. As such, it is not always clear how much power they should be able to wield. One of the tasks of the university community is to assess the relative power its constituents should have. Weighing the interests of the different groups is important to ensure a fair and equitable allocation of power in deciding what path the university should follow.

All too frequently the balance of power is tilted toward the administration, whose interests take precedence—for example, in the eyes of the trustees and the board of directors. Meetings of the board tend to exclude all but a few faculty and students. For that reason, one issue examined in this volume is shared governance. First we need to acknowledge that "the faculty" is not a unified group of individuals on an equal footing. The range extends from tenured full professors on down—full professors to associate and assistant professors who are tenured or tenure track, and from nontenurable contract faculty and visiting faculty to instructors and adjuncts. Achieving shared governance, as we see in part 2, may not be as simple as we might think. Consequently, this needs to be taken into consideration.

One of the pillars of an ethical university is its library system. Access to information and the development of research skills are central to a quality education, as the chapter in this section demonstrates. We should also recognize the contribution to the university community of the adjunct instructors, who carry much of the teaching load. This vulnerable population makes it easier for tenured and tenure-track professors to do research, publish articles, and participate in university committees and professional associations. The ethical issues that arise warrant recognition.

Another vulnerable population are student athletes. Cases of abuse have been brought to light by high-profile examples. Look, for example, at the sexual misconduct of assistant coach Jerry Sandusky at Penn State (Viera 2011) and the University of Michigan's Dr. Robert Anderson, accused of sexually assaulting hundreds of athletes in the 1980s, with the personal toll lingering for decades (Kozlowski 2020). Concerns facing students are threaded throughout this text: each of the three parts includes discussions of issues centering on their interests.

The number of students either committing harm or being harmed is not insignificant, as the class action lawsuits demonstrate. For that reason, universities have a moral obligation to care for their students and minimize harm. Here is where campus security and police come into play. Although one option is "defunding the police," the reality is that some form of policing—even by security without guns—is likely to stay a fixture of the university. As a result, the ethical university needs to make sure campus police don't overstep their boundaries.

Other challenges facing universities are explored in part 3. Some center on addressing trauma; others look at pedagogical issues and the fairness of the grading scale. Another challenge is answering the question, What are the obligations of aging faculty when it comes to retirement? Tenured faculty are not normally required to retire at a particular age. However, they may be morally obligated to do so—to step aside so younger faculty have more opportunities for advancement. Yet another concern has to do with international students and faculty. This issue was brought to the fore when the COVID-19 pandemic led to restrictions regarding travel and access to teaching and studying. A final consideration is the corporatization of the university. This developed as a result of treating the university as a business rather than as an institution of higher learning—and contributed to a decrease in transparency in decision-making. These are not incidental matters, as we see in this text.

There is a great deal to be said for a defensible set of values and beliefs and being able to articulate why we do what we do. Having a sense of what makes for moral character and what virtues should guide us is vital for an ethical university.

WORKS CITED

Kozlowski, Kim. 2020. "How UM Failed for Decades to Heed Warnings about Doctor's Alleged Sex Abuse." *Detroit News*, October 21, 2020. Updated December 10, 2021. https://www.detroitnews.com/in-depth/news/local/michigan/2020/10/21/how-university-michigan-failed-doctor-robert-anderson-alleged-sex-abuse/4894925002/.

Teays, Wanda. 2000. "Introduction." In Bioethics, Justice, and Healthcare, edited by Wanda Teays and Laura M. Purdy. Belmont, CA: Wadsworth/ Thomson Learning, xi-xviii.

Viera, Mark. 2011. "Former Coach at Penn State Is Charged with Abuse." *New York Times*, November 5, 2011. https://www.nytimes.com/2011/11/06/ sports/ncaafootball/former-coach-at-penn-state-is-charged-with-abuse.html.

Part I

ETHICAL FRAMEWORKS

Scandals and Historic Injustices at Universities

An Argument for Greater Accountability

Alison Dundes Renteln

ABSTRACT

While universities have always played an exalted role in society, they have recently fallen from grace. Universities face tremendous challenges in the twenty-first century as leadership sweeps sexual misconduct and many forms of discrimination under the rug. This chapter offers a survey of egregious scandals and historic injustices that threaten to undermine the legitimacy of colleges and universities in the long run. One main problem is the lack of accountability that is a consequence of reliance on self-regulation. To achieve urgently needed accountability, an independent agency should be established to evaluate complaints about serious misconduct.

Keywords: accountability, administrative bloat, affirmative action, due process, injustices, pay equity, quotas, scandals, self-regulation, sexual assault, sexual harassment, slavery

THE ROLE OF THE UNIVERSITY IN THE TWENTY-FIRST CENTURY

Universities in the United States are unquestionably in crisis. In the twenty-first century, public confidence in the legitimacy of academia has been seriously shaken. In this chapter, I consider major deficiencies that are readily apparent in higher education in the hopes that we may identify possible solutions. This requires examining the purpose of academic institutions. It is necessary to consider the university as an ethical system that requires functioning grievance mechanisms in order to enforce crucial principles that structure its main activities (Tesar, Peters, and Jackson, 2021).

While other volumes consider university ethics (e.g., Kennan, 2015), this book differs by including the voices of scholars from diverse fields other than education. Solving the difficult problems will require experts from many different disciplines. All the diverse stakeholders should be consulted about necessary reforms because the fate of universities is too important to be left to one field alone. Furthermore, given that academic institutions face various challenges, different types of approaches may be needed depending on the nature of the problem.

Why do universities exist, and have the justifications for their existence changed over time? Although originally they were established for the benefit of only the upper class, in modern times the movement to democratize education emerged. Access to education was thought to be crucial for upward social mobility.

One of the main shifts has been away from thinking that colleges and universities provide opportunities to expand the intellectual horizons of students and to teach students how to think critically as well-educated citizens. With the rising cost of tuition, families began to insist that their children graduate with clearly identifiable skills to land well-paying positions. This drastic change in the perception of universities' role has had unfortunate consequences—for example, contributing to the erosion of liberal arts education at many institutions.

A vast literature exists on the history of universities. The purpose of this analytic essay, instead, is to consider some of the scandals and historic injustices that are salient this century. A survey of these reveals many of the shortcomings of university administration and compels us to reconsider what steps should be taken to improve leadership in the academy.

Before turning to some of the specific illustrations, I wish to offer preliminary thoughts about the disconcerting trends at universities. One worry is the influence of management consultants, who are paid exorbitant fees to advise university leadership on the proper course of action. This practice of relying on consultants seems to coincide with a remarkable decline in the power of academic senate organizations and the erosion of shared governance.

Another cause for concern has been the tendency of universities to invite more individuals from the business world to serve on boards of trustees rather than those with substantial experience in university life (Franke, 2022). This propensity for university boards to be dominated by those from the corporate world has generated substantial criticism (Washburn, 2005). Despite their expertise in corporate affairs, they often lack sufficient familiarity with the intellectual life of the university. One manifestation of the influence of the business world is the increase in the number of deans (i.e., "administrative bloat"). Deans also speak in the jargon of the business world—strategic plans, business models, "teams," and so on. Grant proposals are expected to be formulated as business plans.

This coincides with the reduction in the number of tenure-track and tenured faculty. In the past, tenured professors could assume they would enjoy academic freedom, so they could publish controversial scholarship and could speak out without fear of retaliation. As some universities shifted their priorities from academic pursuits to fundraising (euphemisms include "advancement" and "development"), they have reallocated budgetary resources from academic programs to fundraising programs.

Universities have also witnessed mergers—for example, many language departments were combined into a single department of modern languages. Claiming the lack of funds, despite growing numbers of administrators and multimillion-dollar salaries for coaches, universities have closed departments such as the German departments at the University of Southern California and the University of Vermont (Jasnik, 2008; Galloway, 2020). Some lament this trend and suggest it reflects a failure on the part of administrators to remember what the primary function of a university actually is.

Sadly, there is no accountability in universities and hence no way to reverse such irresponsible budgetary decision-making. There is simply far too much emphasis on fundraising at the expense of other priorities at universities. One practice has been allowing donors to influence major decisions about hiring and curriculum. Another development has been the near obsession with indicators that measure success in quantitative terms. This ranges from relying on numerical scores in teaching evaluations, which are themselves increasingly outsourced to private companies, to promotion reviews that depend too much on citation count.

Colleges and universities are experiencing a crisis of confidence. Some ask if colleges are worth the cost. At the same time that questions are being raised about the benefit of a college degree, some incredible scandals have emerged. There are so many types and examples of misconduct that many may wonder about the accuracy of these accounts. It is simply the case that one could not make this up.

The failure of administrators to take action to protect faculty and students forces us to ask if universities deserve our support. Unless they are prepared to reexamine their priorities, make significant structural reforms, and share power with the constituencies for whom universities exist, they are probably doomed. Scandals and injustices affect the legitimacy of academic institutions and suggest that administrators no longer have the right priorities.

I will advance the argument that self-regulation is inherently ineffective. The fact that there is no independent oversight of administrative decisions has resulted in this situation, where faculty and students are often in precarious situations. After reviewing egregious examples of university failings that led to scandals and historic injustices, we might consider what type of independent agency should be established to review allegations of misconduct. Setting up a body that has the power to redress grievances without imposing overly punitive sanctions may be a viable solution to the current crises we observe in universities.

SCANDALS

A scandal in the "ivory tower" is a public episode that reveals poor judgment on the part of decision-makers. Some of these have involved serious harm to students and faculty. Universities should strive to protect their students and not violate the principle of nonmaleficence (i.e., do no harm). I turn now to a few examples of egregious misconduct.

Sexual Assault/Molestation

At the University of Southern California (USC), the only full-time gynecologist at the student health service, Dr. George Tyndall, sexually abused approximately seventeen thousand young women who were his patients between 1989 and 2016 (Ryan and Hamilton, 2021). Ryan and Hamilton explain how women sued in different groups and received vastly different amounts. Some felt they were misinformed by USC leadership about their options—a class action versus a settlement.

Tyndall not only examined women in an entirely unprofessional manner but also made lewd and racist comments. Moreover, he took numerous entirely inappropriate photographs of his patients (not for medical purposes), which he stored in his desk on campus. Although many complaints were made to university offices, tragically, USC failed to take action. It was only after decades of abuse that a courageous nurse, Cindy Gilbert, reported the gross misconduct to the rape crisis center and the matter became known to the public. In an appalling decision by USC, Gilbert was subsequently fired for being a whistleblower.

The *Los Angeles Times* published a series of articles about the way USC dealt with this matter. Students filed multiple lawsuits against the university, which cost the university over $1 billion. A documentary, *Breach of Trust* by USC student Mishal Mahmud, provides a compelling account of this morally reprehensible conduct, both by the doctor and by university administrators. Another physician, Dr. Kelly, was accused of improper conduct when examining male patients (Sequeira, 2018). To be fair, University of California, Los Angeles, also had a doctor who was found to have engaged in indecent behavior (Winton, 2021).

When USC finally removed Tyndall, the university did not report him to the medical board to seek revocation of his medical license. He also received a large severance package, which gave the impression that he was being rewarded for his despicable behavior.

Students have also experienced sexual assault in other parts of university life. Athletes on teams have been touched improperly by coaches. Women have been victimized in fraternities. One particularly disturbing incident was the drugging and rape of women at a fraternity at USC in 2021. After the first incident, USC did not take action, and another woman was subject to multiple-perpetrator rape. While Greek life remains a central part of campus life at many college campuses, it cannot be allowed to jeopardize the health, well-being, and lives of students. Universities have failed miserably in their efforts to regulate the egregious conduct of fraternities.

Universities prefer to avoid negative publicity, as this could affect recruitment, reputation, and donations. Despite these considerations, it is certainly reasonable to expect that administrators would take action to prevent other students from coming to harm. The failure of USC to act on information that was reported to offices on campus is inexcusable.

Sexual Harassment

I turn now to cases of sexual harassment at universities. In the 1970s, the concept of sexual harassment as a form of sex discrimination was established. It was defined in two forms: *quid pro quo*, where a tangible benefit or denial of one was tied to an explicit request for the performance of sexual favors, and misconduct that causes a "hostile work environment" as set forth in the landmark US Supreme Court case *Meritor v. Vinson* (1986). Criticisms of the decision include the fact that the court accepted the notion that a woman's dress, demeanor, and fantasies were admissible evidence to ascertain whether she had been sexually harassed (i.e., whether the advances were "unwelcome"). At least the court did realize that the requirement that the plaintiff should file a complaint with the perpetrator's supervisor might be impossible; after all, sometimes the supervisor is the sexual harasser.

A striking example of a university's failure to act in the face of overwhelming evidence of misconduct is Harvard's treatment of Professor Jorge Dominguez of the Government Department. Three of the four publicized cases of sexual harassment at Harvard in the 1980s involved tenured professors of government (Goss, 1985). The other faculty were Douglas A. Hibbs and Martin Kilson. Despite all the negative publicity, the problem persisted. In 2022, another scandal emerged; this time it concerned a prominent professor of anthropology, John Comaroff (Kim and Xu, 2022).

Dominguez was first accused of sexual harassment in 1983, and this was reported in the campus newspaper, the *Harvard Crimson* (Goss, 1985). The university put him on leave to obtain counseling. After receiving a paid year off, Dominguez returned to Harvard and was later promoted to vice provost of international affairs and director of the Weatherford Center for International Affairs. Despite the complaints about his unwelcome advances, according to public accounts, Harvard did not take any steps to remove him from his positions.

Media coverage had detailed Dominguez's actions for decades beginning in the 1980s. However, it was not until the article "She Left Harvard. He Got to Stay" was published in the *Chronicle of Higher Education* focusing on the harm to Professor Terry Karl that Harvard apparently began to reconsider his status (Bartlett and Gluckman, 2018). Students organized a social media campaign, #DominguezMustGo (Fu and Wang, 2018). Student journalists Fu and Wang observed that "the first *Chronicle* article sent shockwaves across the campus." Dominguez resigned in disgrace (Saul, 2018).

Eventually, the dean of graduate study, Claudine Gay, sent out a memo to the Harvard faculty saying that the Title IX office had completed its review, and, as a result, Dominguez's emeritus status had been revoked and that he was no longer allowed on the Harvard campus (Gay, 2019; Stockman, 2019). While this was commendable, it was three decades after his conduct was first announced in public.

To its credit, Harvard did take steps to convey a clear message to the university community that such conduct would no longer be tolerated. While it took forty years for this to occur (Fu and Wang, 2018), it signified that university ethics would no longer condone such egregious conduct.

Even though Harvard acted to deny Dominguez access to campus, to the surprise of some, he remained a member of professional associations such as the American Political Science Association and the Council on Foreign Relations. As of January 18, 2022, only the Latin American Studies Association had revoked his membership (Anon., 2020). While revocation of membership cannot really remove the traumatic experience this faculty member caused his former colleagues and students, at least it represents a psychological sanction that signifies the mobilization of shame.

Sometimes administrators misbehave and the university fails to remove them from their positions. For example, the USC dean of the medical school, Carmen Puliafito, a prominent ophthalmologist, was using methamphetamine and other drugs, sometimes while he was seeing patients (Pringle, Ryan, El Mahrek, Hamilton, and Parvini, 2017). Puliafito was cavorting with young women, one who almost died in a hotel in Pasadena. It was hushed up. He received a multimillion-dollar severance payment, and USC did not report him to the medical board. The next dean, Rohit Varma, another ophthalmologist, did not last long because he had been sued for sexual harassment years earlier (Parvini, Ryan, and Pringle, 2017).

Universities should act in accordance with the ethical principle to do no harm (nonmaleficence). They have the responsibility of protecting faculty, students, and others from sexual assault and sexual harassment. It is incomprehensible that administrators in some prestigious institutions who knew, according to written documents and published records, for decades that faculty and students were coming to harm neglected to act in the face of overwhelming evidence of egregious misconduct by physicians in student health and faculty. Failure to intervene when complaints are submitted, for decades, is negligent and reprehensible.

Access to Universities

Another scandal in the twenty-first century has been the undermining of the right to education as a human right. Although it is well known that families with means make gifts to universities, particularly if the parents are alumni/ae, in the hopes that their offspring will be admitted, in recent years these efforts to secure access to elite universities have involved the crime of fraud. One was the high-profile Varsity Blues scandal.

Parents paid lavish amounts to Rick Singer, a college adviser, who promised to help students gain access to their preferred elite colleges (Rubin, 2019). His modus operandi included creating fake profiles for students that listed activities in which they had not participated. As this constituted fraud, it was treated as a criminal matter. Some of the parents, including celebrities, were prosecuted and sentenced to several years in prison.

While this unethical behavior deserved to be sanctioned, some might consider the punishment excessive. Wealthy parents often make significant gifts to a university, and this is not subject to any sanction. Although these gifts usually do not involve fraudulent acts, they are nevertheless clearly a form of influence. Under what circumstances do large gifts cross the line and constitute bribery?

Another example of improper influence was the plan to admit Sebastian Ridley-Thomas, the son of a Los Angeles councilman, to the USC School of Social Work, provide a full scholarship, and hire him to teach in exchange for "steering county money to the university" (Finnegan and Hamilton, 2021). Ultimately, this was determined to be a form of unacceptable arrangement, which resulted in charging both Dean Marilyn Flynn and Mark Ridley-Thomas with bribery, conspiracy, mail fraud, and wire fraud. Flynn resigned and Mark Ridley-Thomas was suspended. Their trials in federal court were scheduled to begin in late 2022.

In contrast to those gaining access to universities through connections, some universities have provided access to education for local communities. Some elite private universities have been shamed by media coverage showing that they admit primarily students from extremely affluent families. The *New York Times* reported on a study released by the Equal Opportunity Project at Harvard University (Anon, 2017). It noted that thirty-eight colleges in the US had more students from the top 1 percent income echelon than the lower 60 percent, and this included Ivy League schools such as Brown and Dartmouth. USC has had a long-standing program, the Neighborhood Education Program, that provides courses for students near the campus. If they excel, they may receive scholarships to attend USC. Public attention increasingly focuses on the failure of urban universities (e.g., Columbia University) to share their massive resources with local communities (Bellafante, 2021).

State universities have taken the lead, proving that members of marginalized communities can earn college degrees if programs exist. A prime example is that of California State University, Los Angeles, which established a bachelor's degree program for the incarcerated that has the same courses that students on campus take. Championed by the provost and executive vice president, Dr. Jose A. Gomez, this program has been hailed as a great success and model for other institutions to emulate. The program was launched in 2016 with support from President Barack Obama's Second Chance Pell federal pilot program and the Andrew W. Mellon Foundation. After almost forty students graduated, it expanded to other prisons, including those with female inmates. This initiative demonstrates that a university can guarantee access to education for all, regardless of financial status, and also shows that many opt to take advantage of such opportunities (Beck, 2021).

Hearing of examples like that of California State University, Los Angeles, some may question whether urban universities are doing enough to help their local communities. Indeed, if they are truly committed to providing affordable education, universities will develop new programs to increase access to a university education. New initiatives such as the nonprofit National Education Equity Lab, established by CEO Leslie Cornfeld, are also showing ways to address this need. The Equity Lab enrolled more than three hundred high school students from "high-poverty high schools" in eleven cities in the US in the Harvard course Poetry in America: The City from Whitman to Hip-Hop (Green, 2021).

The experiment has demonstrated the falsity of the claim of administrators at top schools that students from less affluent communities lack adequate preparation to enter Ivy League schools. As Cornfeld put it, "Our nation's talent is evenly distributed; opportunity is not" (quoted in Green, 2021). In the twenty-first century, the ethical university will endeavor to build successful programs that support the communities surrounding their campuses, at home and abroad (e.g., satellite campuses).

One of the silver linings of the COVID-19 pandemic has been the increased use of online lectures. With so many courses available online, there really is no excuse for universities to limit access to knowledge acquisition.

Universities could allow all interested students to take courses, and if they can complete the work satisfactorily, give them the opportunity to earn a college degree. If the right to education were provided cost-free or at low cost, as has historically occurred in other countries, universities could be truly transformative and make the American dream a reality instead of an illusion. As the right to education is a fundamental human right, guaranteed in international law, universities have a duty to provide access to their educational resources. This includes qualified faculty, libraries, mentoring, and all the other aspects of university life.

AFFIRMATIVE ACTION AND REEXAMINING "MERIT"

One way that universities have tried to open up access is through affirmative action. This has been controversial in part because it sometimes involves quotas and reconsideration of what constitutes "merit" (Folely, 2021). I analyze each of these in turn.

A quota is defined as a fixed number of spots. In the US, these are familiar to us in education and immigration, and the policies were generally created to block access. In the early part of the twentieth century, they were used to exclude individuals from universities and entry to the United States. As Prell-Riv observes, "The student of racist and antisemitic quotas has provided one important avenue to understand how higher education enforced the closed borders of the nation against those who were not white, Protestant, or native-born. Private colleges, particularly in the Ivy League, became ideological bastions of racial hierarchy, defined not only by who was excluded but by the ideas about eugenics that were taught there" (2021, pp. 159–160).

Much ink has been spilled over the Ivy League's well-known practice of employing quotas to limit the number of students of Jewish heritage entering colleges (see, e.g., Karabel, 2005). According to some commentators (Biemiller, 2017; Oren, 1986), quotas restricting the number of Jewish students at Yale University lasted until the 1960s! Similarly, the US government for a long time has had quotas for migrants seeking to come to the US that depended on their countries of origin. One such law was the 1924 Immigration Act (Gould, 1982, pp. 157, 231–232). These quotas were notorious because they relied on eugenics, the pseudoscientific theory that some races and nationalities are inferior because of defective "germ plasm" (Haller, 1963).

When quotas have been used to block access to universities and the US, they have been treated as legal. However, when they are used to open up institutions by guaranteeing some spots to members of disenfranchised groups, those, somewhat surprisingly, have been deemed invalid. When universities have acknowledged having specific numerical quotas, this was challenged in court and held as unconstitutional. In the famous case *Bakke v. U.C. Regents*, the US Supreme Court, in a fragmented decision, rejected specific numerical quotas but allowed the consideration of race and ethnicity as a factor to be considered just like musical talent or geographical origin. In this respect, the US differs from other countries where numerical quotas have been allowed to open up access to marginalized communities. India serves as an example here of the implementation of specific numerical quotas. Even though this practice has also been questioned in India, it shows the potential use of quotas to empower Dalits and those belonging to lower castes.

Some did not accept the logic of *Bakke* because they thought that admission decisions should be "color-blind," so they continued to challenge the consideration of identity-based characteristics. In subsequent litigation, the question was whether universities were giving too much weight to race and ethnicity as compared to other characteristics. In the Michigan cases *Gratz v. Bollinger* and *Grutter v. Bollinger* (2003), the Supreme Court held that, whereas giving bonus points to members of a few groups (Blacks, Latinx, and Native Americans) was not justified in undergraduate college admissions processes, this was appropriate for law school admissions.

As legal philosopher Ronald Dworkin (1985) noted, the crux of the matter is determining what constitutes "merit." Although it is reasonable to allow some flexibility in judging criteria for admissions, discarding standardized tests, partly because of documented cultural bias, could risk giving the children of wealthy families more access. He challenged the conventional wisdom that merit should be conceptualized purely as grades and standardized test scores because those reflect privilege; those who excel often happen to be born into families that support their educational goals. If admissions committees see fit to take other factors into account to improve society as a whole, they can play the role of social engineers. Furthermore, it would be unreasonable to give free rein to admissions committees. What if they were to give preference to taller individuals based on studies that purport to show that height correlates with success (Judge and Cable, 2004)?

Asian Americans filed a lawsuit against Harvard alleging that the extant affirmative action policies resulted in discrimination against Asian Americans. Although this matter has not been settled yet, it involves serious questions about which groups should receive preferential consideration and what types of information admissions committees should take into account.

The debate about affirmative action also requires some discussion of favorable treatment given to athletes and the children of alumni. Why should universities admit those who will contribute to the success of sports programs or students whose families have been generous? In the context of equal access to education, it seems disingenuous to disregard policies that privilege athletes and children of alumni. Even if these types of admissions programs are consistent with a "business plan," they are arguably unfair and violate principles of equal access. It is worth asking whether these practices can continue to be justified.

Sometimes when efforts to facilitate access for financial reasons are publicized, it has proven to be highly detrimental to the reputation of a university. For instance, USC suffered when the *Los Angeles Times* published a sensational in-depth story demonstrating the actions of the university president to facilitate entrance to a wealthy member of a family from Qatar (Ryan and Hamilton, 2020). Despite the improper influence documented by the university, the faculty received little assurance that similar practices would cease.

HISTORIC INJUSTICES

Universities historically were conceived of as places where individuals could engage in contemplation. Academic institutions were designed in large part to train individuals to be virtuous citizens, create new forms of knowledge, and apply innovations to improve the quality of life for everyone in the larger society. This idealistic view of higher education has been called into question by increased scrutiny of the origins of universities in the US.

Some of the most prestigious colleges and universities were built by slaves. Lately there has been a reckoning of this past exploitation. Although this fact is not a secret (Esquith, 2010, p. 75), public attention has increasingly focused on the failure of universities to acknowledge they were complicit in the exploitation of slaves. When this came to light, a sustained conversation began about what responses were required—such as apologies, reparations and in what form, and reconsidering public monuments and the naming of public spaces.

Brown University was one of the first to conduct an investigation into the role slavery played in its construction and issued a report in 2006 and a second expanded edition in 2021 (Anon., 2021a). In her contribution to *Slavery and the University: Histories and Legacies* (Harris, Campbell, and Brophy, 2019), Ruth Simmons, the president of Brown University, considers the role universities should take in reckoning with the past. Although it is difficult to accomplish, Simmons supports actively working on reparations. Her poignant statement is compelling:

> The fact that universities are coming under widespread public attack in spite of the immense public good they did is a product of many factors. But I believe that much of the problem reflects universities' own failings, including our adoption of some of the worst habits of large organizations: elitism, predominating self-interest, failure to uphold our stated values, and a mystifying reluctance to stand up to entrenched power and question the status quo. If we truly believe that the Academy exists to promote human welfare and follow the path of truth, then our first task is confronting our own compromises and corruption. (Simmons, 2019, p. 221)

At Georgetown University in 2015, the Working Group on Slavery, Memory, and Reconciliation was convened; it included students, faculty, staff, and alumni who were charged with assessing and acknowledging historic injustices on the campus. The working group outlined a set of recommendations, including the removal of images and names of those who promoted slavery. At the same time, Georgetown established the Institute for the Study of Racial Justice, created the Department of African American Studies in 2016, and authorized the hiring of new faculty with expertise in this area.

Even after the abolition of slavery in the United States, universities continued to exclude minorities and women until the late nineteenth and early twentieth centuries. While African Americans attended historically Black colleges, they began to graduate from "primarily White institutions" in the twentieth century (Bradley, 2018, pp. 25–26). As women were also not admitted to many elite institutions, they mainly attended women's colleges. Yale and Princeton began to accept female students in the mid-1970s. Although women had access to courses taught by Harvard professors for decades, they were not permitted to attend lectures on the Harvard campus. The professors crossed the street to deliver them again at Radcliffe College.

Harvard University, the oldest college in the US, has sometimes been regarded as a model for American education (Bailyn et al., 1986). Consequently, it is striking that it has been remiss in admitting female students on an equal basis in the late 1980s, hiring few women on the tenure track (Smith, 1986, p. 289), and failing to promote highly talented women (AAUW, 2004). Of 356 women on the faculty, in 1980 only 12 were women. Luminaries who taught there (e.g., Professor Theda Skocpol) were denied tenure by a close vote of all-male colleagues in the Department of Sociology. Subsequently, Skocpol received several offers of tenured positions at several top-ranked universities across the country and accepted one at the University of Chicago.

Eventually, Harvard's grievance system reached its conclusion that Skocpol had been treated unfairly, and she was offered a tenured position there (Sanger, 1985). After she returned to Harvard, she was later appointed dean of the graduate school, elected president of the American Political Science Association, and was recognized as one of the most prominent social scientists of her day.

Other universities have also been known to deny tenure to women who had impeccable credentials—for example, Maia Cross in the School of International Relations (see Junn and Cross, 2020; AAUW, 2004). The data reflects favoritism for white males. In some instances, those up for promotion appear to be subject to double discrimination because they are women and minorities. This phenomenon is consistent with the insights found in the literature on intersectionality. Junn and Cross offer quantitative analysis of patterns of promotion success at USC. They find "highly disparate (much higher) rates of tenure for white males compared with all other scholars, including white women, men of color, and women of color." They explain the methodology they employed for data collection, how to recognize "red flags" of discrimination, and strategies universities "may use to deflect and ignore charges of discrimination" (2020, p. 97).

Another injustice that persists at universities concerns inequities in salaries. Many faculty suffer because of what is known as "salary compression"—that is, new faculty are hired at higher salaries that reflect the cost of living, while longtime faculty do not receive cost-of-living increases. In addition, women are sometimes hired at lower starting salaries than men because they are less aggressive in negotiations, and they may not receive perks such as large research accounts for labs, named chairs, leadership positions with course releases, and so on. The lower salaries have long-term implications for women when they come to retirement age. The unfortunate reality is that universities often fail to make salary adjustments in the absence of lawsuits, media coverage, or outside offers.

Even if universities try to make salary adjustments, there are long-term consequences. Raising a woman's salary incrementally does not address the impact of having had a low salary for years. This differential in salaries drastically affects women, as a practical matter. Not only does the disparity represent a lower salary for decades, but also, because of the effect of compound interest, the actual value is substantially higher. For instance, assume a salary difference between male and female assistant professors of $10,000. If that $10,000 were invested by female faculty at a rate of 3 percent per annum (assuming 4 percent inflation), at the end of ten years it would be worth $128,000. After twenty years invested, it would be worth $287,000. This form of gender inequity has serious consequences for retirement plans.

It is easier for faculty at public universities to challenge salary inequities because they are published. Those at private universities are not allowed to know what others earn. Unless colleagues share this information in an effort to promote equity, it is problematic for those who suspect they are grossly underpaid to seek salary adjustments. The US treatment of gender pay equity does not compare favorably with the policies of other countries (Chen, 2011).

Faculty who are not tenured receive much lower salaries and heavier teaching loads. This results in a caste system of sorts, which is demoralizing for the instructors on the clinical and teaching tracks. The trend toward hiring more faculty who will never be considered for tenure has devastating implications for academic freedom.

Tenure is designed to ensure that faculty at universities and colleges can publish controversial research, at least after they receive tenure. For those in positions in which they are not destined to be tenured, it is difficult to seek redress of grievance. The lack of tenure inevitably stifles faculty in this category because they lack job security. What accounts for this trend toward fewer and fewer tenure-track positions? It appears to be consistent with the goals of corporatization of universities because the faculty are converted to at-will employees. This should give us pause. If universities are no longer safe spaces for faculty and students, this will surely undermine the learning experience of future generations.

When professors say something provocative, they may face serious repercussions. One example occurred at USC in 2020. At the Marshall School of Business, an adjunct professor who had taught a cross-cultural communication course for fifteen years used an example he had consistently included. He explained that the Mandarin term *nei ge hr* was sometimes a "filler" like *um* or *er* for those who speak Chinese and that some might misconstrue this as an ethnic slur, the "N" word, which is extremely offensive (Armour, 2020); it sounds similar. After the class, some students of color complained to the professor and the dean and posted a clip from the class on social media. In the aftermath of this incident, the dean removed the professor from the course, and he did not expect to be invited back to USC (Agrawal, 2020).

The example shows the failure to provide due process. The dean, according to all public accounts, did not consult the students or faculty member before taking his decision. Chinese students at USC wondered if they, too, would be reprimanded for "speaking their own language on campus." A group of one hundred USC alumni, mostly Chinese by ethnicity or nationality, wrote to USC to support the professor's explanation of the term (Agrawal, 2020). Although the faculty member might have been prudent to update his lecture notes and discontinue use of this example during the era of Black Lives Matter, the university's response nevertheless appeared to be excessively punitive.

Unfortunately, even holding a tenured position in no way ensures that a faculty member is protected. In one case, a tenured professor, Daniel Pollack-Pelzner, who specialized in Shakespeare studies and was a faculty trustee, publicly criticized other members of the board of trustees at Linfield College in Oregon, where he taught. He accused the group of making anti-Semitic remarks and accused one of sexual misconduct. After he spoke out, the president of the university, Miles K. Davis, terminated his position (Levenson, 2021). This ignored longstanding principles such as the protection of academic freedom and the corollary freedom of expression that is supposed to be guaranteed.

SOLUTIONS

Universities have to serve many constituencies, and their interests may not always seem aligned. How should they balance the competing demands? The primary mission of a university is to educate the next generation and to instill values of civic virtue. The students should be considered the primary constituency. While decisions, particularly those made under pressure, will sometimes be erroneous, enshrouding the decision-making process in secrecy is a recipe for disaster. While mistakes will inevitably be made, the test of good leadership is how the leaders respond to serious problems.

The problem we face now is a failure to act and to take responsibility for wrongdoing. Whether we are discussing scandals, historic injustices, or other types of misconduct, the academy has demonstrated persistent cowardice in the face of the human suffering of individuals whose lives are closely tied to the university. To many who followed the scandals and dramatic revelations of injustices, it was truly incomprehensible that university leaders would not take steps to rectify the problems brought to their attention.

Some contend that universities, like the rest of society, have a fear of litigation. The mere threat of lawsuits may cause administrators to conceal wrongdoing in the hopes that it will escape detection. Indeed, they appear to bargain in the shadow of the law (Mnookin and Korn-hauser, 1979). Insult is added to injury when administrators fail to take responsibility for their misjudgment.

For some of the controversies that universities encounter, litigation may not represent the ideal solution. The law is a blunt instrument, and some individuals may not wish to report wrongdoing for fear that the consequences for perpetrators will be too severe. When families are permitted to give buildings to the university, it seems harsh to put some of the parents in federal prison for attempting to gain access for their children. While it is wrong to try to bribe admissions officers, the selective enforcement of laws prohibiting improper influence is problematic.

This survey of scandals and historic injustices shows that in some cases universities fail to act, or when they do, it is too little, too late (Blinder, 2022). In other situations they act too rapidly and do not provide due process. A major flaw is that the grievance mechanisms are ineffective. The staff who work in universities are hired by university leaders and receive their salaries from the institution. Their allegiance is to the university, and they almost never act in ways to protect those who submit complaints. We see this over and over again; self-regulation seems doomed to fail.

In order to have an effective mechanism to evaluate claims of egregious misconduct, there must be an independent agency empowered to consider them. It should be funded by the state or private foundation without ties to the university in question.

Another important change is the creation of a much larger student health care system that guarantees students and faculty mental health support. Similarly, it should be off campus if possible, to ensure privacy so seeking support will not affect professional or student status at the university.

With respect to governance, faculty should play a much more central role. The board of trustees should be comprised of at least half faculty and also have student representatives. The terms should be limited to several years at a time. No one should have a life term. Those who wish to serve should have to take an exam or otherwise prove they understand the purpose of a university and the ethical principles central to its mission—do no harm and the right to education as a human right.

To ensure access to education, tuition should be reduced. This is conceivable if administrative bloat is reduced and if fewer lawsuits occur. Ideally, college and university education should be available to all students.

In this chapter I have identified some instances of misconduct at great universities. The failure of leaders to do what is required as a matter of ethics compels us to rethink our processes for holding them accountable. Until an independent agency is established that is not funded by the universities and not beholden to the corporate board of trustees, meaningful change will be elusive.

WORKS CITED

AAUW (2004). *Tenure Denied: Cases of Sex Discrimination in Academia.* Washington, DC: AAWU Education Foundation; AAUW Legal Advocacy Fund.

Agrawal, Nina (2020, September 5). Controversy over USC Professor's Use of Chinese Word that Sounds Like Racial Slur in English. *Los Angeles Times.* www.latimes.com/california/story/2020-09-05/usc-business-professor -controversy-chinese-word-english-slur.

Anon. (2020, January 20). LASA Membership of Jorge Dominguez Revoked. https://lasaweb.org/en/news/lasa/statement/sexual/harassment/jorge/ dominguez/

Anon. (2021a). *Brown University's Slavery and Justice Report* (2nd edition). https://slaveryandjustice.brown.edu/report/2021-report. (Accessed January 2, 2022.)

Anon. (2021b). Working Group Report. www.georgetown.edu/slavery/history/ #working-group-and-report. (Accessed January 2, 2022.)

Armour, Jody (2020). *N*gga Theory: Race, Language, Unequal Justice, and the Law.* Los Angeles: Larb Books.

Bailyn, Bernard, Donald Fleming, Oscar Handlin, and Stephan Thernstrom (1986). *Glimpses of the Harvard Past.* Cambridge: Harvard University Press.

Bartlett, Tom and Nell Gluckman (2018, March 9). She Left Harvard. He Got to Stay. *Chronicle of Higher Education* 64 (26), pp. A14–16, A18, A20, A22– 23. www.chronicle.com/article/she-left-harvard-he-got-to-stay/?cid2=gen _login_refresh&cid=gen_sign_in.

Beck, Jillian (2021, October 7). Incarcerated Students Earn Cal State LA Degree at First-of-Its-Kind Commencement in a California State Prison. *Newsroom Cal State LA.* https://news.calstatela.edu/2021/10/07/incarcerated-students -earn-cal-state-la-degrees-at-first-of-its-kind-commencement-in-a-california -state-prison/.

Bellafante, Gina (2021, December 12). Do Urban Colleges Give Back Enough? *New York Times*, p. 35. www.nytimes.com/2021/12/10/nyregion/urban -universities-neighborhoods.html.

Biemiller, Lawrence (2017, February 26). Slavery Isn't the Only Historical Blemish That Colleges Have Had to Confront. *Chronicle of Higher Education.* www.chronicle.com/article/slavery-isnt-the-only-historical-blemish -that-colleges-have-had-to-confront/.

Blinder, Alan (2022, January 19). University of Michigan Will Pay $490 Million to Settle Abuse Cases. *New York Times*. www.nytimes.com/2022/01/19/sports/ncaafootball/michigan-abuse-settlement-robert-anderson.html.

Bradley, Stefan M. (2018). *Upending the Ivory Tower: Civil Rights, Black Power, and the Ivy League*. New York: New York University Press.

Chen, Cher Weixia (2011). *The Jurisprudence of Gender Pay Equity*. Leiden: Martinus Nijhoff.

Dworkin, Ronald (1985). *Bakke's Case: Are Quotas Fair? A Matter of Principle*. Cambridge: Harvard University Press, pp. 293–303.

Esquith, Stephen L. (2010). *The Political Responsibilities of Everyday Bystanders*. University Park: Pennsylvania State University Press.

Finnegan, Michael and Matt Hamilton (2021, October 26). USC Former Dean Pleads Not Guilty in Mark Ridley-Thomas Bribery Case. *Los Angeles Times*. www.latimes.com/california/story/2021-10-25/usc-dean-flynn-bribery-plea.

Folely, Nadirah Farah (2021, October 25). Why Do Colleges Use Legacy Admissions? 5 Questions Answered. *The Conversation*. https://theconversation.com/why-do-colleges-use-legacy-admissions-5-questions-answered-169450.

Franke, Katherine (2022, January 18). Columbia Has Lost Its Way. *The Nation* www.thenation.com/article/society/columbia-university-strike/.

Fu, Angela N. and Lucy Wang (2018, May 23). Forty Years in the Making: Dominguez and Sexual Misconduct at Harvard. *Harvard Crimson*. www.thecrimson.com/article/2018/5/23/the-dominguez-case/.

Galloway, Anne (2020, December 3). UVM to Eliminate 23 Programs in the College of Arts and Sciences. *VTDIgger*. https://vtdigger.org/2020/12/03/uvm-to-eliminate-23-programs-in-the-college-of-arts-and-sciences/.

Gay, Claudine Dean (2019, May 9). Letter to the Members of the Faculty of Arts and Sciences Community. Harvard University. [Subject: Outcome of Title IX Investigation].

Goss, Kristin A. (1985, October 4). Sexual Harassment: Lesson or Legacy? *Harvard Crimson*. www.thecrimson.com/article/1985/10/4/sexual-harassment-lesson-or-legacy-pin/.

Gould, Stephen Jay (1982). *The Mismeasure of Man*. New York: W. W. Norton.

Gratz v. Bollinger (2003). 539 U.S. 244 (2003).

Green, Erica L. (2021, February 18). A College Program for Disadvantaged Teens Could Shake Up Elite Admissions. *New York Times*. www.nytimes.com/2021/02/18/us/politics/college-admissions-poor-students.html.

Grutter v. Bollinger (2003). 539 U.S. 306 (2003).

Haller, Mark H. (1963). *Eugenics: Hereditarian Attitudes in American Thought*. New Brunswick, NJ: Rutgers University Press.

Harris, Leslie M., James T. Campbell, and Alfred L. Brophy (Eds.) (2019). *Slavery and the University: Histories and Legacies*. Athens: University of Georgia Press.

Idelson, Holly A. (1983, September 28). Harvard Disciplines Professor for Sexual Harassment. *Harvard Crimson*. www.thecrimson.com/article/1983/9/28/harvard-disciplines-professor-for-sexual-harassment/.

Jasnik, Scott (2008, April 11). Das Ende for German at USC. *Inside Higher Ed.* www.insidehighered.com/news/2008/04/11/das-ende-german-usc.

Judge, Timothy and Daniel M. Cable (2004). The Effect of Physical Height on Workplace Success and Income. *Journal of Applied Psychology* 89 (3), pp. 428–441.

Junn, Jane and Mai'a K. Davis Cross (2020). Investigating Discrimination: Injustice Against Women of Color in the Academy. In Kieu Linh Caroline Valverde and Wei Ming Darioties (Eds.), *Fight the Tower: Asian American Women Scholars' Resistance and Renewal in the Academy* (pp. 96–109). New Brunswick, NJ: Rutgers University Press.

Karabel, Jerome (2005). *The Chosen: The Hidden History of Admission and Exclusion at Harvard, Yale, and Princeton.* Boston: Houghton Mifflin.

Kennan, James F., SJ (2015). *University Ethics: How Colleges Can Build and Benefit from a Culture of Ethics.* Lanham, MD: Rowman & Littlefield.

Kim, Ariel H. and Meimei Xu (2021, March 9). In the Wake of Comaroff Harassment Scandal, Harvard AAS Graduate Students Demand Sweeping Reforms. *Harvard Crimson.* www.thecrimson.com/article/2022/3/9/aaas-grad-student-letter/.

Levenson, Michael (2021, May 1). Linfield University Fires Professor Who Spoke Out about Misconduct Cases. *New York Times.* www.nytimes.com/2021/05/01/us/Linfield-university-professor-fired.html.

Mnookin, Robert and Lewis Kornhauser (1979). Bargaining in the Shadow of the Law: The Case of Divorce. *Yale Law Journal* 88 (5), pp. 950–997.

Oren, Dan A. (1986). *Joining the Club: A History of Jews and Yale.* New Haven, CT: Yale University Press.

Parvini, Sarah, Harriet Ryan, and Paul Pringle (2017, October 6). USC Medical School Dean Out amid Revelations of Sexual Harassment Claim, $135,000 Settlement with Researcher. *Los Angeles Times.* www.latimes.com/local/lanow/la-me-usc-dean-harassment-20171005-story.html.

Prell, Riv-Ellen (2021). Antisemitism without Quotas at the University of Minnesota in the 1930s and 1940s: Anticommunist Politics, the Surveillance of Jewish Students, and American Antisemitism. *American Jewish History* 105 (1/2), pp. 157–188.

Pringle, Paul, Harriet Ryan, Adam El Mahrek, Matt Hamilton, and Sarah Parvini (2017, July 17). An Overdose, a Young Companion, Drug-Fueled Parties: The Secret Life of a USC Med School Dean. *Los Angeles Times.* www.latimes.com/local/california/la-me-usc-doctor-20170717-htmlstory.html.

Rubin, Joel (2019, August 30). How Rick Singer Tried to Rope in USC Legend Pat Haden into the Admissions Scandal. *Los Angeles Times.* www.latimes.com/california/story/2019-08-30/rick-singer-pat-haden-usc-admissions-scandal.

Ryan, Harriet and Matt Hamilton (2020, July 16). The True Story of the Heartthrob Prince of Qatar and His Time at USC. *Los Angeles Times.* www.latimes.com/california/story/2020-07-16/qatar-prince-usc-ucla-la.

Sanger, David E. (1985, January 8). Harvard Reverses Tenure Decision. *New York Times*, p. A11. www.nytimes.com/1985/01/08/us/harvard-reverses-tenure-decision.html.

Saul, Stephanie (2018, March 17). Resignation at Harvard over Claims of Abuse. *New York Times*, p. A15.

Sequeira, Kate (2020, February 1). Dennis Kelly Surrenders Medical License Following Health Concerns. *Daily Trojan*. https://dailytrojan.com/2020/02/01/dennis-kelly-surrenders-medical-license-following-health-concerns/.

Simmons, Ruth (2019). Slavery and Justice at Brown: A Personal Reflection. In Harris et al. (Eds.), *Slavery and the University* (pp. 215–223). Athens: University of Georgia Press.

Smith, Richard Norton (1986). *The Harvard Century: The Making of a University to a Nation*. New York: Simon & Schuster.

Stockman, Farah (2019, May 4). Harvard Sexual Harassment Case Elicits Calls for an External Audit. *New York Times*, p. A13.

Tesar, Marek, Michael Peters, and Liz Jackson (2021). The Ethical Academy? The University as an Ethical System. *Educational Philosophy and Theory* 53 (5), pp. 419–425.

US Supreme Court (1986). *Meritor v. Vinson*, 477 U.S. 57 (1986).

Washburn, Jennifer (2005). *University, Inc: The Corporate Corruption of Higher Education*. New York: Basic Books.

Winton, Richard (2021, December 9). New Lawsuit Alleges Sexual Battery by Top UCLA Doctor Who Ran Student Health Center. *Los Angeles Times*. www.latimes.com/california/story/2021-12-09/lawsuit-alleges-sexual-battery-by-ucla-doctor.

2

Ethical Foundations for Institutional Integrity

Wanda Teays

ABSTRACT

In this chapter, I give an overview of the major ethical theories as a framework for assessing the ethical challenges facing universities and laying a groundwork for academic integrity. I proceed by setting out a few cases giving rise to ethical concerns and then apply different ethical theories to examine the likely options. This survey and application includes teleological ethics (which prioritizes end goals and consequences), deontological ethics (which prioritizes moral duty and obligations), virtue ethics (which prioritizes moral character), and feminist ethics (which prioritizes relationships and moral agency). Each theory has a role to play in our coverage and assessment of university ethics, so each provides a foundation for our analysis.

Keywords: academic integrity, categorical imperative, deontological ethics, feminist ethics, justice theory, moral agency, principle of utility, teleological ethics, utilitarianism, virtue ethics, virtues

INTRODUCTION

It seems like every week or two, scandals involving universities are in the news, casting a shadow over students, faculty, and staff. Administrators are put on the spot: ignoring moral crises may be appealing, but that is not really an option. The glare of the media and the outpouring of concern makes it clear that shoddy ethics just won't do. From admissions bribery to sexual assault, from cheating scandals to firing tenured faculty, the issues are all over the map.

And so it is that moral reasoning is put to the test. Universities should not downplay the challenges they face—or not for long. It is vital that we think carefully about the basis of decision-making and institutional integrity. Students, faculty, and administrators, as well as parents and the community at large, should be able to trust that the groundwork is solid.

There are three aspects to accomplishing this goal: (1) moral navigation—having an ethical framework to guide the decision-making; (2) moral leadership—overseeing decisions with integrity and insight; and (3) moral reflection—working together to address the issues we confront while keeping institutional integrity at the forefront.

Let's start by looking at three scandals and see how ethicists might respond.

FIRST CASE: DISHONEST STUDENTS

What should universities do when students violate academic integrity?

Described as the biggest academic scandal in nearly fifty years, fifty-nine cadets at West Point confessed to cheating on their calculus exam in the spring 2020 semester (Shanahan 2020). That they all signed an honor code obviously lacked the moral force to prevent dishonesty. The sheer number of cheaters is staggering—a call for West Point to figure out what went wrong. And it's clear: something went wrong.

→ Honor codes only go as far as they have credence. Signing our names to an academic integrity declaration means nothing if our actions fall short.

SECOND CASE: ABUSIVE PERSONNEL

What should universities do to protect their students?

In November 2020, the University of California reached a $73 million settlement with seven victims of sexual assault and misconduct on the part of UCLA gynecologist Dr. James Heaps. He abused female patients over a span of thirty-plus years, resulting in a class action lawsuit involving thousands of women (Holcombe and Moon 2020). The lack of care, the betrayal of trust, and the abnegation of fiduciary duties makes it clear: something went wrong.

And it doesn't stop there. In March 2021, the University of Southern California (USC) reached the largest settlement in the history of

American universities concerning the sexual abuse of student patients. The perpetrator was another gynecologist, Dr. George Tyndall. "[The settlement] awards an additional $850 million to hundreds of women, bringing the total payout to more than $1 billion when combined with a previous class-action lawsuit. The lawsuit claims the university knew about the complaints against him, yet did nothing to protect students" (Yuccas 2021).

Then there are the sins of the past. January 2022 saw a $490 million settlement by the University of Michigan—more than a thousand people claimed sports doctor Robert E. Anderson sexually abused them during physical exams. Anderson was on the university's staff from 1966 to 2003 and died in 2008. Survivors said "they repeatedly complained about the doctor to coaches, trainers and administrators, to no avail" (Anderson and Svrluga 2022).

→ Mechanisms must be in place to deter abuse by university doctors and other personnel. Students should be able to trust that their best interests are at the foreground.

THIRD CASE: DISHONEST PARENTS AND STAFF

What should universities do when parents commit bribery to get their children admitted?

In November 2020, a Maryland businessperson was accused of bribing a fencing coach to get his two sons admitted to Harvard (Levenson 2020). The coach is now a *former* fencing coach at the university. It was said to be quite the haul—at least $1.5 million in bribes, including payments for a car and a house.

Coaches aren't the only ones sucked into admissions scandals. In March 2019, fifty people were arrested due to an admissions scheme involving such top schools as Georgetown, USC, UCLA, Yale, and Stanford. Among them were actress Lori Loughlin and her husband, Mossimo Giannulli. They reportedly paid admissions counselor and mastermind Rick Singer $500,000 to get their two daughters admitted as crew team recruits, even though neither one rows. Presumably, the coach was not disturbed by this fact. Loughlin was sentenced to two months in prison, community service, and a $150,000 fine. Actress Felicity Huffman also served a prison sentence for paying $15,000 for a proctor to change (inflate) her daughter's SAT score (Gross 2020). The admissions scam organizer, Singer, reportedly made $25 million over a seven-year period (Amore 2021).

Dishonest parents not only fail as role models; their actions harm others. They put honest students at a disadvantage when buying their children's way into a university. Their moral deficiency is matched by that of corrupt coaches, admissions counselors, and staff who succumb to the bribery.

→ Universities need to make it clear that the path to admission is not paved in gold, that qualifications, not money, are what matter. Policies and their enforcement are needed to prevent parents and university personnel from crossing ethical boundaries.

ETHICAL FRAMEWORKS

Central to institutional integrity is *academic* integrity. Academic integrity committees bring to light the various forms dishonesty can take. The range of violations include plagiarism and cheating, buying or selling exams and essays, forging transcripts or faculty signatures, passing oneself off as another on exams, changing grades by hacking into university databases or stealing faculty grade books, creating fraudulent student IDs, reusing essays for another class, and so on. And that does not count other forms of misconduct, such as misrepresentation on résumés and scholarship applications, faking letters of reference, stealing university property, and offering bribes or sexual favors in exchange for higher grades.

When looking at the scandals facing higher education, a number of values stand out. Some prominent ones in the ethical scaffolding are:

- The value of beneficence—do good
- The value of integrity—be honest
- The value of nonmaleficence—do no harm
- The value of justice—be fair
- The value of courage—stand up for what is right
- The value of care—show empathy, protect the vulnerable

To get a handle on university ethics, it is useful to look at the major ethical theories. Each theory puts a set of values at center stage. Beneficence is a major concern of teleological ethics, with its emphasis on the best consequences. Integrity is central to deontological ethics, with its emphasis on moral duty, obligations, and individual rights. Nonmaleficence is a key concern of Ross's prima facie duties, which are applied on a case by case basis. Justice is fundamental to John Rawls's focus on human rights. Courage is at the center of virtue ethics, which prioritizes moral character. And care, hand in hand with justice, is a primary concern of feminist ethics.

These ethical theories provide powerful vehicles for analysis and reflection. Each one shines a light on conceptual and experiential challenges facing universities and helps us examine the ethical dilemmas we face. They fall under one of two categories: metaethics, which looks at conceptual issues regarding ethical theory, and normative ethics, regarding value judgments and ethical decision-making.

Metaethics targets the nuts and bolts of ethical theories. This includes ethical frameworks, definitions, moral concepts, personal worldviews, and value-laden terms. How we define and compare such concepts as "good" versus "bad," "virtuous" versus "vicious," and "honorable" versus "dishonorable" comes under scrutiny in metaethics. Another function of metaethics is analyzing competing ethical theories and codes, noting any differences, assessing their value as theoretical models, and contrasting their principles. This includes evaluating the criteria for moral agency, rationality, competence, and moral duty.

In normative ethics, the boots are on the ground. Here is where we apply ethical theories, evaluate moral reasoning in context, arrive at decisions, offer advice, and make value judgments. This brings ethics into the world, where we consider what is right or wrong in particular situations. This is the practical side of ethics. We assess ethical dilemmas, weigh the various factors, contemplate options, and arrive at a plan or course of action. So, for example, when deciding what to *do* about the West Point cheaters or the parents bribing admissions counselors, we are in the realm of normative ethics.

MORAL AGENCY AND CULPABILITY

Of fundamental importance to moral reasoning is what it means to be a moral agent—someone capable of ethical decision-making. Only then can we hold people responsible for their actions. The two criteria of moral *agency* are free will and rationality (competence). They are necessary and sufficient conditions. If we cannot act on our own volition or if we lack the mental wherewithal to think clearly, we may not be considered responsible (or fully responsible) for our actions.

To be held responsible for our actions and intentions, we must be free to decide and act. This is the criterion of *volition*. For example, some participants in the January 6 attack on the Capitol argued that they were under duress or could not easily extricate themselves without considerable risk. If this limited their ability to act freely, then they deserved leniency in terms of accountability—or so they contend.

The second aspect of moral agency is *rationality*. To be held responsible for our decisions and actions, we must be able to tell right from wrong and articulate a coherent and consistent set of values. A great deal turns on competence. If either free will or competence is in dispute, accountability may collapse altogether. Normally, only competent adults are considered moral agents; children and juveniles are not usually thought competent and, thus, lack the moral status of an adult. Instead, the spotlight of responsibility falls on their parents or guardians.

MORAL STATUS

Moral agency has a pivotal role in determining moral *status*, which sets out rights and interests. Some theorists, like ethicist Immanuel Kant, think moral agency determines moral status; so only competent adults would qualify for full moral status.

Dilemmas involving students who are minors also tread into the domain of moral status. Consider the free speech controversy involving cheerleader Brandi Levy. Her profanity-filled post on her off-campus Snapchat (social media) site resulted in her being suspended from the high school cheerleading team. The case made it up to the US Supreme Court (see *Mahanoy Area Schools District v. B.L.*). As Mark Joseph Stern (2021) observes, "This case is certainly easy for Justice Clarence Thomas, who believes that students have virtually no free speech rights in or outside of school because, according to the justice's own historical research, minors had no such rights when the First Amendment was ratified in 1791."

Nevertheless, the court ruled in Levy's favor, with Justice Thomas voicing the sole dissent. Speaking for the majority, Justice Breyer stated, "It might be tempting to dismiss B. L.'s words as unworthy of the robust First Amendment protections discussed herein. But sometimes it is necessary to protect the superfluous in order to preserve the necessary." (2021).

THE MAJOR ETHICAL THEORIES

There are four major ethical theories, each one has had a significant effect in shaping the values and principles that govern our lives and our institutions. They lay a foundation for deciding what we consider right and wrong and how we ought to treat one another. Examining the ethical theory undergirding a university is therefore of pivotal concern. The major ethical theories are each distinct in the following ways: teleological ethics prioritizes goals and outcomes; deontological ethics focuses on intentions and moral duty; virtue ethics emphasizes moral character; and feminist ethics focuses on caring and just relationships. Each one provides a useful conceptual framework for examining higher education institutions.

Ethical theories provide a structure, expectations, and parameters for decision-making and evaluating academic integrity. The ethical theory behind a university's principles and regulations sets the direction of actions and policies and is instrumental in justifying the course taken. As a result, the importance of these ethical frameworks should not be underestimated.

Let us now turn to an overview of the different ethical theories. One or more may play a significant role in a university ethics and the policies it puts into place.

TELEOLOGICAL ETHICS

Teleological ethics focuses on goals and consequences rather than intentions or means to an end. It is often referred to as consequentialist ethics due to its emphasis on objectives. The overriding concern is to maximize benefits (gains) and minimize harms (losses). Individual interests may thus be sacrificed for the good of the majority. Their mantra is "the most for the most." So, for example, a university may cut the number of faculty or eliminate entire departments to strengthen overall financial stability or bolster long-term goals. Desirable consequences drive the decision-making.

Teleological theories fall into three main categories: (1) ethical egoism, (2) ethical (or cultural) relativism, and (3) utilitarianism. Though similar in prioritizing end goals, they differ in scope. All three teleological theories subscribe to the principle of utility—that we should choose the act that would result in the best consequences. They differ in terms of *whose* interests should prevail and whose benefits should take precedence. This is where the targeted population comes into play.

Ethical Egoism

Ethical egoism has the smallest population in mind. It focuses solely on the individual, putting self-interest above all else. The modus operandi is "look out for number one." Everyone else's interests recede, unless there are personal advantages to factor them into the equation. Any concern for the welfare of others, any altruism, is not on the radar. Their mantra is "me above thee."

Citing foremost proponent of ethical egoism Ayn Rand, philosopher Stephen H. C. Hicks (2021)observes that self-interest rightly understood is "that one's own life and happiness are one's highest values, and that one does not exist as a servant or slave to the interests of others." Ethical egoists would condone such thinking.

Applying the Theory

In the absence of personal gain, don't count on ethical egoists to stick their neck out. That means long-term consequences may not merit the attention of ethical egoists. However, if things go south further down the road, regrets may rise to the surface about the best course of action. If it is not beneficial to speak up, however, ethical egoists would likely stay silent. Personal advantage overrules any qualms about violating a moral principle.

Stepping on others' toes or crossing ethical boundaries is of little concern so long as there's no significant downside. For example, the fencing coach who weighs the monetary benefits of a bribe may perceive little risk in taking the payoff. Both the dishonest parent and the coach put self-interest above principle and fall prey to ethical egoism.

In the case of the West Point cheaters, a student who is an ethical egoist may perceive benefits to being a whistleblower, thereby bringing the dishonesty to the professor's attention. On the other hand, joining the cheaters may be attractive to those who have no allegiance to honesty and think they won't get caught—a riskier proposition. One of the tasks of a university is to steer them away from cheating and help them see that they have more to gain in the long run by taking the high road of academic integrity. Institutional integrity is bolstered by this latter scenario.

Ethical Relativism

Ethical relativism, the second type of teleological ethics, foregrounds the interests of a particular group to which the members are affiliated. The "group" could be a culture, subculture, professional organization, academic department, religious organization, political activist group, neighborhood, gang, cult, terrorist cell, or so on.

There may be shared principles and values, but the bottom line is that the group's interests prevail and should be maximized. Those who adopt this value system leave their independence and, to some degree, their rationality at the door. They have relinquished their power over decision-making. What benefits the group may entail personal sacrifices on the part of its members. Their mantra is "us above me." Adopting such priorities and conforming to the group's standards can result in questionable or even dangerous results.

At an extreme are those who risk their careers, or even their lives, to honor the group's values and beliefs. That's the dark side of this theoretical framework. On a more positive note, ethical relativism allows for multiple points of view to reach expression. This could offer advantages for less powerful groups (e.g., ethnic or religious minorities, gays and lesbians, political factions, small departments) relative to those with more status and clout. Misguided members may then be led away from a destructive or morally bankrupt mindset that would not be in the group's interest.

Applying the Theory

Even if they have doubts or disagree with a course of action, ethical relativists will not be inclined to buck the system to further their specific interests. The group's interests, conventions, and standards rule. As a result, an administrator, staff, faculty member, or student who is personally opposed to a policy may nevertheless go along with it, if doing so conforms with the group's wishes. Ethical relativists may then adhere to institutional policies and priorities even at personal cost. For example, adjunct faculty may accept employment conditions and remuneration that causes them to live in near-poverty conditions rather than speak up or form unions to challenge the status quo. The collective interests of adjuncts keeping their jobs (even if it entails increased class enrollment or cutbacks on benefits) may take precedence over the interests of particular adjunct faculty.

Students may also align their interests with a group. In the West Point case, a student may be persuaded by their buddies to actively participate in or enable cheating by turning a blind eye and not disclosing it to the instructor. Tossing aside any reluctance is deemed a small price to pay for membership in the group. But there are risks, including forsaking one's own integrity. On the other hand, a group of honest students may be sufficiently forceful or persuasive to keep fellow students from falling off the path of virtue.

Utilitarianism

The most influential form of teleological ethics is utilitarianism, which has a greater target population. Utilitarians put societal or institutional interests above those of any individual. The driving force is to maximize benefits and minimize harms for the greatest number of people. If a minority suffers, so be it; that's just a form of collateral damage. The majority rules, with potential consequences deemed more important than moral obligations. Utilitarians favor a cost-benefit analysis, with the highest ratio of gains over losses. Weigh the potential consequences and then select the best of the lot. The ends thus justify the means.

The foremost utilitarians are John Stuart Mill and G. E. Moore. Their versions of the principle of utility are:

> Mill: Choose that act that will result in the most happiness and least unhappiness for the greatest number of people.
> Moore: Choose that act that will result in the most good and least evil for the greatest number of people.

Both prioritize the society over the individual; their goal is the most for the most—the majority. Societal benefits rule.

Applying the Theory

Utilitarians seek to maximize gains for the greatest number of people. Consequently, whether an administrator or faculty member should support a course of action (such as a tuition increase or a response to staff misconduct) may depend on short-term versus long-term gains. In the short term, increased tuition may bring about positive results for the institution but may negatively impact enrollment or public support in the long run. Furthermore, leniency shown to a staff member who crosses a moral boundary may have undesirable consequences further down the line. In that sense, tunnel vision has its risks. As a result, utilitarians might come to regret downplaying long-term risks when prioritizing short-term benefits.

Utilitarians are caught on the horns of a dilemma. Since long-term consequences are not as easy to predict as what can be accomplished in the short term, they tend to be a lesser concern. Utilitarian administrators might then tolerate the suffering of a minority of students if tuition increases would further the end goals of the institution and address the needs of the present. If some suffer in the bargain, that's the way it goes, so long as the majority would benefit.

There are two forms of utilitarianism: act and rule. Both seek to maximize benefits and minimize harms, but they differ in scope. The focus of act utilitarianism is much narrower than that of rule utilitarianism. Act utilitarians would have us choose what leads to the best consequences overall for the most people *directly affected* by the act in question. It may just be a family, class, campus club, or passengers on a plane, for example. The cost-benefit assessment of the dilemma facing the specific group shapes the decision. Act utilitarians proceed on a case by case basis and do not see the case as a precedent; the resolution is not meant to have a broader application.

For example, an act utilitarian would look at the case of the cheaters on the calculus exam in terms of the participating cheaters, the instructor, and, to some degree, the other students in the class. The circumstances of those particular individuals would be factored into any recriminations or punishment. There would not be any policy decision for future cases of academic dishonesty.

In contrast, rule utilitarians seek to maximize good and minimize harm for the greatest number of people, not just those directly affected. Rather than proceeding on a case by case basis, they approach the ethical dilemma in terms of its wider application to the society or institution. The goal here is to set future policy: consider each case a potential precedent, thus generalizing the decision ("rule") to all similar cases.

Academic integrity boards and grievance committees are often proponents of rule utilitarianism, since they operate with a much broader scope. In dealing with the West Point cheaters, for example, they would seek a policy decision warning *all* would-be cheaters against such misconduct. And in dealing with cases of staff misconduct on the part of the institution, as with the fencing coach or doctors, administrators would weigh long-term consequences in setting policy. Rule utilitarians would focus on the specific situation as well as future cases involving such misconduct.

The next ethical theory is in direct contrast to utilitarianism and other consequentialist theories. Let's see how.

DEONTOLOGICAL ETHICS

Deontological ethics emphasizes moral duties and obligations rather than end goals. In that sense, this theory is the flip side of teleological ethics. Ethical decisions are approached in terms of principles, ethical codes, and moral duties, as with "Don't lie to your friends," "Return what you borrowed," "Never drive drunk," and so on. In contrast to utilitarians, deontological ethicists believe that *intentions* should inform actions—potential consequences should not guide decision-making. Moral obligations rule.

Deontological ethicists are more concerned with individual rights than societal benefits. Human rights are at center stage. This is the case, even if the society as a whole might benefit from sacrificing a minority for the common good. Deontologists would condemn those who disregard human rights in trying to maximize scientific knowledge or social benefits, as with the Tuskegee syphilis study, the Willowbrook experiments on children, and the human radiation experiments.

Similarly, universities have an obligation to provide health services that students can trust. Deontological ethicists would be appalled by Drs. Heaps, Tyndall, and Anderson sexually abusing students getting physical exams or seeking medical care. They would deplore the lack of integrity of doctors using patients for their own abusive ends and, thus, failing to honor their fiduciary duties to the students.

Kantian Ethics

Immanuel Kant is *numero uno* in deontological ethics. His main concern is the individual moral agent and respect for persons. In Kant's view, human dignity is identified with the capacity for rationality. Moral agents must be competent and have free will. Excluded from the set of moral agents are children, juveniles, and mentally impaired adults.

At the center of the Kantian universe are two ethical principles that he considers moral *commands*. Kant sees them as iron-clad rules to be followed—without exception. Such commands are then *imperatives*. They are:

> The categorical imperative: act in such a way that you would have it become a universal law.
> → Universalize ethical decision-making
> The humanitarian principle: always treat others as an end in themselves, never merely as a means.
> → Treat others with respect and human dignity.

The Categorical Imperative

Before settling on a decision, ask yourself, "What if everyone did this?" If it would be acceptable for all to follow suit, then the action is morally permissible. Otherwise not. Only if it's okay for everyone to make the same choice ought you to proceed; you can't be an exception to the rule. Strive to be a moral role model—that is the thrust of the categorical imperative. Kant would likely endorse the use of honor codes to underscore academic integrity and make transparent the responsibility on the part of all who sign their acceptance.

The Humanitarian Principle

Kant's second formulation of the categorical imperative is the humanitarian principle: we should always treat others as ends in themselves, never merely as a means. Treat others with dignity and respect, and honor individual human rights. Kant would be disgusted by students who buy exams or cheat, thus using their fellow students as a means to an end. And he would be horrified by the coaches and the university doctors who exploit the privileges of their office and parents and staff who turn to bribery as the path to admission.

Another case brings both of Kant's imperatives to the fore. This involves the USC Song Girls cheerleaders and their coach Lori Nelson. She reportedly enforced a contract with restrictions causing some of the "girls" to have eating disorders and depression, according to journalist Ryan Kartje (2021). He describes a "toxic culture" that included "Nelson rebuking women publicly for their eating habits, personal appearance and sex lives." Kartje (2021) notes, "Each of the 10 women who spoke to *The [Los Angeles] Times* said Nelson policed their appearance and scrutinized their public personas in ways that went well beyond traditional dance squad rules. That oversight was written directly into the Song Girls contract obtained by *The Times*. It stipulates squad members must stay within five pounds of their audition weight, and any changes to their appearance must first be approved by Nelson herself."

Kant would not want to universalize such a policy. Furthermore, those who had knowledge of the contract and did nothing also violated the categorical imperative. Evidently, "Nelson resigned from her position as coach, accusing the university of discrimination, harassment and retaliation in her resignation letter" (Kartje 2021). From her perspective, things did not end well. That much is clear.

Confronting Kant's Rigidity

For Kant, there are no exceptions to his two principles. This is further complicated by Kant's emphasis on the principle of veracity, to be honest no matter what unfortunate consequences may be unleashed. However, that may not be a principle we would always want to follow. So how do we tone this down? Why not allow for an escape hatch if things go south?

One such option is philosopher Sissela Bok's solution. She thinks "do no harm" needs to be factored into the equation. Her recommendation is that the principle of nonmaleficence should overrule the principle of veracity. If telling the truth would result in grave harm, then we should either stay silent or tell a lie. A rigid commitment to honesty should never take precedence over nonmaleficence. The categorical imperative is normally worth following, but there simply are times when tempering our behavior—and honesty—would be in order.

Applying the Theory

Both the humanitarian principle and the categorical imperative call us to act in a way that we would willingly have others follow. The result is an unequivocal guideline not to violate human rights.

A Kantian would not tolerate the cases of misconduct that we have considered. Both of his moral imperatives have been violated. Under no circumstances should we turn these actions into universal law. Kant would come down hard on the cheating students, the bribing parents, the greedy coaches, and the abusive doctors. In his view, if they got no more than token punishment, the door would open for other types of dishonesty—and this could never be justified.

W. D. Ross's Prima Facie Duties

Deontological ethicist W. D. Ross agrees with Kant on the importance of moral duty but recommends a broader focus than obligations of the present. Factoring in the past and future, he contends, will provide a more balanced approach to ethical decision-making. We may, for example, see a need for reparations for past harms—such as slavery or the abuse of Native American children in boarding schools. Similarly, future generations may need to be factored into moral decision-making, as would be the case in long-range planning for the institution.

Ross sets out what he calls prima facie duties. On the surface they are of equal value, but they may not all be relevant to the case at hand. We would just want to use the duties that apply to the particular dilemma. He thinks it will be intuitively obvious which duties should guide the decision-making. Use them and shelf the rest. Ross's prima facie duties are:

1. Honesty and promise-keeping
2. Beneficence (do good)
3. Nonmaleficence (do no harm)
4. Justice
5. Gratitude (loyalty)
6. Reparations (compensate for harm done)
7. Self-improvement

These duties are in no particular order—they are of equal merit until we apply them. Select the duties on a case by case basis. Ross values honesty, for example, but justice or nonmaleficence may take precedence if telling the truth would result in serious harm.

Applying the Theory

Followers of Ross would argue that the duties of integrity, nonmaleficence, and justice would direct the fencing coach to reject the bribe and report it to university authorities. In addition, Ross would agree with Kant that the West Point cheaters, the Song Girls' coach, and Drs. Heaps, Tyndall, and Anderson exhibited deplorable behavior. The cheaters violated Ross's duty of integrity, and the coaches and doctors seemed oblivious to nonmaleficence and justice. They also need to work on self-improvement and act more professionally. Finally, the duty of reparations would support sanctions or punishment to acknowledge the harm done and arrive at some form of compensation—as was done in the cases of sexual abuse.

John Rawls's Justice Theory

John Rawls is another deontological ethicist who emphasizes moral duty. Like Kant, he focuses on human rights and seeks to universalize ethical decision-making. Like Ross, he thinks justice is an important moral duty. And so he wants to address injustice within social institutions and further human rights.

To accomplish this goal, Rawls offers this advice: distance yourself from any personal attachments and affiliations (nationality, religion, political party, race, gender, etc.). Level the playing field to create a system of justice and fairness. A "veil of ignorance" should be adopted to eliminate sources of bias and prejudice from how we think and behave. In that way we might arrive at a social contract that minimizes forms of injustice.

Rawls sets out three principles to help construct a society based on justice and fairness:

Principle of equal liberty: each person is to have an equal right to the most extensive system of basic liberties compatible with a similar system of liberty for all.
→ Universalize human rights.
Principle of equality of fair opportunity: offices and positions are to be open to all under conditions of equality and fair opportunity so that persons with similar abilities and skills should have equal access to offices and positions.
→ Provide equal opportunities.
Difference principle: social and economic institutions are to be arranged to maximally benefit the worst off.
→ Favor the least advantaged.

Applying the Theory

Like Kant, Rawls seeks a system of human rights where moral agents have equal standing. Honoring those rights is of paramount importance. He would agree with Kant and Ross that honesty is a significant moral obligation; we won't have a system of equal opportunities if some get away with lying, cheating, bribery, or abuse. For Rawls, fair opportunity is fundamentally important to justice. His difference principle would have universities give special consideration to those who are most disadvantaged. This may call for affirmative action or scholarships and loans to help students struggling with financial hardships or other types of adversity.

Our next ethical theory also sees justice as fundamentally important but focuses more attention on the individual than on the society.

VIRTUE ETHICS

Virtue ethics is so named because it puts the spotlight on moral character. Ethics superstar Aristotle sees virtues as paving the way to the good life, one of flourishing and well-being. In contrast to teleological (goal-based) ethics and deontological (duty-based) ethics, living a virtuous life free of vices should be our guide.

Aristotle is the heart and soul of virtue ethics. That said, he is not alone. Confucius also favors a life of virtue but puts more emphasis on relationships and the roles we play in our professional life (as a teacher, librarian, attorney, etc.) or in our relationships (as a husband or wife, son or daughter, etc.).

Aristotle looks at rational individuals (moral agents) and asks us to examine our moral character. Make adjustments as needed. That is the path to finding purpose in our lives. Aristotle emphasizes two kinds of virtues—intellectual and moral virtues:

Aristotle's intellectual virtues are:

1. Artistic knowledge and creativity
2. Analytical and logical knowledge
3. Practical wisdom ("street smarts")
4. Philosophical wisdom (about ultimate things)
5. Understanding and comprehension (for making judgments)

Aristotle's moral virtues are:

1. Courage
2. Self-control
3. Generosity
4. Magnanimity
5. Pride
6. Even temperament
7. Honor
8. Integrity
9. Wit
10. Friendliness
11. Modesty
12. Righteous indignation

To get there from here, we need to practice a life of moderation. Seek the mean between the extremes of too little (deficiency) and too much (excess). Of course, moderation is not always the best choice. In the face of injustice, the correct response might be "righteous indignation"—moral outrage and the courage to take action.

Generally, however, Aristotle recommends the middle path. Keep in mind the moral spectrum of *deficient* → *mean* → *excessive.* For example, *courage* is the mean between cowardice and recklessness, *generosity* is the mean between stingy and wasteful, and *friendliness* is the mean between coldness and fawning. It's not always easy to avoid the extremes, but we should strive to do so in order to achieve moral excellence.

Applying the Theory

Seek a life of excellence by cultivating virtues and avoiding vices. For Aristotle, we would then be rewarded with *eudaemonia*—happiness and self-fulfillment. That means not simply avoiding wrongdoing. We also need to stand up to those who pressure us to kiss our values goodbye. Aristotle would say the entire crew of West Point cheaters, bribing parents, morally deficient fencing coaches, disgraceful doctors, and the weight-obsessed cheerleading coach fall short on the integrity scale. They all need ethical rehabilitation.

Fortunately, it's never too late to turn things around, but that requires making a habit of virtuous actions, of doing the right thing. For that reason Aristotle would praise the victims of the abusive doctors who expressed righteous indignation and courageously reported the abuse. Bringing the violence to light took courage. Their moral character was strengthened by their actions.

Let us now turn to the last ethical theory meriting our consideration.

FEMINIST ETHICS

Feminist ethicists view relationships as a central force in moral reasoning. In contrast to deontological and teleological theorists, they do not consider moral duty or consequences to be at center stage. They would second Aristotle's concern with moral character and justice while putting a greater emphasis on community and relationships. As philosopher Anne Donchin (2015) points out, "Human agents are not fundamentally single-minded, rational, self-interested choice-makers but social beings whose selfhood is constituted and maintained within overlapping relationships and communities."

Mary Anne Warren takes issue with ethicists like Kant who emphasize rationality while overlooking or downgrading relationships. Agreeing that relationships should be integral to moral status and moral reasoning, Virginia L. Warren argues,

> The dominant trend in philosophical ethics has been to regard people as best able to decide what is moral when least tied to place and time, when least connected through ties of partiality to family and community. Ideal moral decision-makers are viewed as common denominators—e.g., rational egos (Kant) or calculators of utility— who are more likely to adopt the proper universal perspective when the veneer of particularity is stripped away. . . . Persons whose unique experiences have been largely omitted from the dominant culture— e.g., women, Blacks, gay males, and lesbians—may find the stripping

away of particularity from the moral observer to be anathema to self. (1992, 33)

Because of this theoretical shift, feminist ethics is often called care ethics or ethics of care. Rita C. Manning's two elements demonstrate why this is the case:

Manning's elements of an ethics of care are:

- A disposition to care: We are called to attend to others' needs. Caring is a goal, an ideal.
  → People are disposed to care about one another.
- The obligation to care for: Caring for another requires action, not just intentions. Caring for others can be expanded to communities, values, or objects.
  → Responding to the needs of others is a moral obligation.

Manning also highlights the role justice plays—a position that Aristotle and Rawls would commend. Weigh both care and justice in ethical decision-making. Pay attention to rules and rights, though not to the exclusion of relationships. Conceive of ethics as a social institution whose chief function is to justly promote the well-being of all (Virginia L. Warren 1992, 33).

Feminist ethicists address the shortcomings of deontology and utilitarianism by taking ethics off its pedestal and into the context of our lives. Our unique circumstances merit recognition. It's not that principles *don't* matter; it's that other concerns also count when plotting a moral course. Ethicist Rosemarie Tong says power, not just care, should play a central role in moral reasoning. She observes, "Whereas a care-focused feminist approach to ethics emphasizes values that have been culturally associated with women (e.g., nurturance, care, compassion), a power-focused feminist approach to ethics emphasizes the need to eliminate those social, economic, political, and cultural systems and structures that maintain patriarchal domination and work against the establishment of a gender-equitous world" (1997, 48).

Factor in a disposition to care without losing sight of working for justice. In that sense feminist ethics is closer to virtue ethics in highlighting moral character while shining more light on the role relationships play in ethical decision-making.

Applying the Theory

First, feminist ethics would advise us to honor our obligations to care for others and think long and hard before casting them aside. So, for example, Drs. Heaps, Tyndall, and Anderson's mistreatment of student patients clearly violates any ethic of care. The class action lawsuits are no surprise in attempts to seek justice.

Second, feminist ethicists would have us pay close attention to power dynamics and guard against actions that further oppression. They would disapprove of wealthy parents bribing officials to admit their children into a university. Poor students pay the price and suffer disadvantages due to financial misconduct on the part of the wealthy and the corrupt college officials who acquiesce. All students lose out when dishonesty eats holes in the moral fabric of the university.

CONCLUSION

Philosopher Martin Heidegger once observed, "Every inquiry is a seeking. Every seeking gets guided beforehand by what is sought" (1962, 24). As we have seen in this chapter, our goals play a role in the direction we take and the values that shape our policies. Central to the university is institutional integrity. It links all the values together and lays a foundation that gives the university its identity and reputation.

If we want to maximize social benefits, teleological ethics may dominate our approach. If we want to be guided by moral duty rather than consequences, deontological ethics will point the way. If we seek the fulfillment of a developed moral character where virtues keep vices at bay, we will prioritize virtue ethics. Alternatively, we may want to factor in a disposition to care along with justice and draw from feminist ethics in constructing university policies.

We can put academic integrity to work. An ethical framework gives us the tools to address whatever moral deficiencies—and scandals—challenge the stability of the institution. The cracks in the ivory tower can be repaired, and an ethical university be achieved.

WORKS CITED

Amore, Samson. "'Operation Varsity Blues': Rick Singer Actually Tried to Pitch a Reality Show about Admissions Scam." *The Wrap*, March 18, 2021. www.msn.com/en-us/tv/news/operation-varsity-blues-rick-singer-actually-tried-to-pitch-a-reality-show-about-admissions-scam/ar-BB1eHxRw.

Anderson, Nick and Susan Svrluga. "University of Michigan Agrees to $490 Million Settlement in Sex Abuse Scandal." *Washington Post*, January 18, 2022. www.washingtonpost.com/education/2022/01/19/michigan-settlement-robert-anderson-sex-abuse/.

Aristotle. *Nicomachean Ethics*. Translated by W. D. Ross. http://classics.mit
.edu/Aristotle/nicomachaen.html. (Accessed January 28, 2021.)

Aristotle. *Poetics*. The Internet Classics Archive. http://classics.mit.edu/
Aristotle/poetics.html. (Accessed January 28, 2021.)

Birsch, Douglas. *Ethical Insights: A Brief Introduction*, 2nd ed. Boston:
McGraw-Hill, 2002.

Donchin, Anne. "Feminist Bioethics." Stanford Library. December 16, 2015.
https://stanford.library.sydney.edu.au/entries/feminist-bioethics/#Car
Eth29.

Fernandes, Deidre. "Colleges Are Under Pressure to Hold Accountable Those
Who Sought to Overturn Election, Attended Capitol Riot." *Boston Globe*,
January11, 2021. www.bostonglobe.com/2021/01/11/metro/colleges-under
-pressure-hold-accountable-those-who-sought-overturn-election-attended
-capitol-riot/.

Gross, Elayna Len. "Lori Loughlin Starts Prison Sentence for Role in College Admissions Scandal." *Forbes*, October 30, 2020. www.forbes.com/
sites/elanagross/2020/10/30/lori-loughlin-starts-prison-sentence-for-role-in
-college-admissions-scandal/?sh=247e93b34b0b.

Heidegger, Martin. *Being and Time*. Translated by John Marcquarrie and
Edward Robinson. New York: Harper & Row, 1962.

Hicks, Stephen H. C. "Ayn Rand." *The Internet Encyclopedia of Philosophy*.
https://iep.utm.edu/rand/. (Accessed April 29, 2021.)

Holcombe, Madeline and Sarah Moon. "University of California Reaches a
$73M Settlement Against Former Gynecologist Accused of Sexual Miscon-
duct." *CNN*, November 17, 2020. www.cnn.com/2020/11/17/us/university
-of-california-settlement-gynecologist/index.html.

Kartje, Ryan. "USC's Song Girls Project a Glamorous Ideal; 10 Women
Describe a Different, Toxic Reality." *Los Angeles Times*, April 22, 2021
(updated June 14, 2021). www.latimes.com/sports/usc/story/2021-04-22/
usc-song-girls.

Levenson, Eric. "Maryland CEO Paid Former Fencing Coach $1.5 Million in
Bribes to Get His Sons Accepted to Harvard, Feds Say," *CNN*, November
16, 2020. www.cnn.com/2020/11/16/us/college-admissions-scam-harvard/
index.html.

Mahanoy Area School District v. B.L. , 594 U.S. (2021).Opinion of the Court
(Breyer).

Manning, Rita C. *Speaking from the Heart*. Lanham, MD: Rowman & Littlefield, 1992.

Nietzel, Michael T. "More Than a Hundred University Faculty in Pennsylvania to Lose Their Jobs." *Forbes*, October 31, 2020. www.forbes.com/
sites/michaeltnietzel/2020/10/31/more-than-a-hundred-university-faculty
-in-pennsylvania-to-lose-their-jobs/?sh=5f83205f2de5.

Ormseth, Matthew. "Admissions Scandal: Socialite Sentenced to 5 Weeks in
Prison." *Los Angeles Times*, July 15, 2020. www.latimes.com/california/
story/2020-07-15/admissions-scandal-newport-beach-mother-sentenced-to
-in-prison.

Shanahan, Ed. "More Than 70 West Point Cadets Are Accused in Cheating Scandal." *New York Times*, December 21, 2020. www.nytimes.com/2020/12/21/nyregion/west-point-cheating.html.

Stern, Mark Joseph. "The Supreme Court Is 'Frightened to Death' by the Case of a Foul-Mouthed Cheerleader." *Slate*, April 28, 2021. https://slate.com/technology/2021/04/supreme-court-free-speech-Ii-levy.html.

Teays, Wanda. *Doctors and Torture: Medicine at the Crossroads*. Cham, Switzerland: Springer Nature Switzerland AG, 2019.

Tong, Rosemarie. *Feminine and Feminist Ethics*. Belmont, CA: Wadsworth, 1993.

———. *Feminist Approaches to Bioethics*. Boulder, CO: Westview Press, 1997.

Warren, Mary Anne. *Moral Status*. Oxford: Oxford University Press, 1997.

Warren, Virginia L. "Feminist Directions in Medical Ethics," in *Feminist Perspectives in Medical Ethics*, edited by Helen Berquaert Holmes and Laura M. Purdy. Bloomington: Indiana University Press, 1992.

Yuccas, Jamie. "USC Agrees to Pay More Than $1 Billion to Women Alleging Sex Abuse by Former Gynecologist." *CBS News*, March 26, 2021. www.cbsnews.com/news/george-Sexall-usc-settlement-sex-abuse-lawsuit/.

3

Privacy, Play, and the Digitalization of the University

Glen Miller and Cora Drozd

ABSTRACT

The digital age, which started with the invention of computers in the 1950s and their rapid, widespread adoption, coincided with advances in social sciences that brought to the fore a new set of privacy concerns. As the concept of privacy evolved into its twenty-first-century form, legislators, policymakers, judges, and scholars have developed concepts such as information self-determination, contextual integrity, and intellectual privacy to express the importance of context and who determines it. Context is a prerequisite for intellectual play—the ethical, social, and epistemic experimentation that is central to personal and intellectual development in the Western university.

Digitalization disrupts and often destroys contextual boundaries and the spaces for play that they create. Digital objects are quasipermanent, and they exist outside the control of their creator. Their creation and transmission, especially through social media, transforms one's potential audience, previously limited to those in the same place at the same time. The awareness that audience includes those on social media leads to curated acts and utterances and, perhaps counterintuitively, restricts opportunities for identity experimentation. The digital transformation requires a careful consideration of how university faculty and administrators assess the success of their institutions; it also calls for pedagogical design informed by the principles of information privacy and information self-determination, and pedagogical activities that enable students to develop a modern version of the "sensus communis" as part of "contextual literacy" so that they are able to flourish in a digitalized world.

Keywords: digital objects, digitalization, Hans-Georg Gadamer, identity, intellectual development, lateral surveillance, privacy law, profilicity

The increasing technological mediation of discourse that previously occurred in campus halls, quads, and classrooms has also transformed it. Much of what used to be communicated orally or in written comments on paper now is shared through technologies including learning management systems (e.g., Blackboard, Canvas), email, and, especially in the COVID-19 era, Zoom and Microsoft Teams meetings; student interaction outside the classroom—with peers and professors—has similarly moved more online than off and more asynchronous than before; and many faculty, whose work is now assessed in part with learning analytics, now are active participants in social networks such as Facebook and Twitter.

Strong economic forces are fueling these transformations. According to digital technology and educational policy expert Ben Williamson,

> Contemporary higher education (HE) is undergoing significant trans-
> formations as digital technologies, data analytics, metrics and
> other techniques of evaluation are advanced across the sector by
> governmental and businesses [sic] actors. Processes of marketiza-
> tion, privatization and consumerization of HE mean universities are
> increasingly focused on achieving market value through competition,
> performance ranking, consumer demand, and return on investment,
> often enabled by digital technologies and infrastructures of measure-
> ment. Data, metrics, performance rankings and accountability ratings
> have become driving "engines" of HE, cultivating powerful effects
> on how universities are evaluated and valued. (Williamson 2020, pp.
> 50–51, citations removed)

One measure of the inertia and magnitude of the economic forces at work is the existence, as of October 2021, of thirty-two EdTech "uni-corns"—start-ups valued over US$1 billion—collectively are worth $97 billion (HolonIQ 2021).

These technological transformations in the university mirror what has been happening in society, where mass and social media has changed how we get our news, how we meet and communicate with others, and how we work. The general trend is to adopt as much technology as we can as fast as we can to achieve efficiencies and conveniences without thinking of the long-term implications, including those having to do with privacy. These implications have particularly serious ethical, social, and epistemic implications in universities due to their institutional social role. Especially in the West, universities evolved to provide a space for individuals to explore (to play, in a sense) as they determine the projects they wish to pursue and what they wish to believe. In the past, this exploration took place in a situation of what could be called relative or practical privacy, as acts and utterances were confined to particular contexts, to those present at a particular time or those who had physical access to a paper. Digitalization alters these contextual barriers, usually lowering them and at least potentially allowing the redeployment of recordings of speech and acts in other contexts.

Making sense of these transformations of the space in which students and faculty work requires an interdisciplinary analysis that uses resources from legal scholarship, communication and media studies, science and technology studies, and sociological research, supplemented by insights from philosophy of technology literature. Our investigation begins with a brief historical review of major legal and conceptual innovations (such as information self-determination, contextual integrity, and intellectual privacy) that have occurred in the United States and Europe as digitalization has increasingly altered privacy expectations and constraints. These concepts undergird the social function of a Western university that gives its participants space to "play," to experiment with different ethical, social, and epistemic commitments as they imagine and begin to pursue various possible futures. Play is impacted by digitalization, and we sketch out the characteristics of this change with a focus on how it affects universities. We conclude with a few proposals that can help faculty and students better navigate the digitalized space and consider how to generate contexts that will help students and faculty develop in their thinking and as individuals, and also to reconsider how various contexts advance, impede, or even run counter to the aims of the university as an institution.

PRIVACY

Privacy is political in two related senses of the term. Historically, it has been political in the sense that it primarily had to do with relations between individuals and institutions—first governments (think the techno-totalitarian government in George Orwell's *1984*) and more recently private corporations—where significant economic and technical power asymmetries exist. Privacy also has a normative political sense: it has to do with what persons or entities *should do* when they have a capability to capture, use, or disseminate information about another person or entity.

Privacy law in the US can be traced back to Samuel Warren and Louis Brandeis's influential *Harvard Law Review* article that developed "the right to be left alone" (1890, p. 193) and privacy protection grounded in the Fourth Amendment to the Constitution, which protects individuals, especially their possessions, from unreasonable government searches and seizures. The European legal foundation for privacy is derived from Article 8 of the European Convention on Human Rights, drafted in 1950, which promises everyone a right to privacy in their personal life and in their correspondence and prohibits interference by public authorities except when faced with an overriding societal interest. The form and importance of privacy was transformed in the 1960s with the related developments of computers and the social sciences that made it possible to collect, analyze, and disseminate vast amounts of data from and through increasingly complex and interwoven socioeconomic networks. The ideas that shape privacy norms today have been developed by scholars, citizens, legislators, judges, and policymakers who have sought to address practical concerns as technology has advanced.

Since the 1960s, privacy concerns have focused on protecting data and freedom of expression. The United States Census Bureau, which had accumulated extensive data on citizens and pioneered many techniques to analyze this data, became a lightning rod in the debate about potential data misuse, abuse, and threats of emerging technologies. This debate resulted in the elevation of data protection to the congressional agenda. From 1965 to 1974, nearly fifty congressional hearings and reports examined privacy issues related to information and communication technologies and privacy, and in *Katz v. United States*, the Supreme Court expanded the scope of the Fourth Amendment to afford protection to personal communications when one has a "reasonable expectation of privacy," even when in a public space.

The idea of *information self-determination*, a term coined by Alan Westin, sought to balance interests in self-expression and freedom from surveillance while simultaneously expanding the scope of privacy to encompass more than a civil liberty that protects individuals from their government. Information self-determination is "the claim of individuals, groups, or institutions to determine for themselves when, how, and to what extent information about them is communicated to others" (Westin 1967, p. 7). In this framing, privacy possesses an empowering, participatory character that affects governmental and nongovernmental entities. This idea has been codified in policy and legal realms as a right of ownership in personal data, either because it is an extension of "personhood" (Radint 1982) or because it has economic value (Lessig 1999).

Similar ideas were enshrined in a patchwork of laws in various European countries that led to the European Union's 1995 Data Protection Directive. One of the most influential data privacy texts, the directive requires EU nations to protect the privacy of "data subjects" by requiring that personal data collection and use be limited to transparent and legitimate purposes, that the data be accurately maintained, and that the subject be anonymized when possible. The directive applies to corporations as well as governments. These protections are codified as rights in Article 8 of the 2009 EU Charter of Fundamental Rights, which states that everyone has the right to personal data protection, the right to access data collected on them, and the right to correct this data if it is in error. The European Union's 2016 General Data Protection Regulation expands citizen rights to include "the right to be forgotten," which is most closely linked to a European Union Court of Justice decision in *Google Spain*, in which a man sought to remove records of his insolvency from Google's search results. The court more or less reframed the right as a "right to practical obscurity" and granted this request, ruling that the individual's desire for the (accurate and public) information to recede in the public memory should override Google's right to publish it.

As *Google Spain* and the US privacy debates of the twentieth century showed, privacy is not an absolute right but rather one that must be balanced against other competing goods, such as freedoms of expression, association, observation, and security, for individuals as well as institutions, and, to a lesser degree, the efficiencies of contemporary life. In balancing these rights, the *contextual aspect* of privacy has become increasingly important. Controlling context is essential for vulnerability (boyd 2010), and our attention to context is present in what Helen Nissenbaum calls "personal information flows," which are governed by norms that depend on the data subject, the sender and recipient, the type of information being conveyed, and the medium of the message (Nissenbaum 2011, p. 33). Nissenbaum argues that people should aim to maintain and respect "contextual integrity," adherence to the norms of communication, even though internet technologies have removed conventional contextual boundaries. The sector-specific nature of many US privacy laws, such as the Health Insurance Portability and Accountability Act and the Family Educational Rights and Privacy Act, can be seen as attempts to develop context-dependent legislation.

Recent Fourth Amendment jurisprudence has aimed to determine the degree to which a speaker's context rights should be protected and whether information accumulated from various contexts and at different times should be analyzed piecemeal or as a collective. Third-party doctrine, developed in *United States v. Miller*, holds that an individual takes the risk that "in revealing his affairs to another, that the information will be conveyed by that person to the Government." Mosaic theory, developed in *United States v. Maynard* and *United States v. Jones*, proposes that some aggregations of information drawn from different social or temporal contexts may deserve Fourth Amendment protections even if none of the discrete elements on their own would.

Context awareness is relevant for the university as well. On the one hand, the development of a rich (nonproprietary) intellectual commonwealth depends on disclosure and broad dissemination of ideas. One of the enumerated powers that the United States Constitution gives the federal government is the ability to enact legislation on trademarks and copyrights, to provide an incentive for individuals to share their innovations and creations so that they are not kept secret or private. Modern universities fulfill the dual elements of this aim: in their research function, they create knowledge that is then disseminated widely through publications and their teaching function, contributing to the global intellectual commonwealth while also reducing advantages that members in private organizations have over those not in their organizations.

On the other hand, exploration and experimentation, fundamental to the development of a rich intellectual commons, usually flourish when individuals can act with limited visibility. Neil Richards (2008) has coined the term *intellectual privacy* to explain the dependence of the intellectual commons on individual privacy. Intellectual privacy includes elements such as freedom of thought and belief, time and space to think free from intrusion and surveillance, and confidentiality of communication. Some nascent ideas can only develop or develop best outside of the public gaze. Intellectual spaces that "insulate an individual's reflective facilities from certain forms of manipulation and coercion" are important for the development of ideas and character traits (Schwartz 2000, p. 1653). Put another way, they provide the space for intellectual play.

PLAY

The importance of play in the Western tradition can be traced back to Aristotle, who considered it a necessary and pleasant activity (2002,

Nicomachean Ethics X 6; 2012, *Politics* VIII 3). At first glance, this embrace may be surprising due to his focus on the development of virtue and goal-oriented work: play is an intentional deviation from these ends. It is a curious suspension of concerns that "deserve respect" (*spoudaios*) and ultimately lead to the eudaimonic life. Aristotle deems play important because, when pursued in right proportion, it provides a relief from the stresses of "serious" goal-oriented work that allows for its eventual success. One vacations so that one can work better or smarter.

Aristotle's limited treatment of play does not explain how this "medicine" operates and understates its importance in personal development, a shortcoming that has drawn attention from a number of recent theorists. Drawing from a metaphorical analysis, Hans-Georg Gadamer describes play—whether of people, animals, forces, light, or words—as a "to-and-fro movement that is not tied to any goal that would bring it to an end" (2004, p. 104). Even when limited to humans, play takes many forms: it includes some conversational exchanges, puzzle games such as solitaire or Yahtzee, sports games such as soccer and golf, and theatrical plays. All are activities constructed by humans that, at their best, entirely engage their participants: in good play, its possibilities and challenges can be said to "master the players" (Gadamer 2004, p. 106).

Play is a decontextualization from serious or actual circumstances and commitments, or, put slightly more precisely, it is an artificial and temporary recontextualization. Detachment from quotidian concerns and continual social and economic demands provides a new vantage point that yields a new perspective of one's self and situation, of those with whom one interacts, and of human existence in general, that is impossible when one is locked into particular commitments. Play also provides distance to view one's inherited prejudices and dominant cultural assumptions. It often spurs the imagination to generate different possibilities of action and being. As Gadamer puts it, "The being of all play is always self-realization, sheer fulfillment, energeia which has its telos within itself" (Gadamer 2004, p. 112). Much of life is play—that is, it is self-presentation, not self-preservation, and a human can be thought of as *homo ludens* (cf. Huizinga 1955) as much, if not more, than as *homo sapiens* or *homo faber*.

At least in the Western world, the university has been an institution that has historically provided space for intellectual play. To some extent, it is buffered from immediate market pressures felt by firms that produce commercial goods and services. Students are physically "decontextualized" from their childhood friends and institutions as they matriculate to campus. Ideally, they are exposed to a wide variety of ideas and people (both faculty and students) from many disciplines and backgrounds in their coursework and extracurricular activities. It is a chance for students to take distance from what they have largely imitated and inherited up to that point in their lives, to think critically before affirming or denying prior beliefs and commitments. The concept of academic freedom has been developed to protect the right of faculty to pursue interesting lines of research regardless of their commercial appeal or political popularity and to teach as they see fit. Along the same vein, the term *academic exercise*, sometimes used as a pejorative by those in the business world, expresses the sense of freedom for play that is possible for students in their coursework. At least in the ideal, student and faculty work is judged based on quality and creativity of the research and the development of ideas rather than on how they align with dominant social opinions or even those of the instructor in the classroom or the editor of a journal or book series.

The freedom to play in the university arose in part due to the construction of manifold and distinct contexts for expression and action. Each course is its own context, guided by the instructor but, at least for the liberal arts, also shaped through the interactions between faculty and students and between students. The context persists for a few months (a quarter or a semester) before a new set of courses and contexts is constructed. Departments are usually mostly self-governing, and their members often employ a variety of pedagogical approaches and pursue diverse research projects, even under the same disciplinary banner. For better or worse, most academic publications, which have a form of permanence, and conference presentations are given to small audiences and attract minimal attention from those not in one's field, which allows risk-taking and catalyzes new ideas there is a practical obscurity that has resulted in practical intellectual privacy which is further encouraged by tenure protections. Students have the ability to choose their majors and electives, and they can participate in any of a multitude of student groups that operate independently, with different objectives and memberships, or they can start new ones.

These conditions provide the opportunity for students to "try on" different identities or personalities in different activities, to imagine and to start to pursue a variety of different futures (and, relatedly, to reject others). Taking on various forms of playfulness in various settings contributes to the reflective determination of identity, defined as asking and answering "questions about how I am going to live my life which touch on the issue of what kind of life is worth living, or what kind of life would fulfill the promise implicit in my particular talents, or the demands incumbent on someone with my endowment, or of what constitutes a rich, meaningful life—as against one concerned with secondary matters or trivia" (Taylor 1989, p. 14).

There is no one set of questions that one can pose or answers that one can find: the problem is underdetermined, as a mathematician or an engineer would say, and the process of finding these answers is iterative, unfolding as an individual's drive, social responsibilities and possibilities, and station in life change over time.

Contextualization meant that students could run multiple experiments simultaneously: one could be an active member of student groups supporting socialism while developing arguments against it in their papers for economics or political philosophy courses, and one could be the "devil's advocate" in an organization of atheists. One can play in various ways at the university: one kind of play is the exchange of conversational banter, which is often clever and collegial, pleasant yet not necessarily contributing directly to any task at hand. Another is trying to improve one's skills or master some task, such as public speaking or designing heat exchangers. In this way it is similar to practicing and playing basketball (especially if one is not aiming to be a professional). Play in the form of a theater takes on a unique form, where one takes on a disguise and participation is judged according to how well one morphs into a character that one did not script, a role usually unrelated to one's identity off the stage. "A person who plays such a game denies, to all appearances, continuity with himself. But in truth that means that he holds on to this continuity with himself for himself and only withholds it from those before whom he is acting" (Gadamer 2004, p. 111). Playing in different "games," as it were, provides varying levels of distance and reflective insight.

The role of the audience is the last aspect of play that is worthy of attention. Gadamer notes that in some play "openness to the spectator is part of the closedness of the play" (2004, p. 109). This openness can be seen clearly when theatrical players break down the "fourth wall" and communicate directly with an audience. It is also seen in the transition from Olympic wrestling to professional wrestling, where crowd engagement is essential. In the past, one's audience was almost entirely those present, in the same social and temporal context, for an event: a classroom setting served as a distinct audience composed of relatively autonomous individuals, as did an academic conference.

Prior to the widespread adoption of digital technologies, spaces for play were bounded by time, place, and community. These contextual elements provided the interpretative grounding for experience and discourse—how to make sense of the people and ideas that are exchanged. The space of play has been radically changed in the last twenty years due to digitalization, which alters and often obliterates context. A life that has an online component no longer has discrete contexts. It is "radically heterogeneous," in a sense a "totality of experience" (Nissenbaum 2011, p. 38, italics removed).

DIGITALIZATION AND THE UNIVERSITY

Digital technologies are not the first technology to affect spatial, temporal, and social continuities—writing technologies famously drew Socrates's ire in the *Phaedrus*—but their ubiquity and power are especially suited to disrupt them. Albert Borgmann (2009) has called these disruptions *commodification*, which often accompanies the more common meaning of the term, bringing something into the market that previously was not, in order to improve convenience and availability. Put in contemporary terms, digital objects "scale well" and can be monetized. While not all commodification is problematic, commodification explains what is lost in certain activities when they are decontextualized—perhaps one loses focus on the task at hand, concern for another, or a sense of how the present fits into the "grand scheme of things"—a concern that is multiplied when almost everything is decontextualized.

Digitalizing interactions in the university, for example, in a student discussion board or on a Zoom or Teams meeting, leaves them prone to decontextualization. In some ways, this shift is not bad: students can contribute to discussion boards when they have energy and have had time to think through their comments, not just when they are physically in the classroom. But this upside comes with a downside: every digital utterance, either orally in classroom discussions or in written form, can be reappropriated by anyone who has access to it whenever they choose. This mode of distributed data collection and dissemination has been called "coveillance" (Mann, Nolan, and Wellman 2003, p. 338) or "lateral surveillance" (Andrejevic 2005, p. 481), as there is no power differential between the individual surveilling and the individual being surveilled, unlike the top-down surveillance by governments or corporations that originally drew legislative and judicial concern in the United States.

In the terminology of Jean-Gabriel Ganascia, these forms of observation are part of "sousveillance," a more general term that embodies all forms of observation, whether it be downward, upward, or lateral, that arises when "everybody is able to take pictures and record the sounds of everyone else and then disseminate them freely on the

Internet" (2010, p. 3). Most regulations and laws were constructed to address questions of top-down surveillance—for example, the United States Family Educational Rights and Privacy Act prevents instructors and staff from disclosing information about student educational records—and do not address these new concerns.

Digitalized objects also become part of "social memory" that has a technological dimension. Human memory has primary retention—perceptions I experience remain present in mind, usually from the recent past—and secondary retention, what I remember experiencing, a recollection. These retentions are imperfect, singular, corruptible over time, and contextualized. Technology makes possible "artificial memory," which is reproducible, long-lasting, and decontextualized, characteristics taken to an extreme in their digital form, called "tertiary retention" by Bernard Stiegler (1998).

The Janus-face of retention is protention, which follows a similar structure but is directed toward the future rather than the past. Primary protention is what we anticipate in the immediate, whereas secondary protention is what we think will happen a little later. (To use one of Stiegler's examples, think about a song: one can often unthinkingly anticipate the next note or two, the primary sense, but one can also imagine how the song would change the mood of a situation, the secondary sense.) Yuk Hui rightly argues that tertiary protention becomes increasingly important in a digitalized space. Whereas interests, desires, and ideas were previously largely the product of an individual's imagination, supplemented by a smaller group of influencers and experiences, they are now shaped by (and often determined by) digital technology. More frequently, technology determines the song that I am listening to and the ones I will know.

As Hui points out, "(1) Tertiary protention tends to depend on tertiary retention, for example, the relations given by digital objects, those traces we have left, such as pictures, videos, or geolocations; and (2) orientation becomes more and more an algorithmic process that analyzes and produces relations to pave the way for the experience of the next now or the immediate future" (2016, pp. 221–222). As noted above, the digitalization of the university provides more tertiary retention resources. Orientation obviously affects identity, most clearly in terms of what one attends to and pursues.

Digitalization also allows for efficiency and scale of dissemination never seen before. The printing press allowed for a message to be reproduced reasonably efficiently; mass media provided a few-to-many mode of one-way information transfer in which a few voices were amplified using a megaphone, a model that persisted with Web 1.0.

But with the advent of Web 2.0, with social media users serving as both producers and consumers of information, a many-to-many information ecology has evolved, one where the boundaries between media streams are easy to cross.

Digitalization also causes dual temporal transformations. Its first aspect is well known: now almost all communication occurs in "real time." The acceleration of exchanges between individuals increases the risk of reciprocal escalations. As René Girard notes, there is a reason that "justice is slow, and 'drags along' in both divorce and the most odious criminal cases. The slowness, which does not seem justified on the surface, is entirely reasonable from an anthropological point of view: it serves as a brake on reprisals, it is a crucial 'friction' that slows down relations, thereby preventing them from degenerating into reciprocity. . . . Life is livable only if reciprocity does not appear" (2010, pp. 60–61). Instantaneous communication, when compounded with human awkwardness, self-interest, and other moral and communicative imperfections, as well as spatial separation of one's interlocutors, increases the risk of reciprocity.

The second temporal transformation arises due to the perfection of tertiary retention, which stands in contrast to the finitude of human memory. With some exceptions, human memory degrades over time: secondary retention is usually less complete and perfect than primary retention. Moreover, most affective responses weaken over time. An apparent slight can become humorous in retrospect; one can be unsure of exactly what was said, and it could provide the fodder for another conversation (part of the "processing mechanism," as it were) or simply be forgotten. With tertiary retention, screen-based digitalized experiences can always be felt again, in the same manner as they originally were (e.g., seeing an awkward slight on the same social network platform). Fewer events are only experienced immediately by those present: more are recorded by some devices, making them prone to decontextualization, and many events occur only in a digitalized space. Tertiary retention of digitalized impressions effectively erases the benefits of temporal distance: there is no "right to be forgotten" when social memory is constructed by everyone.

For students, these technological transformations have a number of negative consequences. One, they are creating a narrative history constructed by their interactions in various spheres that consists of words and deeds from various contexts, some given intentionally, others not; it is assembled outside of their control; and it has a quasipermanent character. It is easy to see how prudence leads to reticence in classroom or political discussions: to protect against potential reputational harm, losing job opportunities because of "cybervetting," unintentionally offending others due to ignorance, and so on.

But to the degree that the university depends on an open discussion of ideas, especially on sensitive topics, and that individual development also depends on them, these trends are problematic and likely will simply lead to the suppression of unpopular viewpoints or the migration of extreme (or nonmainstream) ideas to niche platforms. Moreover, the quasipermanent character of digitalization limits the freedom of students to experiment with different identities and characteristics as they seek to make sense of who they are, who they want their friends to be, and what they want to pursue when they leave the academy.

Such concerns increasingly shape identity formation and experimentation, which had previously been connected to two different sources: sincerity and authenticity. Guided by sincerity, frequently associated with Eastern cultures and the premodern West, one's identity is determined by one's social roles. Who I am depends on my place in various social systems, especially the family, and by how well I fulfill the expectations that follow from my roles. Goodness is measured by aligning one's will with social expectations. In the modern and individualistic West, authenticity is often considered the definitive principle of identity. It arises from the unique expression of the self. Goodness is measured in terms of self-determination, based on one's desires, at a critical distance from, if not separated from, social forces and expectations. (It is worth noting that "authentic" self-presentation is always already attuned to social reception and responses, in a way even more than one who aims to be "sincere.")

Digitalization and social media create a novel force that affects identity development that has been described as "profilicity" by Hans-Georg Moeller and Paul J. D'Ambrosio (2018). They draw from systems theorist Nicholas Luhmann's insight into the elevation of "second-order observation" as a fundamental characteristic of modernity (2013, p. 114): not only does one observe, but one observes the observers and the observations. Applied to the digital ecosystem, profilicity explains the elevation of what others say about something that they observed (book reviews, movie and teacher ratings, hotel and restaurant ratings) over one's direct experience and judgment (of the book, movie, teacher, hotel, or restaurant). Identity is developed through one's "profile" curated for others. They define the core aspect of profilicity as "(a) distinctness or visibility resulting in *quantitative attention*, (b) a certain 'coolness,' or other forms of 'excellence' resulting in *qualitative acclaim* and (c) coherence with generally expected ethical expectations in a given context (e.g. political, academic or aesthetic) resulting in *normative approval*. The triple-A presentation of identity (i.e., those achieving attention, acclaim and approval) is capable of generating exhibition value" (Moeller and D'Ambrosio 2018, p. 587). Moeller and D'Ambrosio note that acts and utterances are increasingly intended for a mass audience, and those that do not find one have a minimal existence, like the tree that falls in the forest that no observer hears. Performing for the mass audience is the social media version of breaking down the "fourth wall" of play.

While Hui emphasizes how algorithms and one's digital footprint influence one's choices in his development of tertiary protension, profilicity adds another aspect to what one should imagine or anticipate. The connection between retension and protension takes on its unique form in what Facebook founding president Sean Parker calls "social validation feedback loops," in which one's course of action is shaped by feedback (quantitative, qualitative, and normative) received for previous acts and what one has observed others experience for similar acts. To at least some extent, one's acts and utterances are targeted and curated as though one were a media publisher, seeking to draw attention from one's friends and acquaintances, perhaps one's aspirational social class, and from the general public, whose names do not matter but who provide the quantitative juice in terms of views or likes to draw more attention in the immediate future, but especially in the longer term, while at the same time avoiding most negative or critical attention.

The novelty of the form of awareness of the anticipation of the general public's response, as guided by the algorithms that run social media, found in social media can be understood by comparing it to the idea of the *sensus communis* ("common" or communal sense) as it developed in the humanistic tradition. No matter how developed and extensive social sciences may be, they do not replace the importance of developing the virtues of *prudentia* and *eloquentia* (knowing and speaking well on what is true and beautiful, attuned to the response of one's audience). In this tradition, training in the *sensus communis* "the most important thing in education," for this sense "gives human will its direction" and "is of decisive importance for living" (Gadamer 2004, pp. 18–19).

CONCLUSION

For better or worse, the university is becoming digitalized: it has entered into modernity, in Luhmann's sense of the term, fueled by private and public resources. The transformations resulting from the digitalization of the university are reason to reconsider, on the one hand, the push toward quantification, efficiency, and private-public partnership intellectual property production that seems to be driving much of higher education and its technology, and, on the other hand, the way that information self-determination, contextual integrity, intellectual privacy, and play manifest themselves in the activities of faculty and students.

The former is a complicated web of issues that requires consideration on the part of administrators, faculty, and, for public universities, legislators, to consider what should be measured, what cannot be measured with reasonable accuracy, and what cannot be measured at all. Doing so requires "matching the use of numbers with dialogue about the means of their construction" (Frodeman, Holbrook, and Barr 2012, p. 313), an activity always at risk of being short-circuited because its success is hard to quantify and inefficient. At the same time, public-private partnerships, especially in science, technology, and engineering, deserve increased scrutiny, as contributions to balance sheets and annual income statements should be weighed against any impediment to the "creative destruction" of intellectual advantage that arises from the time or resources that they consume (cf. Fuller 2009, p. 4) and, from a big picture, whether they contribute to or detract from the social aims of the university.

The latter (concerns about information self-determination, contextual integrity, intellectual privacy, and play) is less complicated but has less "leverage," in the contemporary vernacular, as it falls within the pedagogical control of faculty. Attending to these concerns opens up a number of opportunities for faculty and students, while at the same time it explains why some pedagogical activities will no longer be effective. For faculty, the blurring of contexts means that the "practical obscurity" that had obtained in the past no longer does. Students have become more apprehensive to share beliefs that differ from what they believe are socially favored, judging reputational risks to outweigh the benefits of what they and their peers may gain from discourse.

Students are well aware of "cancel culture" and know that their reputations can be affected by powerful media entities, which they observed in the coverage of Covington Catholic High School students interacting with Native American activists at Donald J. Trump's inauguration, and the treatment of former New Orleans Saints quarterback Drew Brees, someone with far more social power than they possess, when he voiced his interpretation of the American flag. Pedagogical activities that depend on a robust discussion of diverse ideas should be designed to respect intellectual privacy.

One approach is to have students agree to something like the Chatham House Rule, which allows participants to discuss the ideas in various contexts as long as the identity of the speaker cannot be discerned. It is worth considering whether the benefits of using systems or frameworks that allow discussions to be made anonymously, of developing assignments that will only be shared with the instructor, and of assigning roles that ask students to determine the best possible argument for a position, regardless of whether it matches their beliefs (an example of Gadamer's theatrical version of play), outweigh their harms.

At the same time, the university (especially the humanities) seems like the perfect spot for students to think about what is shaping their beliefs, statements, and acts. Is their identity and orientation determined almost solely by profilicity, making one into a slave to algorithms and social response, rather than as a blend of it with sincerity or authenticity? Is this who they wish to be? Are they taking advantage of their time at the university to explore and experiment, to play, as it were, and to meet others that have different beliefs? Have they thought about what tact, respect, dignity, friendship, and courage entail in an increasingly digitalized world?

Over the last few years, there has been a strong push for informational literacy to help students judge the quality of sources, especially those found online. A parallel push toward what could be called contextual literacy seems as important in helping students thoughtfully determine and pursue their goals: it would require an understanding of the various forces that determine identity, including the *sensus communis*. Instructors may also wish to consider how they can help their students intervene in public discourse and help them find appropriate contexts to do so: students today are more accustomed to public presentation than previous generations were. Perhaps information privacy and information self-determination should become pedagogical design principles.

Undergraduate students often think in terms of diplomas and résumés. Imagine a graduation ceremony in which a student receives, along with their diploma for their academic efforts, a thumb drive that includes their digital footprint as well as their reflection on how their identity has been shaped and transformed during their time on campus. This expansion would effectively create a curriculum vitae appropriate to the digital age, and, if universities have adapted to the digital age by crafting new places for intellectual play, would be a mosaic that evokes pride for students.

ACKNOWLEDGMENTS

We thank Thomas Reagor for sharing creative insights and ideas from his research, which significantly improved this chapter. The chapter also benefited from the presentation and discussion of earlier drafts at the 2021 conferences of the Society for Philosophy and Technology and the Society for Ethics Across the Curriculum.

REFERENCES

Andrejevic, Mark. (2005). "The Work of Watching One Another: Lateral Surveillance, Risk, and Governance." *Surveillance and Society* 2(4): 479–497.

Aristotle. (2002). *Nicomachean Ethics*. Translated by Joe Sachs. Newburyport, MA: Focus.

Aristotle. (2012). *Politics*. Translated by Joe Sachs. Newburyport, MA: Focus.

Borgmann, Albert. (2009). *Real American Ethics*. Chicago: University of Chicago Press.

boyd, danah. (2010). "Privacy and Publicity in the Context of Big Data." Speech presented at WWW2010, Raleigh, North Carolina, April 29. Available at www.danah.org/papers/talks/2010/WWW2010.html.

Frodeman, Robert, J. Britt Holbrook, and Kelli Barr. (2012). "The University, Metrics, and the Good Life." In Philip Brey, Adam Briggle, and Edward Spence's (eds.), *The Good Life in a Technological Age*, pp. 307–315. New York: Routledge.

Fuller, Steve. (2009). *The Sociology of Intellectual Life*. London: Sage.

Gadamer, Hans-Georg. (2004). *Truth and Method*. 2nd revised edition. New York: Continuum.

Ganascia, Jean-Gabriel. (2010). "The Generalized Sousveillance Society." *Social Science Information* 49(3): 1–19. doi: 10.1177/0539018410371027.

Girard, René. (2010). *Battling to the End: Conversations with Benoit Chantre*. East Lansing: Michigan State University Press.

HolonIQ. (2021). "Global EdTech Unicorns." www.holoniq.com/edtech-unicorns/. (Accessed October 15, 2021.)

Hui, Yuk. (2016). *On the Existence of Digital Objects*. Minneapolis: University of Minnesota Press.

Huizinga, Johan. (1955). *Homo Ludens: A Study of the Play-Element in Culture*. Boston: Beacon.

Lessig, Larry. (1999). *Code and Other Laws of Cyberspace*. New York: Basic Books.

Luhmann, Nicholas. (2013). *Introduction to Systems Theory*. Translated by Peter Gilgen. Cambridge: Polity.

Mann, Steve, Jason Nolan, and Barry Wellman. (2003). "Sousveillance: Inventing and Using Wearable Computing Devices for Data Collection in Surveillance Environments." *Surveillance and Society* 1(3): 331–355.

Moeller, Hans-Georg, and Paul D'Ambrosio. (2018). "Sincerity, Authenticity, and Profilicity: Notes on the Problem, a Vocabulary and a History of Identity." *Philosophy and Social Criticism* 45(5): 575–596.

Nissenbaum, Helen. (2011). "A Contextual Approach to Privacy Online." *Daedalus* 140(4): 32–48.

Orwell, George. (1977). *1984*. New York: Signet.

Plato. (1999). *Phaedrus*. Translated by Benjamin Jewett. Champaign, IL: Project Gutenberg.

Radint, Margaret Jane. (1982). "Property and Personhood." *Stanford Law Review* 34(5): 957–1015.

Regan, Priscilla M. (1995). *Legislating Privacy: Technology, Social Values, and Public Policy*. Chapel Hill: University of North Carolina Press.

Richards, Neil M. (2008). "Intellectual Privacy." *Texas Law Review* 87, 387–445.

Schwartz, Paul M. (2000). "Privacy and Democracy in Cyberspace." *SSRN Electronic Journal*. https://doi.org/10.2139/ssrn.205449.

Stiegler, Bernard. (1998). *Technics and Time, 1: The Fault of Epimetheus*. Stanford, CA: Stanford University Press.

Taylor, Charles. (1989). *Sources of the Self: Making of the Modern Identity*. Cambridge, MA: Harvard University Press.

Warren, Samuel D., and Louis Brandeis. (1890). "The Right to Privacy." *Harvard Law Review 193*: 213–214.

Westin, Alan F. (1967). *Privacy and Freedom*. New York: Atheneum.

Williamson, Ben. (2020). "Making Markets through Digital Platforms: Pearson, Edu-business, and the (E)valuation of Higher Education." *Critical Studies in Education*, 62(1): 50–66. https://doi.org/10.1080/17508487.2020.1737556.

Part II

THE COMMUNITY

4

Shared Governance in Higher Education

Darin Dockstader, Matthew Mahrt, and Charles Milne

ABSTRACT

This chapter deals with some broad issues about the role of shared governance in higher education and a case study of one institution's challenges and progress in creating an explicitly defined shared governance policy through the faculty senate democratic process. Part 1 takes a detailed look at the shared governance needs of different kinds of institutions. Shared governance is not typically a one-size-fits-all enterprise, but there are common elements tied to institutional success. Part 2 examines the consequentialist and deontological ethical foundations for true shared governance. These are centered around the common elements tied to institutional success in part 1. Part 2 primarily focuses on potential, but predictable, failures of those elements of shared governance. We learn something important about shared governance practices when we take a careful look at where these can go wrong. Part 3 is a look at the history of shared governance at the College of Southern Nevada. It examines some recent crises in the college's shared governance practices, obstacles faced, and lessons learned. It also tells the ongoing story of attempts to fix that existing institutional problem.

Keywords: administration, categorical imperative, College of Southern Nevada, consequentialist ethics, democratic processes, deontological ethics, faculty senate, Kant, shared governance, strategic planning

PART 1: ACHIEVING AN INSTITUTIONAL MISSION
THROUGH SHARED GOVERNANCE

Incredible diversity exists among American higher education institutions. There are large, prestigious universities with graduate programs and a vibrant research emphasis (Yale, Harvard, Princeton, etc.), state universities with a strong research emphasis and a graduate school, smaller universities and colleges that emphasize undergraduate education with limited research, and community colleges with an emphasis on two-year degrees and transfer to universities in addition to awarding a small number of four-year degrees. The emphasis of these latter institutions is teaching and trade education. Smaller community colleges have primarily two-year degrees and focus on transfer with a heavier emphasis on trade education and certificates. Finally, there are numerous smaller, often private trade schools that specialize in certificates with some two-year degrees.

All these institutions of higher education have the same goal—success in their mission. They have the same perceived problems—finances, governing boards, faculty, administration, students, facilities, staff, and so on. Most have a governing board with fiduciary responsibility for the institution delegating the daily responsibility for the institution to a president, who may, in turn, delegate some responsibility to members of the administration. Even in areas where faculty have primary responsibility (i.e., curriculum, subject matter, methods of instruction, tenure, faculty status), the president has the final decision provided there are compelling reasons (AAUP, 1966, 1990).

Faculty, more numerous than administrators, are tasked with teaching and research. Faculty includes full-time, tenured, nontenured, part-time, and various types of instructors and researchers. The staff carry out the institution's decisions and policies and interface with students. Among the students are individuals taking enrichment courses and degree-seeking part-time and full-time undergraduates and graduates. Students should be involved to some degree in discussions of institutional policy and operation (AAUP, 1966, 1990).

Stoessel (2013) presents a thorough description of the roles of the governing board, president, and faculty in shared governance. Unions also support this view. The American Federation of Teachers (AFT, 2002) states, "We believe that all college and university employees—top tenured faculty, junior faculty, temporary and part-time/adjunct faculty, graduate teaching and research assistants, professional staff with and without faculty rank, the classified and support staff that keep the educational enterprise going—should have a guaranteed voice in decision-making and a role in shaping policy in the area of their expertise." The idea of including others (alumni, businesses, parents, legislators, etc.) has been broached (Keller, 2004) but has led to problems (Heaney, 2010).

A properly crafted mission should be the goal for every institution, regardless of the type. The mission is used to formulate a periodically revised strategic plan that guides the institution and its decisions. Its success depends on the healthy interaction—which we would call shared governance—of the various individuals in light of their positions. Every institution has governance and decision-making, some good and some bad, but not all constitute effective *shared* governance. The responsibility for every major decision lies with the administration in general and the president specifically. Shared governance does not alter this fact.

Decision-making is strengthened if the various groups of employees and students have input into those major decisions. One administrator wrote, "We are in the business of education, however, and one of the best things about working in higher education is that one's colleagues are intelligent, thoughtful, creative people" (Behr, 2016).

The number of faculty usually greatly outnumber the administrators at an institution, and most faculty sincerely care about the institution. The staff may also care about the institution and outnumber the administrators. Often, staff are frontline workers who must carry out the decisions of the faculty and/or the administration with the students and should have input into those decisions. If unions are established at the institution, their inclusion in shared governance must be considered.

We propose that shared governance is giving a guaranteed voice to the various groups—employees, unions, and students—to speak to the major decisions made at an institution (Bergan, 2004). That input can vary with the nature of the decision. Groups should have a larger input into the decisions if they have responsibility for the area, such as faculty and the curriculum. This approach capitalizes on the expertise within the entire organization.

There is no widely accepted definition of shared governance. Traditionally, it has been described as the set of practices or rules that enable administrators, faculty, staff, and often students to participate in important decisions concerning the operation of the institution (AFT, 2002). Such rules and practices for that input and decision-making are often codified in a shared governance *policy*. Shared governance differs substantially among universities and community colleges, with the faculty and administration having distinct areas of authority and decision-making.

Effective shared governance is vital to the success of every institution of higher education. True shared governance entails a participatory process rooted in long-held principles of collegiality and cooperation. It is currently threatened by the growing view of education as a business (Smith, 2015) and by the explosion of online courses and institutions. Smith (2015) presents a concept of faculty governance in matters of curriculum, tenure, research, and so on that fits nicely into the participatory model of shared governance.

However, even with these matters of primarily faculty responsibility, shared governance should be practiced with a responsible administrator having the final say. Bahls (2014) presents four different models of shared governance—as equal rights, as consultation, as rules of engagement, or as a system of aligning priorities. The model presented is like the final one on the list—shared governance as a system of aligning priorities. A number of public and private institutions function this way (AGB, 2016).

The administration bears the responsibility for decisions made and, when the various employee groups know they have significant input into those decisions, they will generally support them. This input must occur early in the decision-making process to be effective shared governance. Substantial input by diverse faculty and staff will shape the decision in ways that would be missing had the administration made the decision without broad shared governance input. Soliciting wide input into decisions will also improve institution morale.

Institutions where the administration makes decisions without faculty or staff input will eventually falter or be radically changed by the board. One of the present authors experienced such an institution, which closed over a decade ago. Another model of not quite *shared* governance is the administration consulting faculty as a mere obligation, even if it affects the academic program (Bahls, 2014, March/April).

There are serious pitfalls and difficulties in developing and sustaining effective shared governance. A lack of understanding of what is shared governance is a serious problem, along with a lack of trust at the institution. A dictatorial administration or one that does not involve substantial input in the decision-making process makes achieving shared governance difficult. A faculty who thinks they should make the decisions is also a hinderance to developing shared governance. Transparency is vital. Progress can only be made when participants know what others think. A reluctant administration that does not trust the employees to provide valuable input will not realize successful shared governance.

A governing board whose members have no experience in higher education can disrupt an institution's shared governance (Scott, 2020). The presence of a substantial number of individuals who transitioned to higher education from business or industry will make the development of effective shared governance more difficult (Waldman, 2019). Faculty unions present difficulties if the union and the faculty senate do not limit their domains of input to issues of compensation, benefits, and workload and to traditional governance issues like curriculum and faculty appointments, respectively (AGB, 2017). If these difficulties exist, the institution should get a consensus of what shared governance is and how to achieve that at their institution from where they are now.

Regardless of the stimulus for the institution-wide discussion of shared governance, there is an opportunity for the institution to consider where they are and what shared governance consists of. We suggest that faculty with tenure lead the process of developing shared governance. Faculty can bring the staff and unions into the discussion and may already be tasked with writing many policies at the institution. If the administration leads the process to develop shared governance, some of the different voices at the institution may be ignored or muted. Governing boards can start the process and provide a framework and description of shared governance, but they should let the individual institutions develop their own shared governance process.

There are numerous beneficial publications on shared governance and examples of shared governance policies on the web pages of various institutions. These shared governance policies reveal an amazing variety of methods to achieve shared governance. Some policies describe the task of numerous committees and their membership, the flow of information, and who makes the decisions but do not always provide the desired shared governance. Others have a framework for shared governance and enjoy an institution-wide commitment to shared governance that ensures it is accomplished.

Several shared governance policies and descriptions of processes used to achieve shared governance are listed in the appendix and references. We estimate that only one out of five American community colleges and universities have a shared governance policy describing its importance and a process for carrying it out in the institution. Some only have a shared governance statement indicating that shared governance is a priority, with a mention of a faculty senate, but there is no process or description of how shared governance is to be carried out.

After examining these shared governance models, it is easy to conclude that no two are alike. Different institutions achieve effective shared governance in different ways. Leach (2008) states that "there is little consensus nationally about what form of shared governance works best." Each institution must start where they are and seek a process that they believe will accomplish shared governance.

One caution, given the variety of shared governance models in higher education, is to avoid merely copying the shared governance approach of another institution. An institution can learn from other models, but every shared governance needs to be homegrown to a large extent (Minor, 2003). The entire institution needs to determine what shared governance is for them. They need to examine how decisions are currently made and brainstorm how significant input can occur into the major decisions made at the institution. These discussions need to be made with representatives of all the various groups present. Discussion without representation by a certain employee group will result in a policy without the support of that group.

At this point, each institution is on their own to write a policy accepted by all that allows input into the major decisions, with the ultimate responsibility for the decision made by the administration. Regardless of the method by which shared governance occurs, it needs to be consistently applied, decisions must be made in a timely manner, and it must be periodically examined and changed to improve the shared governance.

To achieve true shared governance, it is vital that there is mutual trust between the various groups. Even with guarded mutual trust, effective shared governance can be realized. If the various employee groups believe they have the opportunity for input into the decisions and the administration knows they make the ultimate decision and honestly consider the input received, success will be realized. For continued shared governance at an institution, trust needs to grow, commitment to the process must be accepted by all, transparency is vital, and respect must be present. No institution gets it right the first time. Every shared governance policy should have a process to review the past year's shared governance activities by a committee with broad representation which can suggest changes, if necessary, to improve the shared governance.

Good working relationships must be developed. Participants in shared governance should be chosen by the group they represent and must be given the information they need and the time to participate. Including all groups on campus in discussions (fostering inclusiveness) is vital to successful shared governance. Kezar and Holcombe (2017) stress the importance of developing shared leadership by identifying individuals with relevant expertise to develop multiple perspectives on issues that will be considered in shared governance. Shared leadership produces task forces or cross-functional teams to address issues as they occur. Reliable shared governance requires continuous, intentional effort and diligence by all involved to have shared governance function well and persist at an institution (AGB, 2017).

Maintaining excellent shared governance is being challenged on many fronts. Reduced budgets for higher education institutions is a serious problem that leads to shifting teaching to part-time faculty and reduced tenured faculty (McNaughton, 2016). National policy directives, such as increasing graduation rates, puts pressure from many directions on higher education institutions (Claxton-Freeman, 2015). Viewing higher education as a business challenges shared governance in colleges and universities (Scott, 2020). Increased unionization can reduce the involvement of the faculty senate in shared governance (Leach, 2008).

Governing boards have exerted more control of institutions, reducing the effectiveness of shared governance (Smith, 2015). In the early parts of the nineteenth century, community colleges were regarded as qualitatively different from universities and not truly part of higher education. A recurrence of such views would threaten shared governance (Smith, 2015). Increasing numbers of faculty who do not understand shared governance and do not participate weakens shared governance (Waldman, 2019). Wholly online institutions, for-profit universities and colleges, fewer tenure-track positions, and the lack of support for shared governance by accrediting bodies threaten shared governance in those institutions (AFT, 2002). The erosion of faculty participation and the lack of recognition of those participating in shared governance is also a threat to shared governance (AGB, 2017). Board members who do not understand the need for shared governance can reduce the effectiveness of shared governance (AGB, 2017). Administrators who have never been faculty, but are familiar with businesses, can run the institution like a manager and, thereby, limit shared governance (Hass, 2020).

Vibrant shared governance has been shown to help institutions shift in response to emergencies better than those without shared governance (Rosenberg, 2014). It is also wise to rely on decisions made by representative rather than direct democracy, with representatives from all the employee groups; ensure that an elected faculty member serves on the president's senior staff; and provide opportunities for faculty to learn about all aspects of the institution (Rosenberg, 2014).

By contrast, divided governance, where faculty focus on the curriculum while the administration works on virtually all other matters, can result in a situation of little collaboration and leave the institution floundering (Rosenberg, 2014).

To summarize, effective shared governance provides many benefits, including improved morale in those working at the institution. Decisions made with institution-wide input will often have novel, ingenious components and employ multiple perspectives. Those decisions will improve the institution, and the institution will more likely succeed in accomplishing its mission, even in the face of emergencies.

Another important benefit is the improvement of relationships between the groups at the institution. No longer will the groups think only about their own members. They will also think about the institution. Fighting and strained relationships should be reduced, and trust of others will spread throughout the institution. A one-team atmosphere will develop at the institution. Individuals in one employee group will better understand those in different employee groups as they work cooperatively. Individuals at an institution with effective shared governance will be freer to express concerns and questions. Although involving more individuals collaboratively slows down the decision-making process, it provides a more thorough discussion.

Increased involvement of faculty in shared governance will reduce faculty and staff apathy about the decision-making process. In her testimonies to working shared governance, Chancellor Nancy Zimpher noted that shared governance was the driver for their greatest accomplishments (Zimpher, 2012, 2017). An institution is able to accomplish its mission in a spectacular fashion if everyone works together.

How can an institution determine if they have achieved effective shared governance? Those at the institution will know by the changes it produces. Decisions will be made with institution-wide support. Employees will know they had a say in the decision. When crises arise, such as budget cuts or problems with accreditation, the institution will work together to solve the problems. Morale will improve, and periodic institutional climate surveys, like the PACE survey, will be able to reveal change in several metrics. Finally, accreditation teams will mention the effective shared governance and exceptional success in accomplishing the institutional mission in their reports. As Trakman (2008, Page 77) notes, "'Good' university governance also does not simply happen. It is usually the product of painstaking effort to arrive at suitable governance structures, protocols and processes. 'Good' governance is also about timing and judgement: it requires boards of governors to recognize when a governance model is not working, why and how to repair it. Ultimately, governance models are created by people to govern people. They are only as good as they who devise and apply them, as well as those who live by them."

PART 2: ETHICAL FOUNDATIONS OF
TRUE SHARED GOVERNANCE

Part 1 of this chapter looked at a broad range of different kinds of higher education institutions and a broad range of challenges to shared governance within those institutions. The conclusion was that there is no one-size-fits-all model for shared governance. The shared governance needs of one institution will not likely be the same as the needs of another institution. But one shared thread was emphasized. That is the need for shared participation and trust between institutional stakeholders in the early stages of institutional decision-making through to the conclusion and implementation of those decisions.

True shared governance is not just one element of an institution sharing its decisions with others and implementing those decisions without consultation. When this happens, it is typically administration informing other employee groups of decisions that have already been made, without consultation in the process of making those decisions. This is a failure of communication.

In part 2, we want to look more closely at the ethical foundation of shared decision-making in higher education. We will do this from both a consequentialist and a deontological perspective. Evidence of the need for true shared governance is clear in cases where it is successful. Part 1 emphasized the value of shared governance where it succeeds. Here we will look at possible points of failure. Evidence of the need for true shared governance is, maybe, even more clear where it fails.

Consequentialist Analyst

Consequential ethical analysis focuses on a definition of good outcomes as the moral justification of a decision, policy, or action. The following section looks at possible opportunities for successful shared governance through the lens of potential points of failure of shared governance.

There are many things that could be said about the consequences of failed shared governance, and it would be easy to get lost in a sea of case studies. Here we take a different focus. We are interested in thematic elements of the relationship between shared governance and strategic planning and the role of shared governance in specific institutional policy formation and revision. There are at least two levels of consequential analysis that need to be kept in focus when thinking about institutional policy and practice in relation to shared governance. One macro concern is institutional strategic planning and mission in relation to institutional funding. A narrower micro concern is specific policy formation and implementation. We will look at each of these in turn.

Let's start with institutional mission statements and institutional funding. Shared governance needs to start at the ground level of strategic planning and mission definition to ensure that as many obstacles can be identified and eliminated, or at least planned for in advance. It is very common to find institutional priorities that are at odds with one another in this broad macro strategic planning concern. For instance, sparks often fly at the intersection of priorities over student tuition and fees, enrollment numbers, and student completion rates. Maximization strategies for one of these goals can minimize desirable outcomes in other priorities. These potential foundational conflicts emphasize the critical importance of ground-level participation of all stakeholder groups in institutional strategic planning and institutional mission definition.

At the macro level, a primary concern is the relationship among tuition and fees, enrollment, and completion rates.

Student Tuition and Fees

Private institutions, those that do not receive state funding, have always been dependent on student tuition and fees. Some private institutions also have large endowments or grants; others do not. State funding has shrunk as a proportion of public institutions' revenue. In addition, funding formulas for state-funded institutions have become increasingly performance-based, rewarding enrollment and completion targets. This is a trend that started back in the 1980s. It is nearly universal for state-funded institutions today.

The authors of this chapter all currently work at the College of Southern Nevada, which is a state-funded institution with a performance-based funding formula emphasizing enrollment and completion priorities. We are very heavily dependent on student tuition and fees for our operating budget.

Our current state funding formula allows each institution to keep all student tuition and fees collected. (Other state funding formulas may withhold some student tuition or fees.) This revenue can be used at the administration's discretion with very few restrictions. So it is financially incentivized for administration to maximize student tuition and fees. But maximization of student tuition and fees can work directly against both long-term enrollment and future completion goals. The reasons for this should be clear. Performance-based funding formulas tend to emphasize enrollment numbers and completion rates. Increases in enrollments and completion rates are rewarded with increases in state funding allocation.

Looking at long-term enrollment, driving up costs and fees will typically motivate students to seek more affordable alternatives. If you drive up student enrollment costs and fees, you also incentivize stop-out and drop-out decisions on the part of students. For most students, cost is a primary decision factor in where or whether they enroll. Further, if you drive students away from enrollments, you also take a hit in completion rates by default. If students do not enroll at your institution, they will not complete at your institution. So, driving up tuition and fees tends to hurt future allocation of state funding determined by enrollments and completions in performance-based funding formulas. The increase in tuition and fees may counterbalance the loss of funding from enrollments and completions. But this should be an intentional decision, not a fortuitous accident.

These are examples of shared governance decision-making at the strategic planning and mission definition level. Unless all stakeholders are involved with important details in the formulative stages of decision-making, important details will be missed. An institutional mission statement should not just be an elevator speech. It should reflect an integrated plan.

Enrollments and Completion Rates

Increasing enrollments is another way to increase tuition and fee revenue. The more students enroll, the more tuition and fees are collected. This applies equally to private and state-funded institutions. Where state performance funding formulas are involved, there are typically increased state funding allocations attached to increased enrollments. So it is typically an administrative goal to increase enrollments year over year.

This is not universally a problem, but there are possible undesirable consequences for going after increased enrollments if the goal of increased enrollment is not carefully balanced in relation to the goal of sufficient course offerings and student completions, faculty and other staffing, and facilities. It is not enough for an administration to unilaterally set a goal of increased enrollment without understanding what that means for the faculty and staff who will be responsible for implementing and maintaining new enrollment levels.

Student completion rates will suffer if enrollments increase without sufficient increases in the courses they will need to graduate and the ability to staff those courses. There are also increased demands on nonacademic employees and physical space limitations. This is another place where shared governance mechanisms are critical at the initial stages of decision-making. All who will be responsible for handling the increased workloads need to be consulted and included in the strategic planning stages of enrollment initiatives.

Individual Policy Formation

Strategic planning is the macro level of shared governance. Individual policy creation is the micro level of shared governance. The things to be said about individual policy creation are quite similar to what has already been said about strategic planning.

The faculty senate committee process is sometimes criticized for being cumbersome and inefficient. It is, admittedly, a time-consuming process. Committees themselves take time to draft policies. The broader the scope of the policy, the longer it typically takes. Darin Dockstader's personal record was more than two years chairing a committee that drafted a general education policy for our institution, where no such policy previously existed. This was a policy that had far-reaching implications for every degree program in terms of future course offerings, staffing, and enrollment numbers. Jobs were potentially in jeopardy college-wide. So, this was a very controversial project to take on. Even with a big committee that contained a representative from every school and every institutional office, there had to be mass information gathering and a network of communication. The policy went through many drafts, all of which had to be vetted college-wide, then voted in by the faculty senate, approved by general counsel, and signed by the college president.

This is an extreme example. Most policies are not as complicated or time-consuming to create. But there is no way that this policy could have been successfully created or implemented had it not gone through this very time-consuming and detailed process. The committee process is time-consuming. It is rare for a committee to create a policy change or new policy document in less than a month. It is even more rare for a committee to vet that document with the institution at the same time. At our institution, committees and the faculty senate typically meet monthly. Under time constraints things can change, but the standard practice in our bylaws is Robert's Rules of Order, which governs the institutional path of policies. That means any proposed policy must first be introduced at one faculty senate meeting as an information item. An information item generally is not moved to an action item for a vote in that same session. Senators need time to take any possible issues to their constituents for feedback.

Assuming there are no major changes, the policy proposal can come back to the next faculty senate meeting for a vote. If there are substantive changes, then the policy proposal returns as an information item for a second time, only to come back as a possible action item a month later. Assuming that all the background and legal issues have been addressed, the proposed document is then ready for signature from the president. A typical best-case scenario for introducing a new policy or amending an old one is at least three months. It usually takes longer. That is, granted, a long time.

Here is where the "inefficiency" critical argument comes from, and it usually comes from administrators or general counsel. If you have an administrative or curricular goal, you can implement that goal in a week or two if you are not constrained by the democratic faculty senate committee process. The presidents of institutions typically do have the authority to make immediate and universal policy decisions. It is desirable that presidents can do this in crisis situations. But it is fundamentally consequentially desirable that policy creation conform to the democratic committee process in normal circumstances, no matter how long that takes. The inefficiency criticism is spurious.

One of the authors, Darin Dockstader, notes,

> I spent four years as lead faculty for philosophy at the College of Southern Nevada, ten years as a senator in faculty senate, more than thirty cumulative years spent as chair or member of major campus committees, and six years as a faculty senate chair. During that time, I also spent a year as the chair of faculty senate chairs for the state of Nevada, for all of the Nevada institutions of higher education. I also had key roles in the construction of two different seven-year institutional strategic plans. I currently serve in a pilot role as a shared governance liaison. (The liaison role is something that is addressed in more detail in part 3.)
>
> In all that time and in all of those roles, I have never seen attempts to circumvent the democratic committee process (outside of crisis situations) save time or advance the health of the institution. Notably, attempts to side-step the democratic committee process almost never save time. In fact, these attempts to circumvent tend to create

delays because they often overlook critical details that would have come to light if the democratic committee process had been followed. It is often harder to correct these oversights after implementation than it would have been to get the changes or strategies in place prior to policy implementation.

Further, these kinds of blunders compromise trust between institutional units. When trust is compromised, this makes further institutional initiatives harder to accomplish and slower to achieve. So the circumvention of democratic process in one instance has a ripple effect that slows everything down in future instances of policy-related decision-making. Breakdowns of democratic process do not inspire confidence in future applications of that process. When people do not have confidence in a process, they are typically more reluctant to participate in that process in the future

Faculty senates and academic faculty members, governing administrators, department chairs, program directors and lead faculty, administrative faculty, student affairs, and classified staff are all indispensable members of a team of people that have to work together in order to make any institutional change effectual. Because of this reality, all of these stakeholder groups need to be involved at the ground level of decision-making as they will eventually be responsible for enacting the required changes. These are the people who know where the obstacles are and exactly what those obstacles look like. These are the people who can potentially eliminate obstacles before they arise. These are the people who are best able to strategize contingencies for obstacles that may not be avoidable.

It is time-consuming to find out what these obstacles are likely to be. But it is far more time-consuming and difficult to repair the damage that is done by plowing ahead with a poorly defined plan. The most noble goals are typically undermined by poor planning.

Deontological Analysis

Deontological ethical analysis differs from consequential ethical analysis by focusing on the principles motivating a decision, policy, or action. These principles tell us about the duties that we have to one another. The following section looks at what these principles tell us about inclusion in shared governance.

Deontological analysis has its roots in Kantian ethics. Kant's categorical imperative provides us with a test for identifying motives that conform to what duty requires. We don't have to dive deeply into Kantian ethics to see how they apply to shared governance mechanisms. Here is Kant's second version of the categorical imperative: treat yourself and others as ends in themselves and never as a means only. Application of the test relies on the distinction between intrinsic value and instrumental value. Intrinsic and instrumental value are two different ways of thinking that something is important or desirable. If something has intrinsic value, it is valuable as an end in itself. It is valuable for its own sake. Its value is built right in and does not depend on externally defined means to achieve some set of consequences or goals. If something is instrumentally valuable, its value is externally defined. When something is instrumentally valuable, it is good for what it can get you. Its value is found in its utility or as a means to accomplishing some goal.

The categorical imperative applies awkwardly to the principle of inclusion in shared governance, but it does still apply. It was designed to apply to the decisions of individuals—not institutions. But we have a kind of modified Kantian argument for inclusion of all stakeholder groups in the planning stages of institutional decision-making all the way through to the implementation stage of institutional change.

When stakeholder groups are included from beginning to end of the institutional decision-making processes, the intrinsic value of those groups is acknowledged. This by no means implies that every stakeholder group will have their interests honored. But it does ensure that those interests are acknowledged and considered as part of a democratic decision-making process. Democracy never actually ensures that one set of interests will win out. It only ensures that different sets of interests will be equally considered in a collective decision-making process.

When institutional groups are excluded from collective decision-making, they are not treated as intrinsically valuable. They are treated as tools for implementing decisions that they did not help to make. In an institutional setting, the "means only" clause of the categorical imperative clause of the second categorical imperative is not strictly applicable. An employee is not treated as a "means only" since the employee is compensated with a wage that the employee has agreed on. But the emphasis on value has another dimension.

Deontological frameworks have been updated by Rawls and others to deal with social institutions. Rawls's original position thought experiment asks us to consider possible future roles for organizations behind a "veil of ignorance," without the knowledge of what future role we will occupy in the organization in the future. In this thought experiment, we all have an equal chance of being a student, an administrator, a classified employee, an academic faculty member, a leader of faculty senate, a leader of classified employees, and so on.

In this hypothetical decision-making paradigm, we will all have to consider our options "as if" we do not know what those options will be. We all have an equal chance of ending up in any one of these populations. In these circumstances, the best option for any individual is the option that maximizes the broadest range of opportunities for any role that they might play in the future situation.

In these circumstances the best option for an individual is the one that maximizes the broadest range of opportunities for every individual in a constituent social role that the agent might occupy outside of the veil of ignorance. So the best principle is the one representing all the stakeholders. That option maximizes participation of those stakeholders in decision-making. That is the feature of human interaction that defines our duties to one another. The broadest application of this principle is the one that extends an equal voice to all stakeholders.

We will now shift our attention to part 3, which involves an examination of the need for an explicitly articulated shared governance policy at the College of Southern Nevada and the ongoing evolution of that policy.

PART 3: ONE INSTITUTION'S ROAD
TO SHARED GOVERNANCE

To illustrate some problems that must be overcome to achieve good shared governance, we describe the development of a shared governance policy (SGP) at our own institution. In our state higher education system, three bodies of policy govern higher education institutions: (1) policy developed by the state board of regents (BOR), who are elected officials; (2) policy developed by the chancellor/system office; and (3) policy developed by individual institutions. In addition, BOR policy requires institutions to develop a set of institutional bylaws. Institutional bylaws provide an overarching framework for an institution's structure, practices, and policies. Sensu stricto, institutional policies must align with institutional bylaws. In turn, institutional bylaws must align with system policy and BOR policy.

BOR policy establishes a faculty senate at each higher education institution. Senates represent the institution's faculty. While the word *faculty* can be interpreted in various ways, it has commonly been interpreted (e.g., in institutional bylaws) as academic faculty who teach and engage in scholarly activities. Regardless, BOR policy gives faculty senates the right to recommend institutional polices related to mission, faculty welfare, and faculty rights to the president.

Policies approved by the president are binding to all employees of the institution.

Ideally, this scheme of hierarchical policies and bylaws should lead to good, shared governance at an institution via its faculty senate; and, for many years, it led to shared governance that was acceptable at our institution. However, the scheme was developed in an era that no longer exists. During this bygone era, sizes of institutions were comparatively small, administrations were less subservient to performance metrics, and the public did not view higher education as a customer service industry.

Beginning in 2005 or 2006, our system and our institution entered a period of rapid growth in enrollment. This growth accelerated with the Great Recession of 2008, peaking around 2011 or 2012, and was accompanied by a significant change in public attitudes (at least locally) toward higher education. Specifically, the public began to ask how and why students could attend college for years, accrue large amounts of debt, and fail to derive any tangible benefit in the form of earned degrees or certificates. Driven by these changes in public attitudes, our system began a shift away from funding based on raw enrollment (in place since 1968) to funding based on performance.

This shift culminated with the adoption of a new, performance-based funding formula in fall 2012. This formula is used to calculate budget requests made to the state legislature and to distribute appropriated funds to higher education institutions within our system. Under this performance-based funding formula, courses (or more appropriately credit hours) completed and degrees/certificates awarded effectively become commodities that generate revenue for an institution via student tuition and fees and money appropriated from the legislature. Changes in public attitudes and adoption of the performance-based funding formula dramatically altered the landscape of expectations for higher education administrators, almost overnight. In contrast, the day-to-day business of teaching and scholarly activity continued more or less unchanged.

In 2016, our institution lost its vice president of academic affairs. In 2017, our institution lost its president. Because both individuals had previously served in lower-level positions at our institution, they were intimately acquainted with our system's scheme of hierarchical policies and bylaws, and shared governance via the faculty senate. The vice president of academic affairs had previously been teaching faculty and both a faculty senate chair and a department chair. So he also had an intimate acquaintance with our institutional processes. That person moved on to become the president of another institution.

The president who retired had previously served as the vice president of academic affairs, so he was also well acquainted with the academic needs of the institution before becoming president.

Prior to the rollover in institutional leadership, shared governance at the College of Southern Nevada functioned smoothly and was applauded by our accreditors. What we lost with the departure of our previous president and vice president of academic affairs was at least a decade of institutional memory and practice. That institutional memory included shared governance procedures that were not directly codified in policy. These were de facto processes that had organically evolved with the needs of the institution and had the status of standard practice for many years but were not explicitly written down. That was the trigger point that showed the need for an explicit policy about shared governance for our institution.

When the president and vice president of academic affairs departed, they were replaced by individuals from outside our system and our state. The replacements had management styles that were more performance-oriented and more authoritarian than those of their predecessors. More importantly, both replacements came from higher education systems that did not have strong traditions of shared governance via faculty senates. Thus, the stage was set for a crisis in shared governance at our institution.

The crisis developed rapidly. Only three years after the arrival of the new vice president of academic affairs, multiple breakdowns in shared governance had negatively affected numerous aspects of our institution, from procedures for scheduling courses to the overall work climate as measured by evidence-based surveys (e.g., the PACE survey). The breakdowns in shared governance culminated in a traumatic vote of no confidence in the vice president of academic affairs by the faculty senate. Precise effects of this vote are difficult to determine. However, they were not inconsequential. Although we cannot tie the change to the vote of no confidence, the individual who received the vote no longer serves as the vice president of academic affairs.

Beyond the unique personalities involved, there were many proximate causes of the breakdowns in shared governance. Major contributing factors included:

1. Failure of administrators to read and/or understand the policies (at all levels) governing our institution
2. Failure of faculty and support staff to read and/or understand the policies (at all levels) governing our institution

3. Poorly written policies (at all levels) that are vague and thus subject to alternative interpretations
4. Disjunction of policies at different levels such that changes in policy at higher, more inclusive levels (BOR policy) are not accompanied by changes in policy at lower, less inclusive levels (institutional policy)
5. Decisions by administrators to change institutional structure that failed to seek input from faculty and support staff affected by the changes
6. Decisions by administrators to change institutional practices that failed to seek input from faculty and support staff affected by the changes
7. Decisions by administrators to implement new academic initiatives that failed to seek input from faculty and support staff responsible for implementing the initiatives
8. Failure of faculty and support staff to understand the environment that administrators must be responsive to, including needs to maintain funding, meet performance goals, and satisfy conflicting desires of multiple stakeholders
9. Failure of faculty and support staff to understand that administrators are ultimately accountable for performance and funding of the institution

In response to the breakdowns in shared governance and their aftermath, the administration and senate decided to write and implement an institutional SGP. This policy would align with system and BOR policy and provide explicit definitions, principles, and procedures for effective shared governance at our institution.

In its current iteration, the SGP defines shared governance as input by the executive leaders, academic faculty, administrative faculty (administrators below the rank of associate vice president), support staff, and (when appropriate) students into the major decisions made at our institution. Critically, the SGP notes that input must be "substantial" and must occur "early" in the decision-making process, preferably in the initial discussion period. It also clearly states that faculty and support staff "do not have veto power over decisions made by administrators within their oversight responsibilities."

The definition of shared governance in the SGP reflects the basic tenet that breakdowns in shared governance have their roots in profound lack of communication between those responsible for making decisions and those responsible for operationalizing decisions.

Consequently, the procedures for shared governance in the SGP begin with measures designed to facilitate transfer of information from administration to faculty and support staff and vice versa. These procedures include:

1. Establishment of an institutional committees web page that lists all college committees, task forces, and advisory boards, their chairs, their memberships, and relevant minutes of meetings
2. Monthly meetings (or meetings upon request) between the president and the leaders of all major employee groups
3. Establishment of a permanent college strategic plan committee consisting of members from the executive administration and each major employee group
4. Establishment of shared governance liaisons

Of these procedures, establishment of the shared governance liaisons (SGL) is the most pivotal. As originally envisioned, the SGL were to be academic faculty members chosen by the senate. Their task was to attend meetings of the executive administration, where they would act strictly as information gatherers. More specifically, the SGL were to collect information on major changes in structure/practice or new initiatives under consideration and then provide this information to the senate and the employee groups representing administrative faculty and support staff. Having identified changes or initiatives necessitating shared governance, the senate and employee groups representing administrative faculty and support staff would request the formation of shared governance task forces (SGTF).

The SGTF would consist of small numbers of executive administrators, academic faculty, administrative faculty, support staff, and (when warranted) students. Members of a specific SGTF would have expertise on the specific changes/initiative under consideration. Thus, the SGL would gather information that determined when shared governance was warranted, and the SGTF would carry out the actual work of shared governance.

Problems quickly arose concerning the delineation of the SGL, specifically the notion that they would be academic faculty chosen by the senate. While the SGL were intended only to be information gatherers and were required to report to all major employee groups, their role was misinterpreted as one of advocacy that would give academic faculty primacy in shared governance. Consequently, the delineation of SGL was reworked to include one representative from each of the major employee groups: (1) full-time academic faculty, (2) administrative faculty, and (3) support staff. Within each employee group, the SGLs are chosen by a popular vote and serve from June 1 to August 31 of the following year.

In addition to allotting one SGL to each of the major employee groups, the reworked definition expanded SGL responsibilities and clarified the means by which they can gather information. Specifically, SGL were given the ability to act as limited advocates for their employee groups. They were also given responsibilities for coordinating communication between their employee groups and the executive administration and facilitating formation of SGTF. To gather information, SGL are now required to hold regularly scheduled meetings with the executive administration and the intuition's ombudsman. These meetings are ostensibly designed to identify all proposed changes in instructional structure/practice and development of new initiatives that require shared governance.

Finally, the reworked definition of SGL creates the Employee Leadership Council (ELC). This council consists of four academic faculty, four administrative faculty, and four support staff. In the case of academic faculty, two members of the ELC are chosen by the senate, and two are chosen by the academic faculty's collective bargaining representative. The ELC oversees the work of SGLs and can remove them for failure to adequately perform their duties.

In spring 2016, the academic faculty at our institution voted to organize and make an external state professional organization their collective bargaining representative/organization. It is worth noting that the organization in question is affiliated with the American Association of University Professors, an organization dedicated to the advancement of academic freedom and shared governance. It is not affiliated with a national labor union such as the American Federation of Teachers, which is dedicated to improving the wages, benefits, and working conditions of its members. It is also worth noting that the vote to organize passed by the slimmest of margins (50 percent plus one vote, or exactly the margin necessary to organize).

The vote to organize has created additional challenges for shared governance. The first collectively bargained contract did not go into effect until July 1, 2020. In our opinion, it is a disjointed set of policies that reflects the specific concerns/grievances of its negotiators more than a coherent effort to improve wages, benefits, and working conditions for all members of the bargaining unit (all academic faculty). In several areas, the contract appears to conflict with approved institutional policies and/or BOR policies. Other areas seem completely unrelated to wages, benefits, and working conditions, which are the standard purview of collective bargaining organizations.

In our opinion, the collective bargaining organization has demonstrated a marked tendency to conflate its function/mission with that of the faculty senate. Indeed, the collective bargaining representative has claimed it has a "clear mandate" to be part of shared governance as an entity separate from the senate. At the same time, dues-paying members of the collective bargaining organization, including its elected officers, are academic faculty and can be elected members of the senate (up to and including the position of senate chair)—a situation that can lead to conflicts of interest. Regardless, the collective bargaining organization is now a fixture at our institution and must be included in the SGP when and where appropriate.

As noted previously, the collective bargaining organization chooses two of the academic faculty who sit on the ELC. In addition, the collective bargaining organization is allowed to choose one academic faculty member who sits on the Shared Governance Review Committee.

The current iteration of the SGP establishes the Shared Governance Review Committee as a mechanism for annually assessing shared governance at our institution and providing a critical report that is disseminated to all employees at the institution. The report should list all instances where the SGP was not followed appropriately and suggest remediations to prevent future violations. When warranted, remediations should include suggested changes to the SGP itself. The Shared Governance Review Committee consists of two executive administrators, two academic faculty (one chosen by the senate, one chosen by the collective bargaining organization), two administrative faculty (chosen by their employee organization), two support staff (chosen by their employee organization), and two students (chosen by student government).

At the time of this writing, our path to good shared governance is still a long and winding road. The current iteration of the SGP has the backing of (1) the senate, (2) employee groups representing administrative faculty and support staff, (3) collective bargaining organization, and (4) president. However, the need to be more inclusive with respect to the organizations that have an explicit role in shared governance has resulted in an increasingly complex policy that is increasingly difficult to operationalize. Some elements of the SGP have been put into operation. For example, the SGL began performing their information-gathering activities in 2020, and the college strategic plan committee is being formed. However, the policy remains unapproved by the president. The current holdup is related to compensation of the SGL representing support staff for the time they spend performing their SGL responsibilities.

CONCLUDING REMARKS

In this chapter, we have just scratched the surface of shared governance in American colleges and universities. There is a vast body of literature on shared governance. We are confident that every college and university in the country can develop a shared governance that works well and will help the institution excel in meeting its mission. Many institutions need to do this.

We have examined the ethical need for shared governance as a process of inclusion for all stakeholders. All need to be included at the start of the institutional decision-making process. All must continue to be included through to the implementation and management of decisions that come from the democratic process of true shared governance. These ethical priorities are compelling on both consequential and deontological grounds.

Our institutional road to rebuilding shared governance has been rocky. However, the obstacles have hardened the resolve of employee groups and the administration to build an inclusive, shared governance policy. Importantly, this policy has an inbuilt assessment/feedback process that can ensure that policy operates as intended and can be readily adapted to changing circumstances. While the shared governance policy has yet to be approved and will be difficult to fully operationalize, we feel that the end of the road to shared governance is near and that a new journey down a road of refining and improving shared governance awaits us.

We are very close to achieving a shared governance that works for us, and we are not special in the struggle to connect potentially very complicated fields of variables to institutional outcomes. When the policy is signed by our president, you can see it at www.csn.edu/policies-procedures. Hopefully this will have already occurred by the essay's publication. We are optimistic that this will be the case.

REFERENCES

American Association of University Professors (AAUP). (1966, 1990). AAUP statement on government of colleges and universities. www.aaup.org/report/statement-government-colleges-and-universities.

American Council on Education. (2017). Lessons from research and practice. www.acenet.edu/Documents/Shared-Leadership-in-Higher-Education.pdf.

American Federation of Teachers (AFT). (2002). Shared governance in colleges and universities: A statement by the Higher Education Program and Policy Council. www.ulm.edu/.

Association of Governing Boards of Universities and Colleges (AGB). (2016). Shared governance: Is OK good enough? https://agb.org/reports-2/shared-governance-is-ok-good-enough/.

Association of Governing Board of Universities and Colleges (AGB). (2017, March). Shared governance: Changing with the times. www.csusb.edu/sites/default/files/report_2017_shared_governance_2.pdf.

Bahls, S. C. (2014). Shared governance in times of change: A practical guide for universities and colleges. AGB Press.

Bahls, S. C. (2014, March/April). How to make shared governance work: Some best practices. *Association of Governing Boards Trusteeship Magazine.* Association of Governing Boards.

Behr, M. (2016, October 7). Shared governance, shared responsibility: One CAO's lessons learned. *Higher Education Today (American Council on Education).* www.higheredtoday.org/2016/10/07/shared-governance-shared-responsibility-one-caos-lessons-learned/.

Bergan, S. (2004). Student participation in higher education governance.As part of the preparation for its Bologna seminar on student participation in higher education (Oslo 12–14 June 2003), the Norwegian Ministry of Education, Research and Church Affairs commissioned a report from the Council of Europe to survey the state of affairs with regard to formal provision for student participation as well as actual practice.

Claxton-Freeman, A. H. (2015). Higher education governance structures and operational efficiency and effectiveness of 4-year public institutions. [Doctoral Thesis, East Tennessee State University]. https://dc.etsu.edu/etd/2583.

Hass, M. (2020, April 29). Shared governance is a strength during the COVID-19 crisis. *Inside Higher Ed.*

Heaney, T. (2010). Democracy, shared governance, and the university. *New Directions for Adult & Continuing Education 128,* 69–79. www.coe.int/t/dg4/highereducation/Governance/SB_student_participation_EN.pdf.

Keller, G. (2004). A growing quaintness: Traditional governance in the markedly new realm of U.S. higher education. In W.G. Tierney (Ed.), *Competing conceptions of academic governance: Negotiating the perfect storm* (pp.158–176). Baltimore, MD: Johns Hopkins University Press.

Kezar, A. J. & Holcombe, E. M. (2017). Shared leadership in higher education: Important Lessons from Research and Practice. Washington DC: American Council on Education.

Leach, W. D. (2008). Shared governance in higher education: Structural and cultural responses to a changing national climate. http://dx.doi.org/10.2139/ssrn.1520702.

McNaughton, D. (2016). Can shared governance in higher education survive? https://changinghighered.com/shared-governance-in-higher-education -survive/.

Minor, J. T. (2003). Assessing the senate: Critical issues considered. *American Behavioral Scientist 46*(7), 960–977.

"New realm of U.S. higher education." In W. G. Tierney (Ed.), *Competing conceptions of academic governance.* John Hopkins University Press.

Rosenberg, B. (2014, July 29). Shared or divided governance? *Inside Higher Ed.*

Scott, R. A. (2020). Leadership threats to shared governance in higher education. *AAUP Journal of Academic Freedom 11,* 1–17. sharedgovernance/ documents/shared_governance.pdf.

Smith, C. (2015). The decline of shared governance in higher education (a historical perspective). www.kckcc.edu/files/docs/ejournal/volume -three/number-two-oct-2009/the-decline-of-shared-governance-in-higher -education.pdf.

Stoessel, J. W. (2013). Conceptualizing the shared governance model in American higher education: Considering the governing board, president and faculty. *Inquiries Journal/Student Pulse 5*(12). www.inquiriesjournal.com/ a?id=818.

Trakman, L. (2008). Modelling university governance. *Higher Education Quarterly 62*(1-2), 63–83. DOI:10.1111/j.1468-2273.2008.00384.x.

Waldman, T. A. (2019). *The understanding and involvement in shared governance by faculty who have transitioned to higher education from industry.* [Doctoral Thesis, Concordia University, Portland]. https://digitalcommons .csp.edu/cup_commons_grad_edd/409.

Zimpher, N. L. (2012). Shared governance drives our greatest accomplishments. *Faculty Senate Bulletin, Special Issue on Shared Governance.* 4. www.suny.edu/media/suny/content-assets/documents/voices/FS_Bulletin -Fall2012specialissue.pdf.

Zimpher, N. L. (2017). Shared governance: Changing with the times: Case study: State University of New York. Association of Governing Boards. https://agb.org/wp-content/uploads/2019/01/casestudy_suny.pdf.

5

Academic Libraries

Advocating for an Ethical University

Robert V. Labaree and Melissa L. Miller

ABSTRACT

This chapter examines some of the ways academic librarians contribute to the aspirational goals of an ethical university, particularly in relation to supporting positive student learning outcomes, principles of access to information and freedom of expression, and ethical forms of knowledge acquisition, creation, and preservation. Within the profession, however, librarians struggle with numerous ethical dilemmas. Two examples currently debated within the field of academic librarianship are described. Although largely invisible within higher education, both have broad implications for realizing the ethical university.

Keywords: academic librarianship; access to information; critical librarianship; #critlib; crowdsourcing; digital humanities; digital research; diversity, equity, inclusion, and access; ethical conduct; #first-gen; first-generation; freedom of expression; interdisciplinarity; professional standards; social capital

The contributions of academic librarians in advocating for and facilitating ethical conduct within academe is rarely mentioned in studies that examine the intersection of higher education and ethics. Possible reasons for this are likely attributable to long-held beliefs about who librarians are and what they do. Working in a female-dominated academic profession, librarians struggle against deeply rooted paternal structures of leadership, decision-making, and resource allocation (Ballenger, 2010). Depending on the institution, academic librarians lack faculty status or they hold a faculty rank, but their status is not known or understood by other faculty. This can diminish their standing as equal partners in the educational enterprise of the university. Studies also show that librarians are often stereotyped in ways that diminish their prestige as leaders (Gaines, 2014), and, as a result, their professional roles are viewed as supportive rather than as actively engaged in producing original research and new knowledge. Finally, libraries are viewed primarily as service-oriented expenditure centers within the university rather than an academic unit that is different from, but on par with, schools. Collectively, these issues could explain the absence of academic librarianship in studies that examine ethics in higher education.

Yet, the responsibilities of academic librarians to help lead the educational mission of the university can be easily understood within an ethical framework. This may include aspects of critical analysis and evaluation in learning; information literacy instruction focused on copyright law and avoiding plagiarism, building and managing a diverse and inclusive collection of both print and digital materials, cataloging of unique materials that confront institutional bias and structural racism in the assigning of controlled vocabulary used to organize knowledge for subsequent retrieval, and supporting access to information by leading efforts to adopt open access materials to mitigate the exorbitant pricing of scholarly resources. Many of these principles of professional practice are codified in standards of ethical conduct developed by professional organizations, most notably the Association of College and Research Libraries, a division of the American Library Association. These standards are often supplemented locally by regional and state library associations or within individual academic libraries themselves.

In addition to supporting an ethical university, there are forces external to academic libraries that create intransigent, ongoing ethical problems within academic library organizations. Some of these problems are long-standing and reflect, for example, the relationships libraries must maintain with commercial vendors. Other problems, however, have emerged in recent years or become exacerbated by the growing influence of new technologies on all aspects of university life. These ethical problems primarily encompass issues of equitable access to information or result from unpredictable organizational change within higher education institutions. In this respect, we must be reminded that academic libraries do not rest in isolation from their parent institutions but are governed by administrative, legal, and economic decisions that are beyond their control and, in some cases, we argue, that are imposed on them with little or no consultation for the reasons already stated.

The purpose of this chapter is to examine these issues in more detail and, in so doing, illuminate the unique leadership role academic libraries have in promoting an ethical university. We conceptualize ethics broadly so as to encompass the scope of right and wrong applied to the diversity of professional practice within academic librarianship. The first sections of the chapter discuss the ways in which librarians advocate for an ethical university and, in particular, how the work they do facilitates adherence to ethical principles applied to knowledge acquisition and production, pedagogy, and student learning. Next we identify and describe two examples of ethical problems in the field of academic librarianship. These problems are often invisible to the greater academic community, but they are loudly debated within the profession. The topics we examine do not reflect all aspects of ethics and academic librarianship but are selected for the purpose of highlighting issues that have a significant impact on institutions of higher education and, as a consequence, could imperil the aims of supporting an ethical university.

INTERDISCIPLINARITY

Institutions of higher education have placed greater emphasis on interdisciplinary research, teaching, and student learning during the last several decades (Frodeman, Klein, and Pacheco, 2017). Based on a random sampling content analysis of scholarship analyzing the concept of interdisciplinarity, mission statements and the anticipated learning outcomes of integrative curriculum programs in higher education, and value statements from government-supported educational commissions, agencies, and boards regarding interdisciplinary teaching and learning, the movement to break down disciplinary silos can be categorized into at least five categories (Labaree, 2013). First, universities support interdisciplinarity for the purpose of promoting creative or innovative thinking around complex problems. The sample of content reviewed indicated that interdisciplinary-based creative thinking facilitates approaching research problems unconventionally, in the sense that problem-solving requires modification or rejection of previously accepted ideas or assumptions.

This form of creative thinking is also presumed to enhance researchers' ability to formulate original insights or unconventional reasoning, to aid in developing an understanding of higher-order relationships and organizing principles, and to produce a cognitive advancement or unique understanding of a research problem to explain a phenomenon, solve a problem, create a product, or raise a question in new ways (Sill, 2001). Interdisciplinary-based creative thinking is also viewed as generating intrinsic motivation to pursue knowledge and understanding based on the enjoyment of the research process itself rather than relying on or requiring external reinforcement (Miller, 2021).

Second, findings suggest universities pursue interdisciplinarity because it supports integrative learning and synoptic problem-solving. This includes demonstrating a sensitivity to bias, applying assumptions and methodologies from multiple disciplines to develop integrated theoretical frameworks and research design models, and, reflecting Albert Bandura's triadic reciprocity behavioral and personality model (Bandura, 1986), combining academic knowledge and a learner's life experiences to formulate a more coherent and unified sense of self during the act of pursuing knowledge. Interdisciplinarity applied to integrative learning also involves methods of synoptic problem-solving. Selective mission statements that describe the purpose of integrated curriculum include supporting the need to connect and assimilate knowledge across disciplinary boundaries to solve problems. Integrated curriculum also is seen as improving comprehension of global interdependencies that take into consideration more in-depth exploration of topics, issues, and problems within and across disciplinary boundaries.

Third, higher education's pursuit of interdisciplinarity is viewed as critical for improving the ways in which researchers can interpret and communicate something that is unfamiliar or ambiguous by means of comparing and contrasting it to something more familiar and recognizable. As a result, knowledge can be integrated from multiple disciplines to produce a more comprehensive understanding of a particular hypothesis or research problem; obtain a pluralistic sense of the nature, scope, and utility of knowledge and its production; and understand the organization of knowledge in academic subfields and areas of specialization within other disciplines.

Evidence also suggests that researchers are better able to recognize disciplinary strengths, processes, and limitations if they are engaged in interdisciplinary projects. For the student learner, the interpretive power of interdisciplinary thinking in unfamiliar or ambiguous research contexts can be framed around the cognitive flexibility theory of knowledge acquisition developed by Spiro, Coulson, Feltovich, and Anderson (1988). As Newswander and Newswander (2012) state, interdisciplinarity enhances a learner's capacity to restructure knowledge in multiple ways depending on changing situational demands, thereby supporting the ability to construct from these representations an investigative agenda tailored to understanding the specific dimensions of a research problem.

A fourth reason why universities allocate resources to support interdisciplinary initiatives is to promote collaborative inquiry among researchers by demythologizing expertise. The act of collaboration is intended to break down complex problems into more manageable parts. This form of inquiry is also viewed as important by universities because it creates conditions for engaging scholars in seeking new information to clarify new ideas or concepts brought into a research project. As a result, scholars may be more receptive to modifying their own work or research design as a result of interactions they have with researchers in other fields. In addition, value statements about interdisciplinarity often highlight the opportunity to work with and within diverse cultures and communities as a reason why universities support interdisciplinary collaboration initiatives.

Finally, random content analysis of research studies, integrative curriculum mission statements, and value statements of educational organizations indicates that interdisciplinarity enhances comprehension and appreciation of working with complexity. This commitment rests on the assumption that complexity requires studying problems from multiple vectors of analysis in order to find the best solutions. This results in a learner's ability to tolerate and cope with ambiguity, paradox, uncertainty, and imperfectly known relationships. Another presumed outcome of working with complexity is that it encourages agile, flexible, and reflective thinking applied to practice. Researchers become more comfortable with doubt and uncertainty and, as a consequence, build a capacity to perceive value in the highly complex or asymmetrical. Outcomes from interdisciplinary learning also indicate that a variety of cultural, political, ethical, historical, economic, or other contextual factors must be taken into account during the process of researching complicated problems or intractable social issues.

As this evidence shows, interdisciplinary programs and initiatives are intended to enhance learning, teaching, and research throughout the university in ways that address complex problem-solving in today's world. At least, this is the goal. However, traditional curricular, organizational, and bureaucratic structures within higher education are significant barriers to these objectives. As Wallace and Clark (2017) note, "Disciplines are designed to be self-perpetuating, as a means to ensure that they remain the academy's dominant intellectual units" (p. 233). We argue that an exception to these rigid barriers is academic libraries. Academic libraries have always been a bastion in the pursuit of interdisciplinary research and learning. The simple act of browsing the bookshelves is an opportunity for users to come across a book that presents a unique perspective or piques the interest of a researcher to pursue a path of discovery that would have been otherwise invisible. However, as institutions of higher education have pursued a more deliberate emphasis on interdisciplinary knowledge creation, teaching, student learning, outreach, and service, academic libraries have followed with their own interdisciplinary initiatives. This is summarized in Mack and Gibson's book *Interdisciplinarity and Academic Libraries* (2012).

Libraries are the university's knowledge hub for interdisciplinary research and learning because they provide services that aid in accessing information in multiple formats and from multiple sources representing diverse perspectives. Librarians are experts in understanding the organization of information and, therefore, as Mack notes, are well-positioned "to act as negotiator among the multiple vocabularies, literatures, methods, and paradigms encountered throughout the curriculum" (2012, p. 4). During research consultations with students, librarians bring together their own multidisciplinary knowledge, coupled with prior consultative experiences, to help the student explore new pathways of discovery. In the classroom, librarians apply resource-based learning methods to teach students how to use research resources in ways that support multidisciplinary knowledge acquisition. Librarians help students expand the scope of discipline-based assumptions to frame research questions that incorporate interdisciplinary thinking (Jones, 2012). And, as we discuss in more detail in the next part, collections are deliberately built to reflect a diversity of viewpoints. The materials not only represent the core literature of a discipline taught at the university but are acquired and preserved to support areas of disciplinary intersection and convergence (Reynolds, Holt, and Walsh, 2012).

So, how does the library's contribution to interdisciplinarity contribute to an ethical university? Librarians teach methods of critical thinking that help students identify bias throughout the entire life cycle of research. This can include identifying bias in a study's research design, locating gaps in the coverage of prior literature, discerning selection bias of data gathered for analysis, and recognizing inadequate discussion and analysis of findings that lead to erroneous conclusions. Contributions to ethics derived from interdisciplinarity is also reflected in how academic librarians help students discover hidden cultural contexts of research and knowledge production.

This can include, for example, identifying local approaches to examining issues of public concern or locating primary source materials that dramatize the knowledge, culture, and values of, for example, indigenous groups or displaced communities. Librarians provide access to interdisciplinary resources that help break down the privileged position of Western thought. The collections of many libraries include research and conceptual analyses produced within the philosophical, analytical, and methodological traditions of other cultures throughout the world. Finally, we argue that teaching students to view research problems through an interdisciplinary lens supports ethical principles of tolerance, empathy, and mutual understanding because it exposes the researcher to voices that would otherwise be unheard or ignored.

REPRESENTATIVE COLLECTIONS

One of the most visible roles of academic libraries is to identify, acquire, manage, and preserve materials in all forms or formats that support the educational mission of the university. Broadly defined as collection development, this area of a librarian's responsibility is governed by principles of access to information, freedom of expression, and enhancing learning by making available a diversity of perspectives about a topic. In many cases, librarians approach collection development from an anticipatory stance. This requires identifying and acquiring materials that anticipate newly emerging trends in scholarship or reflect the fluidity of interpreting and reinterpreting the past as new evidence is discovered.

The process of collection development at many institutions involves the use of approval plans that set the parameters for what is collected. They are considered an efficient and cost-effective way for libraries to acquire books in large quantities across multiple disciplines. Librarians set the parameters for what books are acquired from publishers based on the research, curricular, and learning needs of the campus community. The approval plan profiles dictate the subject areas and nonsubject categories by which books are shipped to the library or which e-books are entered into the online catalog.

The approval plans also establish nonsubject-area parameters for acquisitions, such as readership level, cost, language, country of origin, and preferred format. Book vendors also provide notifications of publications that reside outside of the approval plan profile but still may be of interest for possible purchase. An example would be a profile that designates notifications for any books in political science costing more than $100. Any books under that price would be automatically shipped to the library. Approval plan profiles must be evaluated regularly to ensure that they continue to reflect current disciplinary needs or to be adjusted as research and teaching priorities change within the university.

While approval plans ensure that a core set of books or e-books are acquired, the profiles cannot be configured so that all relevant titles are known. If funding is available, librarians must supplement the approval plan with direct orders of titles. It is within this work of building collections that librarians must pay particular attention to standards of ethical conduct applied to the selection of resources. Described by Highby (2004), these standards establish principles of neutrality and intellectual freedom. The principle of neutrality applies to all aspects of acquisition, preservation, and removal of items. The neutrality standard states that, while materials should be acquired in support of the institution's educational programs and research priorities, the process of identifying items should not be influenced by a librarian's personal values or beliefs.

The acquisition of titles should be an objective process absent of bias or self-interest. Intellectual freedom is the principle that librarians must acquire materials that they may find offensive or that some patrons may find objectionable. Librarians must take an agnostic stance toward the content of the materials they acquire as long as those materials support the educational and research mission of the university. The overarching objective is to develop collections that reflect a diversity of perspectives, providing students and researchers with the opportunity to acquire the broadest understanding of a subject.

Aside from books and other publicly accessible materials, most academic libraries also acquire special collections. These collections are most often inaccessible to the public because items are rare, valuable, unique, or can no longer be acquired if lost or stolen. As with books, special collections are also acquired based on academic value and the research needs of the university. However, materials may also be purchased or accepted from donors because they bring distinction to the university. As Potter and Holley (2010) point out, "Some especially beautiful or rare items or those connected with famous people may have more value as museum artifacts than as scholarly resources" (p. 149). These materials may not directly support research and teaching on campus, but they are considered valuable because they attract scholars from outside the university.

The Association of College and Research Libraries Code of Ethics for Special Collections Librarians (https://rbms.info/standards/code_of_ethics/) provides the framework for ethical practice among special collections practitioners and archivists. Of particular importance is the principle of intellectual freedom. For example, the library at Michigan State University preserves a substantial collection of primary documents of the Ku Klux Klan. According to the library's website (https://lib.msu.edu/MurrayHongSPC/collections/kkk/), this collection dates from the 1920s and 1930s and includes constitutions, installation ceremonies, advertisements for Klan merchandise, and ephemera that describe the role of women in the Klan. California Institute of Technology archives include the records of the Human Betterment Foundation and the personal papers of its founder, E. S. Gosney. Established in 1929, the foundation advocated the reproductive sterilization of people who were designated as socially and mentally unfit as defined by the doctrine of eugenics.

These two examples reflect special collections that may be viewed as controversial or offensive because the materials deviate from the educational mission of the university. However, acquiring donations such as these reflects a commitment to academic freedom and access to information. It also reflects a commitment to presenting a diversity of viewpoints that help scholars gain a more complete picture of an issue. A collection that represents all sides of controversial issues also provides opportunities to teach key aspects about a subject, thereby ensuring more robust classroom discussions and a more complete understanding of the underlying complexities underpinning a research topic.

The responsibility of academic librarians to develop digital and print collections guided by principles of selection neutrality, intellectual freedom, and diversity of viewpoints supports an ethical university. The primary justification for investing in the acquisition of collections, in all its forms, is to support an institution's research, teaching, and learning priorities. However, within these parameters, librarians are guided by ethical standards of conduct that decree an unbiased approach to obtaining materials. This provides the opportunity for students and researchers to explore all aspects of an issue unimpeded by hidden forms of censorship due to incomplete access to information. Representative collections can also reveal the voices of underrepresented, marginalized, disadvantaged, or excluded peoples and communities, highlighting perspectives and insights that enrich research, teaching, and student learning.

CRITICAL LIBRARIANSHIP

Critical librarianship initiatives continue to be reflected in academic libraries. As described by Emily Drabinski (2019), critical librarianship recognizes and interrogates the structures, such as universities, that generate all aspects of our profession, including us as professional academic librarians, our physical library spaces, and our communities both internal and external. Critical librarianship challenges the status quo and the concentrated systems of power and, at its core, is a commitment to social change that lifts up and amplifies the voices for diversity, equity, inclusion, and access.

Myra Waddell and Elena Clariza (2018) published an article detailing critical digital pedagogy and cultural sensitivity and the meaningful impact this may have on information literacy education in the library classroom. They emphasize that critical digital pedagogy acknowledges technological limitations while aligning the inquiry to the center of the learning process. One of the examples highlighted (p. 230) was "digital storytelling in a humanities classroom." Digital storytelling empowers the student and provides a meaningful and intentional learning experience: "Through digital narrative stories, communities at the margins of society provide counter histories as they share their experiential knowledge" (pp. 230–231).

Another aspect or example of critical librarianship can be found in how academic libraries contribute to the social capital of first-generation college students. *Social capital* refers to the networks of relationships among people who live and work in a particular society, enabling that society to function effectively. The concept has been used by various political and social thinkers. In *The Forms of Capital* (2002, p. 286), French sociologist Pierre Bourdieu distinguishes between three forms of capital: economic capital, cultural capital, and social capital. He defines social capital as "the aggregate of the actual or potential resources which are linked to possession of a durable network of more or less institutionalized relationships of mutual acquaintance and recognition."

When it comes to the success of American first-generation college students, meaningful participation within a "durable network" becomes extremely important, particularly for minority students who may lack economic capital. A pertinent role university libraries will play in growing American first-generation college students' social capital is engaging in dialogue and discourse so as to develop meaningful academic relationships that foster the growth of their students as potential meaning makers in academia. Resulting in an increase in opportunities for growth will be bidirectional and foster belongingness and trust as is such in communities of social capital.

First-generation college students are defined as students whose parents have not earned a four-year degree or higher, and they are an increasing population at private four-year universities (Davis, 2010). Research has shown a gap in the literature addressing the challenges and motivations of first-generation college students engaging and being supported socially, culturally, and academically while in pursuit of successfully earning an undergraduate degree (Pascarella, Pierson, Wolniak & Terenzini, 2004; Gibbons & Shoffner, 2004; Davis, 2010). When compared to other students who are not the first in their families to attend a four-year college, first-generation college students struggle with adapting to the increased level of expectation and lack of support from families and/or in the classroom (Pascarella, Pierson, Wolniak & Terenzini, 2004). Ishitani (2006) found that first-generation college students are more likely to drop out during their second year of study. Several studies have measured precollege variables and academic engagement activities during the early college years, hoping to uncover predictors for attrition and interventions to improve outcomes for first-generation college students (Soria & Stebleton, 2012; Woosley & Shepler, 2011). The problem of second-year attrition for first-generation college students is a serious concern that four-year universities need to address.

Creating both academic and social connections in college is important when engaging in campus activities inside and outside the classroom; this is also referred to as building social capital. Academic and social engagement include but are not limited to the following: academic engagement may be measured by time spent studying with peers, discussing readings with peers or faculty outside the classroom, and performing integrated learning activities like group assignments, peer tutoring, or mentoring; social engagement may be measured by participation in events sponsored by campus groups, learning support groups that include faculty and staff, and cultural organizations and service activities. *Collective efficacy* refers to the beliefs of a group as a community, including the ability to organize and implement the necessary skills to attain common goals. Feelings of success lead to students' achievement, which leads to mastery (Goddard, Hoy, & Hoy, 2004).

DIGITAL RESEARCH, LEARNING, AND TEACHING

The COVID-19 pandemic has placed online learning at the forefront of higher education. For most universities and their academic libraries, the pandemic has caused numerous challenges. However, it has also been an impetus for change and an opportunity to redirect priorities. For academic librarians leading in the areas of strategic research development, critical thinking skills and literacy, and innovative scholarship, including digital scholarship, a new approach is emerging in addressing awareness, access and connectivity to resources, instructional design for online research, learning, teaching, and fostering the success of fellow faculty, staff, and students.

Librarians in academic libraries advocate engagement with students, underserved populations, and their local community as part of their mission. In planning outreach engagement for research, learning, and teaching, librarians must work within the constraints of budget and time for the success of their objectives. Few academic institutions maintain a budget designated for outreach. Therefore, many academic faculty librarians have to do more with less.

One example of innovative technologies used for engagement in research, learning, and teaching, especially for multimedia scholarship, is the digital platform Scalar. Scalar is an open-source online publishing tool that was developed at the University of Southern California (USC) by the Alliance for Networking Visual Culture for the electronic journal *Vectors*. Using Scalar not only provides the opportunity for a strategic approach to not only the digitization of selected artifacts but will also allow everyone to share their research project and exhibition with international academic audiences and beyond via publications, workshops, and conference presentations.

By digitizing and publishing the research and artifacts within Scalar digital exhibitions or books, we can preserve them while providing ease of access and therefore fostering a more inclusive and collaborative community of engagement that includes faculty and students in multidisciplinary fields as well as the public (Mihram and Miller, 2021). The director of the USC Libraries Ahmanson Lab, Dr. Curtis Fletcher, has been a vital resource not only in initially developing Scalar but also in its continued evolution. Fletcher created an innovative series called the Collabortory: "Collaboratories are interdisciplinary, team-based research labs designed to engage students in critical making—activities that bridge critical thinking and digital fabrication. They are polymathic in nature, bringing faculty, experts, artists, designers, and students together at the Ahmanson Lab over an academic year. They are organized around topics, problems or set of questions that are best explored via the hands-on design and production of digital artifacts. Collaboratories are designed and coordinated by one or more USC faculty in cooperation with Ahmanson Lab staff" (USC Libraries, Ahmanson Lab, https://polymathic.usc.edu/ahmanson-lab/collaboratory/current).

Another example of the challenges in cultivating an inclusive environment that fosters equitable access and awareness not only for academic resources but also for arts and cultural initiatives for students, staff, and faculty is through digital newsletters. At USC several subject specialist librarians have developed monthly newsletters featuring events and programming. Those newsletters focus on awareness of internal and external opportunities ranging from academic lectures and discussion panels to free admission to museums and exhibits in the Los Angeles area.

A series called Research, Learning, and Teaching (RLT) was launched in July 2021 by Dr. Melissa L. Miller and Christina Snider of the USC Hoose Library of Philosophy. Between July and December 2021, thirteen RLTs were published and were well received. Many department faculty have embedded them in their course syllabi or course content. This series reaches approximately four hundred constituents (faculty, staff, graduates, and undergraduates) in Dr. Miller's subject areas: humanities, philosophy, religion, anthropology, linguistics, comparative literature, history of science and technology, and classics. The RLT series focuses on one resource at a time with step-by-step training on how to explore the resource. The topics include how to access and navigate particular databases; how to use interlibrary loan and document delivery services or course reserves; how to recommend a book, database, or journal for purchase by the university's acquisitions department; how to access streaming services; how to complete a virtual library orientation; how to renew books online; and many more. The RLTs have proven to be a valuable training tool for student assistants working for academic libraries across the USC Libraries system as well.

In addition, crowdsourcing is a trend that has shown to have a great impact on existing library systems and services. As the number of items digitized and required to be digitized by libraries increases, crowdsourcing is one possible solution to the challenge of providing item-level metadata needed to support the search process and virtual access. Crowdsourcing is a way to invite and encourage volunteer participation from the public at large to create, describe, and be engaged in a variety of projects that may otherwise be too time-consuming or not cost-effective for any one institution to accomplish with their available resources.

Crowdsourcing is defined as a "distributed problem-solving and production process that involves outsourcing a task to a group of people—it allows difficult and time-consuming projects to be tackled a chunk at a time, and by a large group of individuals, working asynchronously and at their own pace" (University of Alabama Libraries, 2014). Rose Holley (2010) expanded the definition of crowdsourcing for libraries. She clarified the difference between social engagement and crowdsourcing: "Social engagement is about giving the public the ability to communicate with any given library and each other; to add value to existing library data by tagging, commenting, rating, reviewing, text correcting; and to create and upload content to add to the collections" (Holley, 2010). Crowdsourcing for libraries is an innovative method of community collaboration, emphasizing the importance of the library as a place of cultural enhancement and engagement.

Holley (2010) asks an important question: "Why should libraries use crowdsourcing?" She answers that question by providing the following list of twelve tremendous benefits to libraries derived from crowdsourcing:

1. Achieving goals the library would never have the time, financial, or staff resources to achieve on its own.
2. Achieving goals in a much faster time frame than the library may be able to achieve if it worked on its own.
3. Building new virtual communities and user groups.
4. Actively involving and engaging the community with the library and its other users and collections.
5. Utilizing the knowledge, expertise, and interest of the community.
6. Improving the quality of data/resource, resulting in more accurate searching, adding value to data.
7. Making data discoverable in different ways for a more diverse audience.
8. Gaining firsthand insight on user desires and the answers to difficult questions by asking and then listening to the crowd.
9. Demonstrating the value and relevance of the library in the community by the high level of public involvement.
10. Strengthening and building the trust and loyalty of library users.
11. Feelings being taken advantage of by students are reduced because libraries are not profit seeking entities.

12. Encouraging a sense of public ownership and responsibility toward cultural heritage collections through users' contributions and collaborations.

An example of crowdsourcing is the New York Public Library's (Howard, 2012) menu project called What's on the Menu? NYPL has a collection of approximately forty-five thousand restaurant menus from the 1840s to the present. Several years ago, the NYPL photographed nine thousand of these menus to be included in their NYPL digital gallery, and volunteers successfully completed the transcription of those nine thousand menus within three months. NYPL has thousands of menus remaining and has consistently been scanning more menus and wants them transcribed dish by dish to enable additional avenues of discovery for research and accessibility. The task of manually transcribing all the menus is too large and time-consuming to accomplish without external resources. NYPL took this opportunity to experiment with broader user collaboration or crowdsourcing to execute the work by inviting the public to contribute to the What's on the Menu? project and begin transcribing their digitized copies of New York restaurant menus.

For the transcriber, the collection is a daily adventure of serendipitous thrills—the antiquated use of *soda fountain* instead of today's *soda, Coke, or Pepsi*; the remarkable preponderance of oyster dishes; the shock that steaks cost twenty-five cents, not twenty-five dollars. For the scholar, it is an invaluable source of historical data.

The final report white paper submitted by NYPL to the National Endowment for the Humanities (Vershbow, 2013, pp. 2–3) highlights how author William Grimes used the collection to produce a culinary history of New York, and Texas A&M marine biologist Glenn Jones scoured seafood menus to study fish populations. What's on the Menu? also inspired users outside academia: New York chefs such as Mario Batali (Babbo, Del Posto, Eataly) and Brooklyn's Doug Crowell (Buttermilk Channel) publicly endorsed the project, and Rich Torrisi of Little Italy's Torrisi Italian Specialties, and David Chang, creator of the Momofuku chain, created special menus derived from items in the collections. To emphasize the user-friendly project and the ease of use of the tools, a class of fourth graders in San Antonio, Texas, used the site to practice keyboarding skills while learning about historical cuisine. By codifying and enhancing digital collections, crowdsourcing spawns new applications for historical information.

The National Endowment for the Humanities originally awarded the NYPL a $50,000 Digital Humanities Start-Up Grant to fund the "development of a prototype interface for a tool that would allow scholars and interested members of the general public to contribute to transcription of materials related to culinary history, using the menu collection" (Vershbow, 2013, pp. 2–3). Due to the success of What's on the Menu?, the National Endowment for the Humanities allowed NYPL to extend and expand their funding. NYPL found cost savings by developing the interface tool in-house instead of contracting an outside company to develop it. Also, NYPL utilized a team of interns to help manage the project.

As libraries face budget cuts across the board, finding innovative and cost-effective methods such as crowdsourcing will help secure future creative works and scholarship with academic librarians and the collections they engage with.

ANOTHER EXAMPLE: DARTMOUTH COLLEGE

The Institute of Museum and Library Services published a press release, "IMLS Awards Crowdsourcing Grant to Tiltfactor Laboratory at Dartmouth College: Tiltfactor will develop crowdsourcing consortium for cultural heritage institutions" (Bullard, 2014, p. 1). The National Leadership for Libraries grant is nearly $100,000 and will be used to develop the Crowdsourcing Consortium for Libraries and Archives. Tiltfactor Laboratory's main focus has been to design and study innovative games for social impact in concert with crowdsourcing. Using their experience combined with national humanities scholars and leading technologies, they will investigate and develop best practices for collecting and implementing metadata and data into existing holdings while increasing patron engagement. The goal of the Crowdsourcing Consortium for Libraries and Archives is to enhance the user experience with digitized collections through crowdsourcing tools and platforms (IMLS, 2014).

Metadata Games is a free open-source digital platform that was developed by Tiltfactor Lab at Dartmouth. Metadata Games has support from the National Endowment for the Humanities and the American Council of Learned Societies. Metadata Games are a group of interactive tagging games designed to utilize crowdsourcing to create the metadata needed to make libraries' and museums' collections searchable online. Tiltfactor's Metadata Games are so successful that a wide variety of institutions are using them:

> Various institutions are using Metadata Games to publicize their digitized collections and gather metadata. The British Library is using

the games to add tags to naval images, 16th–18th century portraits, and old book covers and title pages. The University of California, Irvine Library is doing a project called Anteater Tag (named after UCI's mascot), using Metadata Games to crowdsource information about photographs of UCI from 1963–1982. Other partners include the American Antiquarian Society, the Boston Public Library, and the UCLA Chicano Studies Research Center, and the Yale University Library, and more. (metadatagames.org, 2014)

ANOTHER EXAMPLE: UNIVERSITY OF SOUTHERN CALIFORNIA, LOS ANGELES PUBLIC LIBRARY, AND LOS ANGELES LIBRARY FOUNDATION COLLABORATE

University of Southern California's Annenberg School for Communication and Journalism professor Josh Kun is the creator of the To Live and Dine in LA project, which is the second in a series of collaborations between the Library Foundation and the Los Angeles Public Library. "The project will launch with the publication of the first-ever book on the history of restaurants in Los Angeles written and edited by Kun and published by Angel City Press. Throughout 2015, the Foundation and Library will further celebrate the food history of L.A. with a major exhibition at Central Library and diverse public programs throughout the city that will all help raise awareness of food politics and food insecurity in contemporary Los Angeles" (Library Foundation of Los Angeles, 2014).

Professor Kun directed the To Live and Dine in LA project with the Library Foundation of Los Angeles and Los Angeles Public Library librarians. For this project, the crowdsourcing volunteers were Professor Kun's students. This was a step in the right direction for academic libraries.

BENEFITS OF CROWDSOURCING

During an interview regarding eScience data gathering, Lippincott (2011) commented on how crowdsourcing can be applied to libraries to create meaningful engagement for patrons, illustrating the point of libraries accessing the power of the community. Each library and its community will have different needs that will drive their objectives and goals. Choosing the best fit to facilitate user engagement is a result of asking an important question (Holley, 2010): What do we need help with? Fostering an environment for user engagement and participation through the right crowdsourcing strategies allows for libraries to be the spark for community conversation.

Additional benefits to crowdsourcing are increased search accuracy and lower costs of document transcription. Crowdsourcing is an innovative method to get people using and interacting with library collections. There is potential for multiple benefits with crowdsourcing—for example, financial savings, data accuracy, patron engagement, and increased web traffic. NYPL's advice to another library or archive contemplating such an experiment is to take a step back and look at your collections. What items are unique to your institution? Of those items, which have demonstrated or have potential to demonstrate the most diverse and inclusive appeal? Is there a problem that the public can help you solve to improve access to this collection? Utilize available tools. The appeal of a library's collections and the call of its mission are its most valuable assets.

Crowdsourcing in libraries has the promise to be the next positive and cost-effective disruption libraries should embrace. Social media and technology have improved the connection between libraries and their communities, and by harnessing the potential power of crowdsourcing, libraries will remain the center of community engagement.

OPEN EDUCATIONAL RESOURCES ADVOCACY

Another area where academic librarians contribute to an ethical university is leading the open-access movement in higher education. The development of open-access policies in North America can be traced, in part, to the 2008 National Institutes of Health policy that required all research funded by the institute to be available in the PubMed medical research database within twelve months of commercial publication. That same year, Harvard University's College of Liberal Arts and Sciences enacted an open-access policy that granted the university a nonexclusive license to make the scholarly works produced by the college faculty available for noncommercial use. These materials would reside in Harvard's institutional repository, a digital space created to preserve and make accessible research and scholarship produced by faculty, staff, and students (Fruin & Sutton, 2016). Since these initiatives began, the open-access movement has expanded beyond journal articles to encompass a broad range of information sources, including books, dissertations and theses, audio and visual media, research data, and various forms of gray literature published and distributed outside of the traditional commercial publishing industry, such as government documents, working papers, newsletters, maps, and policy reports from nongovernmental organizations (Mack, 2020).

One major offshoot of the growing open-access movement has been support for the use of open educational resources. As Hess, Nann, and Riddle (2016) state, "Open educational resources are pedagogical materials that are free of charge and openly licensed in such a way that they can be accessed, re-used, and distributed widely by educators, learners, and the general public" (p. 128). The growth of open educational resources has primarily been in response to the rising costs of acquiring scholarly materials. For example, the cost of journals has consistently increased past the cost of inflation while many library budgets remained stagnant or increased only modestly (Schroeder, 2021). The rising cost of acquiring research resources in the STEM fields and the medical sciences has been particularly problematic. In response to pressure from libraries, most large publishers now bundle journals into packages that may lower overall per-journal costs. However, these packages often include journals that do not reflect the research and teaching needs of the university and encourage the proliferation of new journals published to fill smaller and smaller disciplinary niches (Greco, 2015).

Open educational resources are intended to create an alternative to commercially produced academic resources. Besides reducing costs, open educational resources provide greater flexibility in customizing resources for students. Rather than forcing students to purchase expensive textbooks that include content that may not be covered in class, instructors can customize access to content that is most relevant to the needs of the course. In addition, as Hess, Nann, and Riddle (2016) note, "Since most of these resources are under a Creative Commons or similar license, instructors are not only allowed to modify the content, they are even permitted to republish their modifications online, allowing others to use the new material as well" (p. 129).

This means that faculty no longer need to be passive consumers of commercially published research. The nature of open educational resources allows instructors to be active participants in creating new content that can be shared and further modified by others, building a repository of scholarship that provides access to materials that are constantly evolving to meet the demands of new research and emerging trends in pedagogy. Finally, evidence suggests open educational research helps historically underserved or financially disadvantaged students obtain access to information that otherwise could be difficult or expensive to obtain (Jenkins et al., 2020; Riehman-Murphy et al., 2020).

Academic librarians are often the strongest advocates in the university for the use of open educational resources and other types of open-access materials in support of research, teaching, and student learning. There are several reasons why this is the case: academic librarians are best positioned to understand the cost benefits of open-access sources versus acquiring materials from traditional academic publishers, they are well-versed in intellectual property rights and copyright law that must be considered when providing access to digitalized materials in institutional repositories, and they understand hierarchies of knowledge production and the organization of information in ways that help optimize the use of information storage and retrieval systems that incorporate open-access materials (Okamoto, 2013). These actions contribute to the ethical use of university resources because they promote the use of knowledge that can be shared, developed in collaborative ways, and transformed to support new modes of teaching and student learning that would otherwise be difficult or impossible to implement for materials restricted under copyright.

As noted, librarians' advocacy in using open-access materials supports the principles of social justice and access to information because it helps build a bridge of opportunity between students who have the financial means to acquire the research resources they need and those who do not. Open access also provides opportunities to obtain content that commercial publishers are reluctant to acquire because doing so may not be profitable or the information may be in a format that cannot be easily repackaged for publication, such as large data sets.

The topics discussed above demonstrate ways in which academic librarians contribute to an ethical university. For various reasons, these contributions have not been explored adequately in the literature that examines higher education and ethics. Within the profession, however, librarians struggle with ethical issues related to building representative collections that support interdisciplinarity, teach students information literacy and critical thinking skills, and promote universal principles of access to information and freedom of expression. We present two examples of ethical problems in the field of academic librarianship that have implications for realizing the ethical university.

COMMERCIAL VENDORS AND ACCESS

Academic libraries rely almost entirely on commercial vendors to provide online access to information required to support research, teaching, and learning within the university. Despite the inroads made by promoting the use of open-access research resources, the vast majority of scholarly communication made available through the library is disseminated by large private companies that acquire, repackage, and provide digital access to knowledge. The packaging of information accessible to the campus community is most often in the form of databases or digital collections that bundle research and, in some cases, popular literature, data, select open-source materials, and digital media in systems that are searchable using keywords and Boolean logic. These products provide access to research resources within a specific discipline, or their content is aggregated onto platforms that can be searched across multiple disciplines.

At most universities, a significant portion of the library's budget is devoted to subscriptions to these databases. As with other forms of scholarly content, costs increase with each subscription contract renewal. This raises a fundamental question: At what point do the costs of subscribing to these systems outweigh the benefits of having access to the journal articles or other sources they provide? This question is particularly relevant because most of the research made accessible by these companies is created by faculty employed in institutions of higher education, and, therefore, repackaging this work can be viewed as violating the principles of open access. The recent battle between the University of California system and Elsevier, the world's largest publisher of academic research journals, illustrates this.

In a memo dated April 25, 2018, the University Committee on Library and Scholarly Communication of the University of California unanimously endorsed eighteen principles that must be considered when the university negotiates any future journal subscription license agreements with commercial publishers. The principles were intended to underpin future negotiations and "to leverage faculty backing to ensure that UC spends taxpayer money in the most ethically, morally, and socially-responsible way when entering into agreements with publishers" (University of California, 2018).

When the five-year contract that provided access to more than twenty-five hundred journals published by Elsevier ended in 2018, the University of California entered into negotiations that included demands to reduce excessively high journal subscription fees that had become unsustainable in relation to overall library budget constraints and to create open access to all articles published by University of California authors, directly challenging the traditional business model of Elsevier and other large academic publishers (Fox

& Brainard, 2019). After months of negotiations, the University of California dropped Elsevier because the company had refused to meet the institution's demands. As a consequence, Elsevier blocked access by University of California faculty, staff, and students to articles published since January 1, 2019. Although librarians braced for a significant rise in complaints, there was only a slight increase in requests through interlibrary loan services. In addition, rather than being upset, most faculty supported the principles of open access advocated by the university.

After more than two years of negotiations, Elsevier agreed to a new four-year agreement that went into effect on April 1, 2021. The agreement secured universal open access to all University of California research and reduced projected journal subscription costs by integrating library and author payments into a single cost-controlled approach known as the "read and publish" model (University of California, 2021). Announced as a win for advocates of the open-access movement, the deal established that all articles published in Elsevier journals with a University of California corresponding author will be open access by default.

However, the ethical struggle of providing access to essential research remains for most institutions. The University of California leveraged its enormous scholarly output (estimated by University of California to represent 10 percent of all articles published in Elsevier journals) to negotiate a new open-access deal. Most institutions do not possess the same leverage to pursue such a goal. As such, libraries are left with the challenge of managing access to increasingly expensive journal packages or eliminating journal subscriptions that can only be acquired through interlibrary loan services. This increased workload requires investments in additional staffing to meet demands for articles that are unavailable. In addition, although interlibrary loan services are an efficient way for the campus community to acquire materials not held by the library, the acquisition and distribution process takes time and is not a substitute for instant access to digital resources purchased by the library.

Libraries are expected to provide the knowledge content required to support all areas of student learning and faculty research. However, as illustrated by the University of California example, this goal can be undermined when expenditures outpace budget allocations. Librarians and vendors have always had an "awkward collaboration" (Shirk, 1991) that reflects tensions between the profit-seeking motives of private vendors and the academic library as a nonprofit entity required to fulfill its mission to provide access to information. Within this ongoing conundrum, librarians are confronted with ethical issues of honesty, transparency, and good faith business practices that impact providing high-quality services to the university.

LEARNING ANALYTICS AND STUDENT PRIVACY

First identified as an emerging trend by the Association of College and Research Libraries in 2018, the issue of learning analytics was named as a top trend within the field of academic librarianship in 2020 (Benedetti et al., 2020). *Learning analytics* refers to deliberate efforts by universities to gather, interpret, and act on data for the purpose of better understanding student learning outcomes and to use this data to formulate methods of active intervention intended to improve academic success and student retention. As more and more universities pursue learning analytics, academic librarians have begun to contemplate their own role in gathering student data for this purpose. The data from libraries can include, for example, statistics related to student use of the library spaces, instruction, utilization of interlibrary loan and other library services, and the use of online resources, including data concerning student use of vendor products and services.

To help address this issue, the Library Integration in Institutional Learning Analytics project was developed with funding from the Institute of Museum and Library Services (Oakleaf, 2020). The objective of the project was to resolve the following key questions: What should the library's involvement with campus-wide learning analytics look like? How might library engagement in learning analytics change the ways in which students interact with the library? How might involvement in learning analytics highlight the value and impact of library services, resources, and facilities on student learning? And, most importantly, how might library involvement in institutional learning analytics increase student learning and success, "especially [for] those who may be less familiar with the unwritten rules of higher education, including first-generation students, community college students, students of color, students with disabilities, and veterans" (Oakleaf, 2020, p. 11).

The white paper provided a comprehensive overview of the possible ways academic libraries could participate in an institution's learning analytics efforts while at the same time increasing awareness of and discussion about the role of academic libraries in learning analytics across the institution. The project also provided case studies of learning analytics projects involving libraries.

However, the growth in academic library participation in institutional learning analytics initiatives has raised serious ethical concerns among many academic librarians. Particularly concerning were unresolved issues of protecting student privacy and how librarians could fully comply with institutional directives to mine learning analytics data used to evaluate student learning outcomes. Underpinning these concerns are ethical standards governing professional behavior. The second principle of the Association of College and Research Libraries' Intellectual Freedom Principles for Academic Libraries states, "The privacy of library users is and must be inviolable. Policies should be in place that maintain confidentiality of library borrowing records and of other information relating to personal use of library information and services" (Association of College and Research Libraries, 1999). This principle establishes foundational guidance regarding intellectual freedom in an academic library setting and how academic librarians fulfill their responsibilities ethically in providing services to library users. Concomitantly, library administrators may be pressured to participate in institutional learning analytics, particularly at institutions where student retention and graduation rates are low.

In a review of the literature, Jones et al. (2020) identified several key problems associated with practical ethical privacy issues and current data practices in academic libraries related to learning analytics projects. The review highlighted concerns about student informed consent and evidence that academic libraries make decisions about participating in learning analytics initiatives almost completely absent of student consent. Evidence from the literature also revealed that data collection was conducted without established best practices or standards of conduct. This is particularly problematic because the granularity of data gathered is not consistently applied.

As the authors point out, tracking student use of electronic databases could be quantified in terms of use or nonuse, the number of times the student used a database, or timed increments within a specific database. Tracking data could also include whether a student checked out books, the number of books that were checked out, or the types of books checked out and for how long. Studies indicate that academic libraries keep data for long durations with little attention to data security. This includes not just methods of storage security but also securing the transfer of data from one place to another. Related to this, the authors found a lack of specificity around anonymization procedures to ensure that the removal of direct identifiers was implemented to protect student privacy.

The emergence of learning analytics in higher education can be tied to broader issues of accountability in response to external constituents and to rising tuition costs and the student debt crisis. Ethical debates within the field of academic librarianship have expanded and melded with issues such as big data (Currier, 2021; Holloway, 2020) and student attitudes about the use of library search data (Gariepy, 2021). The struggle to maintain adherence to ethical standards of student privacy protection in relation to institutional learning analytics data mining of library systems is likely to continue into the foreseeable future. In an ethical university, these conflicting goals must be addressed through mutually respectful, collaborative discussions about the use of library data that protects student privacy and excludes personally identifiable information.

CONCLUSION

This chapter outlines some of the ways academic librarians contribute to ethical conduct in universities in relation to student learning, access to information, and the work of academic librarians to support the overall educational mission. These efforts contribute to transforming universities into organizations that cultivate ethical forms of knowledge acquisition, creation, and preservation and, in so doing, create the conditions for sustained success. At the same time, as with faculty and other members of the university, academic librarians struggle with a variety of ethical problems within their profession. Two examples are provided to illustrate this, although there are many other problems that can be understood through an ethical framework. Most of these issues are invisible to the wider campus community. Nevertheless, they can have a deleterious effect on realizing the goals of an ethical university and, as a consequence, can undermine the overall integrity and reputation of the university if not addressed in a responsible manner.

REFERENCES

Association of College and Research Libraries. (1999, June 29). "Intellectual Freedom Principles for Academic Libraries." www.ala.org/acrl/publications/whitepapers/intellectual.

Ballenger, Julia. (2010). "Women's Access to Higher Education Leadership: Cultural and Structural Barriers." *Forum on Public Policy Online* 2010, no. 5.

Bandura, Albert. (1986). *Social Foundations of Thought and Action: A Social Cognitive Theory*. Englewood Cliffs, NJ: Prentice-Hall.

Benedetti, Allison, Ginny Boehme, Thomas R. Caswell, Kyle Denlinger, Yuan Li, Alex D. McAllister, Brian D. Quigley, Catherine B. Soehner, Minglu Wang, and Andrew J. Wesolek. (2020). "2020 Top Trends in Academic Libraries." *College and Research Libraries News* 81, no. 6: 270–278.

Bourdieu, Pierre. (2002). "The Forms of Capital." In *Readings in Economic Sociology*, 280–291. Oxford: Blackwell.

Bullard, Giuliana. (2014, August 1). "IMLS Awards Crowdsourcing Grant to Tiltfactor Laboratory at Dartmouth College: 'Tiltfactor Will Develop Crowdsourcing Consortium for Cultural Heritage Institutions.'" Institute of Museum and Library Services. www.imls.gov/imls_awards_crowdsourcing_grant_to_tiltfactor_laboratory_at_dartmouth_college.aspx.

Currier, C. (2021). "Unresolved Privacy and Ethics Issues Related to Learning Analytics in Higher Education and Academic Librarianship." *Emerging Library and Information Perspectives* 4: 117–142.

Davis, Jeff. (2010). *The First-Generation Student Experience : Implications for Campus Practice and Strategies for Improving Persistence and Success*. Sterling, VA: Stylus.

Drabinski, Emily. (2019, April). "What Is Critical about Critical Librarianship?" *Art Libraries Journal* 44, no. 2: 49. doi:10.1017/alj.2019.3.

Fox, Alex, and Jeffrey Brainard. (2019, February). "University of California Boycotts Publishing Giant Elsevier over Journal Costs and Open Access." *Science*. www.sciencemag.org/news/2019/02/university-california-boycotts-publishing-giant-elsevier-over-journal-costs-and-open.

Frodeman, Robert, Julie Thompson Klein, and Roberto C. S. Pacheco. (2017). *The Oxford Handbook of Interdisciplinarity*, 2nd edition. Oxford: Oxford University Press.

Fruin, Christine, and Shan Sutton. (2016). "Strategies for Success: Open Access Policies at North American Educational Institutions." *College and Research Libraries* 77, no. 4: 469–499.

Gaines, Ayanna. (2014). "That's Women's Work: Pink-Collar Professions, Gender, and the Librarian Stereotype." In *The Librarian Stereotype: Deconstructing Perceptions and Presentations of Information Work*, Nicole Pagowsky and Miriam Rigby, eds. Chicago: Association of College and Research Libraries, pp. 85–109.

Gariepy, Laura W. (2021). "Acceptable and Unacceptable Uses of Academic Library Search Data: An Interpretive Description of Undergraduate Student Perspectives." *Evidence Based Library and Information Practice* 16, no. 2: 22–44.

Gibbons, Melinda M., and Marie F. Shoffner. (2004). "Prospective First-Generation College Students: Meeting Their Needs through Social Cognitive Career Theory." *Professional School Counseling* 8, no. 1: 91–97.

Goddard, Roger D., Wayne K. Hoy, and Anita Woolfolk Hoy. (2004). "Collective Efficacy Beliefs: Theoretical Developments, Empirical Evidence, and Future Directions." *Educational Researcher* 33, no. 3: 3–13.

Greco, Albert N. (2015, October). "Academic Libraries and the Economics of Scholarly Publishing in the Twenty-First Century: Portfolio Theory, Product Differentiation, Economic Rent, Perfect Price Discrimination, and the Cost of Prestige." *Journal of Scholarly Publishing* 47, no. 1: 1–43.

Hess, Julia I., Alejandra J. Nann, and Kelly E. Riddle. (2016). "Navigating OER: The Library's Role in Bringing OER to Campus." *The Serials Librarian* 70, no. 1-4: 128–134.

Highby, Wendy. (2004). "The Ethics of Academic Collection Development in a Politically Contentious Era." *Library Collections, Acquisitions, and Technical Services* 28, no. 4: 465–472.

Holley, Rose. (2010). "Crowdsourcing: How and Why Should Libraries Do It?" *D-Lib Magazine* 16, no. 3–4.

Holloway, Kristine. (2020). "Big Data and Learning Analytics in Higher Education: Legal and Ethical Considerations." *Journal of Electronic Resources Librarianship* 32, no. 4: 276–285.

Howard, Jennifer. (2012). Breaking Down Menus Digitally, Dish by Dish. ('What's on the Menu?'). *The Chronicle of Higher Education*, 58 (35).

Ishitani, Terry T. (2006). "Studying Attrition and Degree Completion Behavior among First-Generation College Students in the United States." *Journal of Higher Education* (Columbus) 77, no. 5: 861–885.

Jenkins, J. Jacob, Luis A. Sánchez, Megan A. K. Schraedley, Jaime Hannans, Nitzan Navick, and Jade Young. (2020). "Textbook Broke: Textbook Affordability as a Social Justice Issue." *Journal of Interactive Media in Education* 1, no. 3: 1–13.

Jones, Kyle M. L., Kristin A. Briney, Abigail Goben, Dorothea Salo, Andrew Asher, and Michael R. Perry. (2020). "A Comprehensive Primer to Library Learning Analytics Practices, Initiatives, and Privacy Issues." *College and Research Libraries* 81, no. 3: 570–591.

Jones, Maralyn. (2012). "Teaching Research across Disciplines: Interdisciplinarity and Information Literacy." In *Interdisciplinarity and Academic Libraries*, Daniel C. Mack and Craig Gibson, eds., 167–181 Chicago: Association of College and Research Libraries.

Labaree, Robert V. (2013, October 22–25). "Polymathic Information Literacy Competencies: Deconstructing What It Means to Be Interdisciplinarily Literate." Paper presented at the First European Conference on Information Literacy. Istanbul, Turkey.

Library Foundation of Los Angeles. (2014). "New Library Foundation Project Led by USC Annenberg Professor to Focus on History of LA Restaurants." University of Southern California, USC Annenberg News. http://annenberg .usc.edu/News%20and%20Events/News/140813LAMenus.aspx.

Lippincott, J. (2011, June 22). "Digging into Data, Identifiers, Crowdsourcing & Scientific Data." CNI Conversations podcast. http://cniconversations .wordpress.com/2011/06/23/june-22-2011-digging-into-data-identifiers -crowdsourcing-scientific-data/.

Mack, Daniel C. (2020). "Open Access in the Academy: Developing a Library Program for Campus Engagement." *Grey Journal* 16, no. 3: 181–185.

Mack, Daniel C., and Craig Gibson. (2012). *Interdisciplinarity and Academic Libraries*. Chicago: Association of College and Research Libraries.

Mihram, Danielle, and Melissa Miller. (2021). USC Illuminated Medieval Manuscripts: A second polymathic multimodal digital project. *College & Research Libraries News*, 82(9), 420–. https://doi.org/10.5860/crln.82.9.420

Miller, Melissa L. (2021). *Mind, Motivation, and Meaningful Learning: Strategies for Teaching Adult Learners*. Chicago: Association of College and Research Libraries.

Newswander, Lynita K., and Chad B. Newswander. (2012). "Encouraging Cognitive Flexibility and Interdisciplinarity in Public Administration Programs." *Administration and Society* 44, no. 3: 285–309.

Oakleaf, Megan. (2020, November 18). "Library Integration in Institutional Learning Analytics." LIILA White Paper, Syracuse University. https://library.educause.edu/resources/2018/11/library-integration-in-institutional-learning-analytics.

Okamoto, Karen. (2013). Making higher education more affordable, one course reading at a time: Academic libraries as key advocates for open access textbooks and educational resources. *Public Services Quarterly*, 9 (4), 267–283.

Open Source Crowdsourcing Game Platform. (January, 2014). Retrieved from https://metadatagames.org/#games

Pascarella, Ernest T., Christopher T. Pierson, Gregory C. Wolniak, and Patrick T. Terenzini. (2004). "First-Generation College Students: Additional Evidence on College Experiences and Outcomes." *Journal of Higher Education* (Columbus) 75, no. 3: 249–284.

Potter, Susan, and Robert P. Holley. (2010). "Rare Material in Academic Libraries." *Collection Building* 29, no. 4: 148–153.

Reynolds, Gretchen E., Cynthia Holt, and John C. Walsh. (2012). "Collection Development: Acquiring Content Across and Beyond Disciplines." In *Interdisciplinarity and Academic Libraries*, Daniel C. Mack and Craig Gibson, eds., 97–113. Chicago: Association of College and Research Libraries.

Riehman-Murphy, Christina, Victoria Raish, Emily Mross, Andrea Pritt, and Elizabeth Nelson. (2020). "Bridges to Affordability: Adopting a University OAER Mandate with Local Implementation." *Reference Services Review* 18, no. 3: 339–352.

Schroeder, Sarah Bartlett. (2021). "Publicly Funded Research Behind Private Paywalls: The Open Access Movement." In *SAGE Business Cases*. London: SAGE.

Shirk, Gary M. (1991). "The Wondrous Web: Reflections on Library Acquisitions and Vendor Relationships." *The Acquisitions Librarian* 3, no. 5: 1–8.

Sill, David J. (2001). "Integrative Thinking, Synthesis, and Creativity in Interdisciplinary Studies." *Journal of General Education* 50, no. 4: 288–311.

Soria, Krista M., and Michael J. Stebleton. (2012). "First-Generation Students' Academic Engagement and Retention." *Teaching in Higher Education* 17, no. 6: 673–685.

Spiro, R. J., R. L. Coulson, P. J. Feltovich, and D. Anderson. (1988). "Cognitive Flexibility Theory: Advanced Knowledge Acquisition in Ill-structured

Domains." In *Proceedings of the 10th Annual Conference of the Cognitive Science Society*, V. Patel, ed., 375–383. Hillsdale, NJ: Lawrence Erlbaum.

Waddell, Myra, and Elena Clariza. (2018). "Critical Digital Pedagogy and Cultural Sensitivity in the Library Classroom: Infographics and Digital Storytelling." *College and Research Libraries News* 79, no. 5, doi:https://doi.org/10.5860/crln.79.5.228.

Wallace, Richard L., and Susan G. Clark. (2017). "Barriers to Interdisciplinarity in Environmental Studies: A Case of Alarming Trends in Faculty and Programmatic Wellbeing." *Issues in Interdisciplinary Studies* 35: 221–247.

Woosley, Sherry A., and Dustin K. Shepler. (2011). "Understanding the Early Integration Experiences of First-Generation College Students." *College Student Journal* 45, no. 4: 700–714.

University of Alabama Libraries. (2014). "Crowdsourcing at University Libraries." www.lib.ua.edu/crowdsourcing.

University of California. (2018). "Re: Declaration of Rights and Principles to Transform Scholarly Communication." https://senate.universityof california.edu/_files/committees/ucolasc/scholcommprinciples-20180425.pdf.

University of California. (2021, March 16). "UC Secures Landmark Open Access Deal with World's Largest Scientific Publisher." UC Office of the President. www.universityofcalifornia.edu/press-room/uc-news-uc-secures -landmark-open-access-deal-world-s-largest-scientific-publisher.

Vershbow, B. (2013). "Crowdsourcing Culinary History at the New York Public Library." Final White Paper Report. United States National Endowment for the Humanities.

The Use of Adjuncts in US Colleges and Universities

Michael Boylan

ABSTRACT

This chapter will argue that the present system of college and university adjunct teachers in the United States is highly exploitative and is therefore an immoral institution and should be revised in such a way that the dictum of "just implication of rules" will be upheld. It will be the suggestion of this chapter that such a move will require dismantling the tenure system and creating a new structure of academic employment.

Keywords: adjunct professors, desert theory, employment fairness, just implementation of rules, tenure system

This chapter will only examine nonprofit institutions as it is the opinion of this author that for-profit tertiary institutions are faced with a myriad of conflicts of interest. (But this will have to be the subject of another chapter.) Tertiary education in the university systems of the United States contain public and private institutions. They are highly dependent, monetarily, on either (1) a mixture of subsidies from state legislators and student tuitions (though some public universities also have endowments) or (2) a mixture of student tuition and moneys from endowments. (There are only a select number of universities that have endowments that are robust enough to really make a difference here: 120 top endowments account for 75 percent of all college endowment money (among 5,300 total colleges and universities in the US). Thus, most universities are heavily tuition-driven to keep the doors open (Link A).

To remain financially viable, both public and private universities depend on a class of university employees called adjuncts. Let us pause to define our terms. Within the university system in the US, there are the following job classifications:

1. Full-time positions

   a. Full professor (generally tenured). *Tenure* in the United States, according to the American Association of University Professors, means "an indefinite appointment that can be terminated only for cause or under extraordinary circumstances such as financial exigency and program discontinuation" (Link B).
   b. Associate professor (generally tenured).
   c. Assistant professor (generally not tenured but on a track to apply for tenure within six years).
   d. Term appoints (year-to-year appointments—generally limited to six years).

2. Part-time positions

   a. Straight adjunct positions, which are limited in the number of classes they may teach to two per term (quarter or semester). They may have term-to-term or yearly contracts. There are some other positions, such as postdoctorate positions, but these variants are really term appointments as set out above. The same holds true for visiting professors, *distinguished* or otherwise.

None of these part-time positions are on a tenure track unless they are so converted by the academic institution, which is very rare. In addition to these classifications, there are also chairs or named professorships, which are generally less about teaching and more about money.

The overwhelming number of part-time positions are staffed by adjuncts. There are some adjuncts who have other careers and don't need the money. These people use the university affiliation to promote their other career. These sorts of adjuncts are not the focus of this chapter. It is therefore these individuals to whom this chapter is directed.

WHAT'S WRONG WITH THE PRESENT
SITUATION WITH ADJUNCTS?

In a holistic sense, everything that is wrong about the position of adjuncts in our public and private universities can be termed a violation of the legal and moral dictum *just implementation of rules* or JIR, which states that like cases should be treated in a like manner (Boylan, 2004, pp. 167–168). In this context, let us look at new adjunct hires in the context of new assistant professors (see table 6.1).

Certainly, on the face of it, table 6.1 shows that given similar qualifications, the financial and other tangible rewards of being an assistant professor on the tenure track far outweigh those of the adjunct. Thus, it would seem to be a violation of JIR. Since all violations of the JIR are, at a minimum, immoral, this would suggest that the hiring category of adjuncts is immoral. If we all agree that immoral hiring categories ought to be eliminated, then we must eliminate the adjunct hiring category.

Table 6.1.   A comparison between assistant professor tenure track with adjunct

	Qualifications	Salary	Benefits	Fringes	Job Security
Candidate X (assistant professor)	Generally, PhD Minimum masters	$60–80K	Full package	Office, etc.	Tenure track
Candidate Y (adjunct)	Generally, PhD Minimum masters	$5–28K	None	Limited	Term-to-term

- The AAUP collects data such as salary on full-time professors at two-year, four-year, and masters- and PhD-granting institutions. See Link C.
- These benefits can include health insurance, disability insurance, life insurance, daycare reimbursement, parking discount, etc. The total benefit can be as much as $20,000.
- These fringe benefits generally cannot be quantified in dollars. Rather, it is qualitative. If one has a private office with their name on it (assistant professor) and the adjunct must share an office with five other people, and their name (with the four others) is handwritten on a card taped to the door, there is a marked difference in the respect shown.
- In terms of job security, most tenure-track contracts in the United States are three-year renewable contracts that allow the professor to be considered for tenure in the sixth year for a potential lifetime contract (so long as they can meet classes and turn in grades).

THE QUALIFICATIONS OBJECTION

But some would say that under "qualifications," the new assistant professor (or anyone else on the tenure track line) is not *equally* qualified for the job but rather *more* qualified in that they may have done a superior job in their doctoral education and dissertation or may have studied under a more famous director.

To this I would contend that judging who is "more qualified" at the stage of just having finished their PhD is rather imprecise. This is because of the existence of privilege in the process of candidate X having gone to a more prestigious school and/or studied with a dissertation director who is better known by their research.

These problems include (a) what racial, gender, and social class a person is born into; (b) what kind of school a candidate can get into because of (a); (c) what kind of graduate program a candidate can get into because of (b); and the assumption that working with a dissertation director with a long research résumé ensures that the student of such is groomed to be a good teacher and prone to excellence for future research—all on account of the graduate school teacher/student relationship. The system that supports these notions is assumed to be accurate and fair (see Sackett et al., 2012; Toldson and McGee, 2014; Majors, 2019; Hausman, 2012; Barnes and Mertz, 2012).

There is a strong flavor of a "good old boys" network in US higher education—especially at the most prestigious research universities. Those outside this background of privilege are not given a fair assessment of their qualifications. This, in turn, means they will not be treated equally in the mix of things—JIR will not be in play.

Certainly, one way to partially rectify this unfair situation is to put more emphasis on the road traveled by the candidate rather than on just where the candidate got their PhD and who was their director. I have previously outlined such a system that emphasizes what the candidate themselves has done by their own merit (Boylan, 2014, pp. 187–192).

In my forty-five years teaching in US tertiary education, it has often been my experience that random factors that do not adhere to desert (based on my "road traveled" model as being a better indicator of potentiality) are often the reasons people are hired for tenure-track jobs. These might include whether the candidate looks and/or acts like the person whose job change, retirement, or death created the opening in the first place. Another factor I have observed is an assessment of how well the candidate will fit into the department. If the department consists entirely of straight, white males, then obviously this is a disadvantage to those who are not. Again, this is not hiring based on JIR and desert. Thus, the qualifications objection fails and the truth of table 6.1 holds.

CAUSE OF THE ADJUNCT JOB CLASSIFICATION

One important question that must be asked in order to offer a solution to the adjunct problem is, Why did we do it? Why did we create this exploited class of instructors? It is my conjecture that the origin of the problem is the tenure system that is almost universally in place in US colleges and universities. The tenure system was ostensibly put into place to protect academic freedom. With job protection, professors would be free to speak up on matters of public importance without fear of being fired for their views (Kalenberg, 2016; Rosovsky, 1990, cf. McCumber, 2001). Freedom of speech (aside from libel and slander) is essential for tertiary education, but tenure may not be the only way to achieve this.

In the UK there is free speech for university professors without the institution of tenure (Turner, 2010). It has been my experience that university provosts and presidents who "have it in" for a particular professor—even when they have tenure—can make that professor's life unbearable anyway. Therefore, I do not think that changing the tenure system will mean that administrators will be more likely to violate faculty's freedom of speech because this right is supported by other countries that do not have tenure and because faculty within the United States—even with tenure—are punished by their administrations *right now*. So, for the purposes of this argument, the justification of the tenure system as necessary to protect academic freedom of speech is bogus.

The tenure system creates a two-tiered system of university professors in the United States: those with tenure (or who are on the road to getting tenure) and those without. This creates a system whereby those in the tenure system (those with tenure or those on the road to getting tenure) are treated as above those outside the tenure system (including adjuncts), as per table 6.1. This sense of privilege extends beyond monetary benefits alone—often including connotations of ability and worth as teachers and scholars.

In my experience in the US academic world, such a sense of privilege is very often unmerited. I have seen countless adjuncts in my field of philosophy who are as good as or better than those faculty who are tenured or on the tenure track. If my anecdotal experience is applicable to the wider body of faculty members throughout the United States, then such a state of affairs constitutes a gross violation of JIR.

HOW CAN WE IMPROVE THE SITUATION OF ADJUNCTS?

I believe it is the tenure system that has created this problem. The only solution that I can think of is to dismantle the tenure system for college and university professors in the United States and align ourselves with the employment system that most of the other wealthy countries of the world have adopted.

In brief, here are my suggestions:

1. Instead of classifying employees as tenure track versus nontenure track, which creates the underclass of adjuncts, I propose that employees be designated in two ways:

   a. By their rank: assistant professor, associate professor, and full professor (based on assessable criteria according to excellence in teaching, service, or research).
   b. By the number of courses they teach (in the case of those who highlight their teaching); by the amount of professional service they perform inside and outside the university; and/ or by the quantity and quality of research they engage in (as measured by publications and where they are published and how often they are cited) and speaking engagements (on a sliding scale beginning with conference presentations, then keynote addresses, and finally invited lectures). Instructors who are given more classes to teach or who do more service or who excel in research (in a transparent and measurable way) will be paid more than those who do less. There will have to be some sort of maximums worked into each category—a maximum number of classes that can be taught, a maximum amount of service that can be performed for compensation, and a maximum amount of research that will be compensated. Every instructor will be expected to do *some* teaching, service, and research, but according to the abilities and interests of those instructors, they can feature one of the three areas in order to achieve promotion and fulfill their mission as part of the college or university.

2. Benefits (e.g., health insurance, life insurance, disability insurance, retirement payments, office space, parking privileges, positioning on the university's website) will accrue to all ranks equally. The idea here is that all instructors will, at their respective level, be treated equally.

3. In times of economic distress, all ranks will be treated equally in terms of pay cuts by using percentages (which will give those at the top a higher amount of salary reduction based on dollars paid—since they will be at a higher level to begin with). In other words, a 10 percent cut of a full professor's $200,000 salary would be $20,000, and a 10 percent cut of an assistant professor's $60,000 salary would be $6,000. Though the percentage is the same, the actual dollars would be different. Those with more to begin with will have to give up more.

4. All entry-level employees will be paid at the same rate. They will be given an initial three-year contract that will be extended by five-year intervals thereafter based on positive evaluations. Instructors on the five-year contract schedule will be evaluated every three years. If the instructor is deficient in any respect in their primary area (teaching, service, or research), they will be given notice of the deficiency and two years to correct it before being offered a renewal for another five-year contract. There will be no mandatory retirement age. Obviously, there will be no discrimination based on age, gender (or gender orientation), race, ethnic origin, religion, or political view—this will be contractually guaranteed.

5. All instructors at whatever level will be contractually guaranteed freedom of speech, limited only by the laws of libel and slander.

CONCLUDING REMARKS

Under this system, there will be one platform for everyone. However, it is not pure egalitarianism. Those who have been at the university for a longer time may be paid more. Those at a higher rank will be paid more. Those who hold a chair position in recognition of their outstanding teaching, service, or research will also be paid more. And those who (by their work) outperform others in teaching (by number of classes taught), service (by amount and number of obligations), or research (by a transparent and scalable measurement) may be paid more.

The goal of these reforms is that the adjunct underclass will be eliminated. The financial boon to the university (that allows this to happen) is the elimination of tenure (i.e., the engine that has caused this disparity) and the ability to adjust compensation within each rate class (teaching, service, and research) so long as transparent financial exigency can be met.

There will be new problems for this or any major restructuring of the employment practices in higher education instructional services. It seems to this writer that a good first step is to eliminate the two-tiered system of employment and to take a step toward equity and fairness and thus meet the criteria of JIR.

REFERENCES

Barnes, Katherine, and Elizabeth Mertz. (2012). "Is It Fair? Law Professors' Perceptions of Tenure." *Journal of Legal Education* 61.4: 511–539.

Boylan, Michael. (2004). *A Just Society*. Lanham, MD: Rowman & Littlefield.

———. (2014). *Natural Human Rights: A Theory*. New York: Cambridge University Press.

Hausman, David. (2012). "How Congress Could Reduce Job Discrimination by Promoting Anonymous Hiring." *Stanford Law Review* 64.3: 1343–1369.

Kahlenberg, Richard D. (2016). "Teacher Tenury Has a Long History and, Hopefully, a Future." *The Phi Delta Kappan* 97.6: 16–21.

Majors, Amber T. (2019). "From the Editorial Board: College Readiness—A Critical Race Theory Perspective." *High School Journal* 102.3: 183–188.

McCumber, John. (2001). *Time in the Ditch: American Philosophy and the McCarthy Era*. Evanston, IL: Northwestern University Press.

Rosovsky, Henry. (1990). *The University: An Owners' Manuel*. New York: Norton.

Sackett, Paul R., Nathan R. Kuncel, Adam S. Beatty, et al. (2012). "The Role of Socioeconomic Status in SAT-Grade Relationships in College Admissions Decisions." *Psychological Science* 23.9: 1000–1007.

Toldson, Ivory A., and Tyne McGee. (2014). "What ACT and SAT Mean for Black Students' Higher Education Prospects." *Journal of Negro Education* 83.1: 1–4.

Turner, David A. (2010). "Freedom of Speech: Its Exercise and Its Interpretation." *British Journal of Educational Studies* 58.3: 285–291.

INTERNET LINKS

Link A: National Center for Education Statistics. "Fast Facts: Endowments."
https://nces.ed.gov/fastfacts/display.asp?id=73. (Accessed February 13,
2021.)
Link B: American Association of University Professors. "Tenure." www.aaup
.org/issues/tenure. (Accessed February 7, 2021.)
Link C: American Association of University Professors. "The Annual Report
on the Economic Status of the Profession, 2019–20." May 2020. www.aaup
.org/2019-20-faculty-compensation-survey-results. (Accessed March 13,
2021.)

Rights-Based Approaches to the Treatment of Student Athletes

Jonathan Liljeblad

ABSTRACT

The place of student athletes in university sports programs follows Foucault's notions of power structures controlling bodies and minds, with university sports subjugating student athletes in systems encompassing exercise, nutrition, rest, social life, and academics tied to expectations for behavior. The subordinate positions of student athletes renders them vulnerable to abuse by coaches, administrators, and faculty holding higher positions in the university hierarchy. The present analysis argues for a rights-based approach to prescribe norms regarding the treatment of student athletes, using international human rights as a source to guide standards for appropriate conduct by university sports programs toward student athletes. The analysis draws on the scholarship studying the connection between human rights and sports, extending the literature to identify norms for university sports programs vis-à-vis student athletes.

Keywords: ethics, Foucault, human rights, intercollegiate sports, student athletes, university

The term *student athlete* implies the association of academic experience and sports performance, with both holding comparable priority. In the context of university intercollegiate sports, the notion of student athlete entails a dedication of campus resources addressing both education and sport, so that student athletes are part of both a university's academic systems and a university's sports programs. (Ingersoll 2015; Clift & Mower 2013). At elite levels of sports, such as national intercollegiate competition, university sports programs become immersive institutions regulating student athletes' lives (see for example Grenardo 2016; Ingersoll 2015; Clift & Mower 2013; Kevin Foster 2003).

Such programs involve power structures, with a hierarchy of coaches, staff, faculty, and administrators having authority over student athletes' involvement in sports, athletic training, academic learning, and social life (see for example Ingersoll 2015; Clift & Mower 2013; Kevin Foster 2003). The power hierarchy poses a risk of abuse, with university personnel in positions to use their authority over student athletes in ways that are potentially harmful (see for example Lee et al. 2018; *Lee v. Louisiana Board of Trustees* 2017; Stirling & Kerr 2014).

The issues of student athlete welfare align with larger concerns over the treatment of athletes in organized sports. This has drawn attention to the hazards of organized sports with respect to mental and emotional abuse (Mills & Denison 2013), physical and sexual abuse (MacGregor 2021; Timpka et al. 2019), discrimination (Lee et al. 2018), surveillance and violations of privacy (Teetzel & Weaving 2014), and loss of control over image and reputation (Cho 2015). The literature examines the dangers to youth in organized sports, covering junior levels of primary or secondary school (Ojala 2018; Truscan 2012; Burke & Hallinan 2006) as well as tertiary levels of universities (McDonald & Burke 2019; Nam et al. 2018). It also points out the subordinate status of athletes within the hierarchies of organized sports encompassing coaches, trainers, and governing institutions (MacGregor 2021; McDonald & Burke 2019; Nam et al. 2018; Ojala 2018).

A body of scholarship employs human rights approaches—also called rights-based approaches (RBA)—to address the dangers faced by athletes in organized sports (see for example MacGregor 2021; Adams & Kavanagh 2020; Nam et al. 2018; Schneider 2004; Truscan 2012). It frames issues and seeks to resolve them by applying principles of human rights. For example, Nam et al. (2018) apply RBA to delineate the harms suffered by student athletes and efforts to promote cultural change regarding the treatment of student athletes (Nam et al. 2018). Such work shows how human rights can serve as a guide for university conduct toward student athletes and can constitute a framework of parameters for institutional conduct in university sports programs.

The present analysis follows the above direction, with the following sections exploring the possibilities of RBA in helping to formulate codes of conduct or ethics for the treatment of student athletes in university sports. The scope of this analysis demonstrates the utility of international human rights law as a comprehensive source of norms encompassing the status of student athletes vis-à-vis universities. The discussion begins with a brief review of the literature on the relations between universities and student athletes and the efforts to apply human rights to sports. The analysis demonstrates how RBA provides a normative framework guiding conduct through a mapping exercise. It identifies the components of international human rights law related to student athletes in university sports. The discussion then turns to labor law regarding the welfare of student athletes and larger human rights movements in organized sports. The conclusion finishes by identifying directions for future research.

UNIVERSITY-ATHLETE RELATIONS

Student athletes in universities live an immersive experience, the totality of which encompasses academic study, competitive sports, and social life, with elite student athletes under added pressure due to high expectations for sports performance, heightened public attention, and increased time demands relative to nonathlete student populations (Ingersoll 2015; Jolly 2008; Kimball 2007; Miller & Kerr 2002). Such pressures arise within the scope of university sports programs, which at levels of intercollegiate competition subsume student athletes within systems that direct them toward the goal of maximum sports performance.

To do so, university sports programs subject student athletes to comprehensive structures of training, with set schedules; surveillance of activity; monitoring of physical status; and regimens prescribing specific exercise, nutrition, and recovery (Ingersoll 2015; Teetzel & Weaving 2014; Clift & Mower 2013). In addition, they extend to mental components, with expectations for performance tied to norms of conduct in sports, academics, and larger society (Lee et al. 2018; Clift & Mower 2013; Kevin Foster 2003). While ostensibly aimed at sports, the reach of such structures is expansive in that it results in a confinement of academic study and social life to set windows of time. As a result, university sports programs represent systems of control, with elite levels increasing in the scope and depth of structure in terms of disciplining the daily lives of student athletes.

The qualities of structure and control draw scholarship that applies Foucault's concepts to delineate the relationship of student athletes to sports programs. Foucault's concerns about structures of power that discipline the body and mind of the individual apply directly to student athletes, particularly at universities with sports programs that expect to produce student athletes for intercollegiate competition and professional sports. On a more general level, Foucauldian approaches identify how organized sports subjugate athletes as subjects under mechanisms that control exercise, nutrition, rest, motivations, emotions, and roles (Ojala 2020; Mills & Denison 2013). To a degree, athletes can exercise agency within the structure of organized sports through the acquisition of performance, prestige, or economic capital (de Haan & Norman 2020).

In the context of university sports, however, those forms of capital must be treated in relation to the relative disparities between individual athletes and the university, in that compared to an individual athlete, universities host larger pools of high-performance athletes, hold more established public profiles in larger society, and enjoy greater economic resources. The inequalities render student athletes as subordinate subjects in the power structures of universities. In addition, in setting expectations for student athletes, university sports programs host discourses prescribing norms, which means that their systems of control effectively serve to socialize student athletes toward university-dictated identities (Lee et al. 2018; Sinden 2012; Kevin Foster 2003).

The power structures endemic to university sports programs can be harmful to student athletes. In particular, most proximate to student athletes are their coaches, with coach-athlete relations being sites at risk for coercion, manipulation, and maltreatment in the form of physical, sexual, verbal, and psychological abuse (see for example MacGregor 2021; Kavanagh et al. 2017; *Lee v. Louisiana Board of Trustees* 2017; Mills & Denison 2013; Stirling & Kerr 2014; Stirling & Kerr 2013; Stirling & Kerr 2009; Kassing & Infante 1999). Such harms are not isolated, in that university sports programs may also inflict on student athletes forms of discrimination according to gender, race, sexuality, and other aspects (Adams & Kavanagh 2020; Lee et al. 2018; Osborne 2006; Kevin Foster 2003).

Beyond sports is the larger space of university-athlete relations, which is responsible for locating student athletes within a hierarchy of power under coaches, administrators, and faculty (McDonald & Burke 2019). To the extent that the hierarchy of power involves models or standards of behavior, they have the capacity to create a moral atmosphere normalizing expectations and conduct (McDonald & Burke 2019; Sinden 2012; Stephens & Kavanagh 2003). The consequence is that the dangers of abuse can be systemic, with student athletes holding a subordinate position within a surrounding institution wielding superior power over their existence (Clift & Mower 2013; Burke &

Hallinan 2006; Kevin Foster 2003). The nature of the system does not necessarily address both components of the term *student athlete,* in that the promises of university education and student experience can be illusory in the context of schools that prioritize elite athletic performance for the purpose of winning in competitive intercollegiate sports (Ingersoll 2015; Clift & Mower 2013; McCormick & McCormick 2006).

There are efforts to temper the potential harms to student athletes. For example, literature in diverse disciplines highlights multiple trends to devise forms of coaching less tied to coercion and manipulation, with exploration of various pedagogies, such as player-centered approaches (Bowles & O'Dwyer 2020; Nelson et al. 2014; de Souza & Oslin 2008), conflict management methods (Davis & Jowett 2014), self-reflection (Hansen & Andersen 2014), positive reinforcement (Light & Harvey 2017), empathy (Lorimer 2013), motivation (Mageau & Vallerand 2003), or some combination of the aforementioned ideas (Rhind & Jowett 2010). There are also prescriptive efforts to articulate rules regarding coach-athlete relations and limiting the form and extent of disciplinary methods (Denison et al. 2017; Denison & Mills 2014).

Paying attention to coach-athlete relations, however, is not enough, since coaches are components within larger systems of power maintained by university sports programs. As much as student athletes hold inferior positions vis-à-vis their coaches, they are further subjugated by the institutional environment that hosts them. As a result, goals of mitigating dangers to student athletes should look beyond coaches to consider the pedagogies and conduct of the ensemble of actors in university sports programs as a whole.

It is possible to orient institutional pedagogy and conduct within university sports programs toward normative sensibilities that delineate appropriate versus inappropriate treatment of student athletes. Setting norms essentially means developing an ethics to identify ways to reform power structures that either reduce the subjugation of student athletes or at least limit the harms from dominant actors in power structures on student athletes. However, the promulgation of such ethics poses potential issues. First, the expectation for any given university to formulate ethics involves an inherent conflict of interest in that it calls on the university to impose limits to its own conduct—a dubious prospect in the case of a university that places an imperative on intercollegiate sports and by extension the performance of its student athletes.

Second, the awarding of each university with discretion to fashion its own ethics raises the scenario of an ad hoc environment of different universities exercising inconsistent approaches in the treatment of student athletes. The prospect of inconsistency is problematic because it contradicts the larger goal of protecting student athletes as a class against the potential harms arising from participation in university sports as a whole. Both of the aforementioned issues connect to a common concern over universities creating normative frameworks to guide their treatment of student athletes but in so doing leave open the prospect of other sources for norms.

Potential guidance on the treatment of student athletes outside of universities is available in human rights, with the international human rights system providing a corpus of existing sources in law and scholarship regarding norms in the treatment of human beings. The next section delves deeper into the potential for human rights approaches (or RBA) to help fashion an ethics for the treatment of student athletes in university sports programs.

RIGHTS-BASED APPROACHES

Human rights approaches, alternatively called rights-based approaches, are not new to the topic of sports in general (Giulianotti & McArdle 2006). For example, there is literature that asserts that sports contribute to human rights ideals (see for example Isidori & Benetton 2015; Donnelly 2008; Kidd & Donnelly 2000). Such works assert the role of sports as a practice of humanity, with organized sports serving as a vehicle to promote ideals of human dignity (CAS 2021; UNESCO 2015; Kreft 2014; Schurmann 2012; Giulianotti & McArdle 2006). In addition, there is scholarship that asserts sports as being a human right in that it is an expression of human rights regarding health, participation, and leisure (CAS 2021; IOC 2020; UNESCO 2015; Isidori & Benetton 2015; Donnelly 2008).

In contrast, however, there is also literature that explores the human rights issues posed by sports, with scholarship looking at the ways sports either enable abuses of human rights or serve to erode respect for human rights notions such as dignity, health, inclusion, equality, and fairness (Nam et al. 2018; Giulianotti & McArdle 2006; Bale & Christensen 2004; Kosiewicz & Obodynski 2003). In particular, within the literature on human rights problems in sports is research that observes how organized sports can dehumanize athletes through processes such as objectification of their images and bodies in commercial promotions, commodification in terms of being bought or sold by sports business enterprises, and exploitation or abuse by coaching or training services (Isidori & Benetton 2015; Truscan 2012; Schneider 2004; Redeker 2002).

The concern for athletes drives arguments that draw on human rights to seek protection of athletes arising from their engagement in organized training and competition (see for example Adams & Kavanagh 2020; Lubaale 2019; Nam et al. 2018; Schwab 2018; Shahlaei 2017; Kidd & Donnelly 2000; Barnes 1996). Such arguments use human rights to protect athletes against a range of harms that encompass abuse, trauma, discrimination, violations of privacy, and deprivation of rights to images or bodies (see for example MacGregor 2021; Truscan 2012; Donnelly 2008; Schneider 2004; Kidd & Donnelly 2000; Barnes 1996). To the extent that they refer to the international human rights, they connect to claims of universality wherein human rights apply to all human beings (Schwab 2018; Kidd & Donnelly 2000). Hence, the status of athletes as humans places them within the scope of human rights protections.

To a degree, the extent of protections provided by human rights is limited in that it suffers as a body of law. Specifically, human rights may be expressed in declarations and treaties of international law, but under international law the language of declarations is nonbinding and the terms of treaties only apply to their respective state parties (Cooper 2010). As a result, while advocates for athlete rights seek to draw on the provisions of international instruments such as the Universal Declaration of Human Rights (UDHR), the International Convention on Civil and Political Rights (ICCPR), or the International Covenant on Economic, Social, and Cultural Rights (ICESCR), the reach of such efforts is dependent on the will of states for implementation (HRC 2020; IOC 2020; IOC 2022a; IOC 2022b). Further, even in situations where states commit to human rights, there are additional challenges of states disassociating law from the practices of sports, either by excluding sports issues from legal jurisdiction or reserving sports as the business of self-regulating private-sector industries (HRC 2020; Findlay 2016; Standen 2009; Ken Foster 2003).

However, sport is not purely a legal concern, and as a space of human endeavor hosts activities with the potential to raise normative considerations (Giulianotti & McArdle 2006). In addition, the ideals of human rights are not reserved solely for states but are rather directed at enjoyment by human beings, meaning they are realized through the conduct of people (Cooper 2010; Kidd & Donnelly 2000). As a result, human rights go beyond law to represent a basis for norms determining appropriate treatment between people, such that they can guide mobilization of advocacy and construction of systems for accountability outside of state-based systems (Donnelly 2008).

The following subsections are aimed at outlining the reach of human rights available to address student-athlete issues vis-à-vis universities and so work to demarcate a broader framework for RBA toward ethics of university and student-athlete relations. The discussion finds a framework through a mapping exercise that identifies the components of existing international human rights law related to the diverse concerns of student athletes under university sports programs. The ulterior motive behind the mapping is to present RBA as a relevant guide for ethics in university sports programs, with various provisions in international human rights law providing directions for deeper exploration on specific issues.

Rights to Free Speech, Freedom from Discrimination, Privacy, and Education

With respect to athletes, the literature on human rights and sports highlights specific provisions of international human rights law that enable athlete rights. For some rights, the association between athletes and international law is direct. For example, athlete freedom of speech readily ties into the broader rights to freedom of opinion and expression found in Article 19 of both the UDHR and ICCPR (Shahlaei 2017). Similarly, athlete rights to privacy connect to the general right to privacy given by Article 12 of the UDHR and Article 17 of the ICCPR (Mathieson 2006). The nature of privacy can extend to information that is already public (*Case of P. G. and J. H. v. The United Kingdom* 2001).

Further, athlete rights against discrimination fit within the rights against discrimination on the basis of factors such as race, sex, gender, language, religion, or national origin found in multiple human rights instruments (HRC 2020; Lubaale 2019), including Articles 2 and 7 of the UDHR (UDHR 1948); Articles 2, 3, and 26 of the ICCPR (ICCPR 1966); Articles 2 and 3 of the ICESCR (ICESCR 1966); and the entirety of both the Convention on the Elimination of Discrimination Against Women (CEDAW 1979) and the International Convention on the Elimination of All Forms of Racial Discrimination (ICERD 1965). Of particular relevance to student athletes is the right to education, which is articulated by Article 13 of the ICESCR (Nam et al. 2018; ICESCR 1966).

The aforementioned components relate to the treatment of student athletes across a range of scenarios. To begin, they indicate that university sports programs should allow student-athlete voices, including in protests over social justice issues (Schwab 2018), both in terms of the content of their concerns and their ability to express their perspectives. In cases regarding medical information (Cooper 2010; Porvaznik 1995), they suggest that student athletes should retain the right to control the distribution or use of their personal biometric data. With respect to personal aspects such as names, images, or likenesses (Grenardo 2016; Cho 2015), they also enable student athletes to control them as forms of personal information even if they are known to the public.

For issues of discrimination along factors such as race, gender, and sexuality (Lee et al. 2018; Osborne 2006; Kevin Foster 2003), they call on universities to ensure inclusion across multiple dimensions of student-athlete identity. Moreover, for university sports programs tempted to sacrifice academic concerns in order to meet expectations of elite competition (Ingersoll 2015; Clift & Mower 2013), they remind universities to respect the educational aspects of student-athlete experiences.

Right to Work and Right to Participation

Other rights involve additional construction to reach the standards of international human rights law. For example, professional athletes can argue for a right to work, which encompasses rights to choice of employment, favorable work conditions, remuneration, and to join unions, as expressed by Article 23 of the UDHR and Article 6 of the ICESCR (Schwab 2018; ICESCR 1966; UDHR 1948). In the context of organized sports, however, competition is regulated by governance bodies, posing a potential conflict of interest where a single entity operates as both employer and adjudicator of athlete grievances (Schwab 2018). Bypassing the problem requires a corollary right to effective remedy through legal authorities contained in Article 8 of the UDHR and Article 2 of the ICCPR (Schwab 2018; ICCPR 1966; UDHR 1948).

Beyond professional sports, the right to work may not necessarily apply to all student athletes in that some hold amateur status in terms of participation in university sports without remuneration. But there is an alternative approach through a right to participation (Cooper 2010). It is possible to base arguments on a right to participate in sport by construing sport as a component of culture, which would then allow reference to the right to participate in the cultural life of a community contained in Article 27 of the UDHR and the right to take part in cultural life expressed by Article 15 of the ICESCR (Cooper 2010; ICESCR 1966; UDHR 1948).

The preceding provisions help to guide university approaches across different scenarios regarding their sports programs. For example, in situations regarding university payments to student athletes (Ingersoll 2015), they highlight the need to address employment terms covering student-athlete choice of employer, the conditions of university sports programs as workspaces hosting student-athlete labor, the proportion of remuneration for student-athlete activities as forms of labor services, the allowance of student-athlete unions, and the preservation of legal avenues for dispute resolution. With respect to situations of payments to student athletes from parties outside universities (Grenardo 2016), international human rights law provides space for such relationships in the sense that they prevent universities from using them as an exclusionary basis to deny student participation in sports.

Rights to Life, Liberty, Security, and Health

The above rights entail an antecedent need to ensure the existence of the individual in order to enjoy human rights. At a fundamental level, existence connects directly to the right to life articulated in Article 3 of the UDHR and Article 6 of the ICCPR (UDHR 1948; ICCPR 1966). Human rights, however, goes beyond assurance of life to encompass liberty and security of the person, with Article 3 of the UDHR including it as part of the right to life and Article 9 of the ICCPR adding that deprivations of individual liberty or security require legal justification and legal procedure (UDHR 1948; ICCPR 1966). The scope goes further, with Article 7 of the ICCPR proscribing treatment or punishment that might be "cruel, inhuman, or degrading" (ICCPR 1966) and Article 10 of the ICCPR conditioning infringements on liberty with treatment that retains "humanity and inherent dignity of the human person" (ICCPR 1966).

The concerns posed by the aforementioned provisions echo the core of the UDHR, which places dignity in both its preamble and Article 1 (UDHR 1948). For its part, the preamble of the ICESCR indicates a concern for human dignity alongside a freedom from fear (ICESCR 1966), and Article 12 adds the right to the "highest attainable standard of physical and mental health" (ICESCR 1966).

The above terms point attention to the physical and mental welfare of individuals, with factors for consideration in the status of student athletes in university sports programs. They indicate approaches to cases of punitive exercise, physical harm, and sexual abuse (see for example MacGregor 2021; Drake Group 2019; Timpka et al. 2019; *Lee v. Louisiana Board of Trustees* 2017), with the above provisions directing concerns to whether such scenarios in university sports threaten an individual student athlete's life, physical health, and security of the body. In addition, they proffer responses to aspects involving psychological harms (see for example MacGregor 2021; Madrigal & Robbins 2020; Lee et al. 2018; Gervis, Rhind, & Luzar 2016; Stirling & Kerr 2014) by raising issues regarding treatment offensive to mental health.

On a broader scale, they present a larger guiding principle to filter the actions of university sports programs according to their influence on the dignity of student athletes as human beings. The implication affects universities that immerse student athletes in comprehensive systems of regimentation, surveillance, and control (see for example Teetzel & Weaving 2014; Kevin Foster 2003), in that systems that force the subjugation of student athletes or foster their dependency on university sports programs impair the autonomy of student athletes in ways that may threaten their enjoyment of their own humanity.

The preceding subsections demonstrate how international human rights law connects to the relationship between universities and student athletes, with the discussion of each subsection mapping provisions of international human rights instruments to the diverse issues of student athletes. Through such mapping, the discussion illustrates how an RBA drawn from international human rights instruments provides a framework to guide ethics in the treatment of student athletes in university sports programs. The reference to international human rights law was confined to the UDHR, ICCPR, and ICESCR, but there are additional instruments with provisions offering normative guidance for RBA. For the scope of the present analysis, however, they serve the purpose of demonstrating how RBA can employ international human rights law as a framework to guide the formulation of comprehensive institutional ethics for university sports programs toward student athletes.

COMMENTS

In reflecting on the preceding discussion of RBA in university sports, it should be noted that the above sections were oriented toward identifying a human rights approach capable of articulating ethics for the treatment of student athletes. While it drew on international human rights laws, it looked at them more as expressions of norms within a broader literature connecting them to the operations of organized sports. Hence, it went beyond the scope of purely law-based approaches that might otherwise rely on solely legalistic oversight of university sports programs.

Of particular note is the framing of university sports within labor law, as exemplified by the recent statement from the Office of General Counsel of the United States National Labor Relations Board (NLRB) and the decision of the US Supreme Court in *National Collegiate Athletic Association v. Alston* (NLRB 2021; *NCAA v. Alston* 2021). Comparison of such approaches with the normative human rights considerations in the above sections raises a number of distinctions for clarification below.

To begin, the NLRB statement of September 29, 2021, declares that athletes in intercollegiate sports playing under scholarships in private universities are employees within the definitions of both common law and the US National Labor Relations Act of 1935 and hence are protected by US labor laws on employer-employee relations (NLRB 2021). The NLRB's reasoning views scholarship athletes as providing services in the form of sports performance under the control of university sports programs in exchange for compensation in the form of scholarships covering tuition, fees, room, board, and stipends (NLRB 2021). The NLRB statement also indicates that use of the term *student athlete* constitutes misclassification of university athletes because it leads them to believe that they are not covered by the protection of US labor laws (NLRB 2021).

The semantic concern of the NLRB statement is not inconsistent with the meaning of *student athlete* used in preceding sections in that the NLRB focuses narrowly on scholarship athletes in private universities while the present analysis on RBA deals more broadly with all athletes—both those with scholarships and those without scholarships, and both private and public universities—competing in university sports programs. In essence, the NLRB addresses a subset of the population that concerned the previous sections.

Next, the Supreme Court ruling in *NCAA v. Alston* recognizes university sports as a profit-making business and hence subject to US antitrust laws (*NCAA v. Alston* 2021). Following such reasoning, the decision holds that efforts by university sports organizations such as the NCAA to limit compensation to athletes are a violation of US antitrust laws (*NCAA v. Alston* 2021). Among the consequences of the decision is the opening of remuneration disassociated with academics, including compensation to athletes for use of their names, images, and likenesses by nonuniversity businesses (NCAA 2021; NLRB 2021).

While the ramifications of the Supreme Court decision differs from those of the NLRB in that *NCAA v. Alston* impacts both scholarship and nonscholarship athletes, it also differs in that it focuses narrowly on compensation for student athletes. In contrast, the preceding sections worked more expansively to cover a breadth of issues regarding treatment of student athletes. As a result, *NCAA v. Alston* relates to a subset of the issues covered in previous sections.

Differences in scope aside, the labor law perspectives exemplified by the NLRB and *NCAA v. Alston* further differ from the human rights approach of the present analysis with respect to the alienability of student-athlete protections. The NLRB statement and the Supreme Court decision in *NCAA v. Alston* collectively represent a current culmination of an ongoing movement interpreting student athletes as being employees of universities (see for example Mitten 2017; McCormick & McCormick 2006). To the extent that a proportion of student athletes can be framed as employees, labor law enables treatment of university and student-athlete relations as being labor issues involving labor rights protected by law. However, it also entails implications of an exchange wherein universities as employers provide compensation for services in the form of athletic performance from students as employees.

The nature of an exchange raises the prospects of employer-employee contractual relationships with terms negotiated between parties, which raises potential issues regarding bargaining between universities and student athletes (see for example Garlewicz 2020; Czarnota 2012; Cooper 2010; Schneider 2004). In particular is the disparity in knowledge regarding the parameters of bargaining, with universities enjoying greater expertise relative to prospective student athletes regarding the ramifications of forming relationships between them (Grenardo 2016; Ingersoll 2015). To a degree, labor law may help to mitigate such disparity in that both the NLRB and *NCAA v. Alston* recognize issues of bargaining and power relationships, and the National Labor Relations Act 1935 expressly sets itself to mitigating inequalities in bargaining power (*NCAA v. Alston* 2021; NLRB 2021; NLRA 1935). Despite such intentions, however, existing labor law allows for bargaining that goes so far as to include employee rights, as exemplified by "work-for-hire" models wherein employees provide services but surrender intellectual property rights to the employer (Karcher 2012).

The implication is that rights are alienable and divisible, such that student athletes can release them in whole or in part as components of bargaining with universities. This is problematic in that it impairs larger goals of ensuring protection of student athletes against university sports programs. In contrast to labor law's employer-employee bargaining, a human rights approach sees rights as being inalienable and indivisible, in that human rights encompass a corpus of rights that cannot be released or taken away nor enjoyed separate from each other (see for example OHCHR 2021). As a result, human rights does not allow for bargaining over a collection of rights. In effect, human rights sets a minimum to the scope of protection for a slate of rights that is otherwise not available in a labor law approach.

The above distinctions between labor law and human rights perspectives point to a broader challenge about the limits of approaches based solely on law-based approaches. As demonstrated by the issues regarding NLRB and *NCAA v. Acton*, reducing issues to questions of legality overlooks the limited scope of law. While it is possible to seek additional law, either in legislation or common law decisions, the reference to law incurs an ongoing search for relevant sources for each of any number of scenarios involving university and student-athlete relations. The consequent danger is that anything not deemed illegal is rendered acceptable. Use of RBA, in comparison, allows a normative basis with a broad reach extending beyond determinations of legality. As much as the RBA in the present analysis draws on international human rights law, it does so within a larger human rights literature that recognizes them as reflecting an assembly of norms. Norms are aspirational in the sense of lacking the enforceability accorded to law, but as norms they serve as guides for conduct in potential issues that go beyond the confines of law.

Last, applications of the normative aspects of international human rights law in sports is not without precedent. Specifically, a 2016 report commissioned by the Federation of International Football Associations (FIFA) found that as a private sports organization, it fell under the United Nations Guiding Principles on Business and Human Rights, which calls on businesses to promote respect for human rights in their operations (Ruggie 2016). Following the report, FIFA implemented a policy to respect all international human rights (FIFA 2021). While aimed specifically for FIFA, the report serves to indicate the relevance of existing international human rights norms in guiding the treatment of athletes in organized sports. Hence, as much as there may be a tension between the rights of athletes and the rights of sports governing bodies to regulate their own respective sports competitions (Mathieson 2006), human rights norms can help to demarcate boundaries of athlete protections.

Comparable observations of human rights efforts exist for other sports governing bodies, including the examples of the International Olympic Committee's development of a human rights strategic framework (IOC 2021) and the World Athletics Council's (WAC) launch of a Human Rights Working Group (WAC 2021). Such cases demonstrate that even in situations with self-governing sports organizations, it is still possible to utilize international human rights norms to formulate standards and policies of conduct. As a result, to the extent that university sports programs are involved in governing sports bodies such as the NCAA, there are preexisting models for them to follow in terms of using international human rights law to guide their respective treatment of student athletes.

CONCLUSION AND FUTURE DIRECTIONS

The preceding sections leave a number of potential directions for future study. The discussion limited the scope of analysis to delineating the prospective value of international human rights law in facilitating an RBA toward formulation of an ethics for university treatment of student athletes. Because of its exploratory character, it represents only an initial step demarcating the conceptual basis of a human rights framework for ethics in university sports programs. More work is necessary to further the analysis into practice.

A necessary direction to enable practice is empirical study. Specifically, as much as the prior sections identified provisions of existing international human rights instruments relevant to the relations between universities and student athletes, it would be helpful to investigate cases where human rights norms were transformed into codes of ethics. Doing so would help to discern nuances of implementation from general human rights norms into cognizable standards and clarify the challenges of promoting or enforcing those standards within university sports programs. It may be difficult to find cases of individual university sports programs given the prospective character of the endeavor in the above sections. However, it may be sufficient to use cases of human rights approaches toward ethics among sports governing bodies, with the reasoning that entities governing university sports, such as the NCAA, are analogous to other sports governing bodies, such as the above examples of FIFA, IOC, and WAC. In which case, they provide starting points for investigation, with their experiences providing insights for the NCAA and other university-related sports organizations, as well as their respective associated university members.

Another area requiring study is with respect to potential conflicts between international human rights approaches and domestic law approaches. It is possible for the two to complement each other, in the sense that human rights norms and laws exist concurrently, and both can be applied to the same general purpose of protecting student athletes. The previous sections, however, indicate that the differences between them suggest the possibility of scenarios where the scope and reach of protection under domestic law may not match those within international human rights norms. The consequence is that university sports programs that deploy ethics tied to human rights frameworks face a risk of violating domestic laws. While speculative, such prospects suggest a need for further study to determine the potential risks of conflict and to ascertain potential strategies to counter them.

In closing, the work of the previous sections sought to explore the potential for RBA to direct institutional university ethics toward student athletes, with the analysis demonstrating how international human rights law can serve as a normative basis for a framework guiding conduct in university sports programs vis-à-vis student athletes. The discussion employed a mapping exercise that illustrated an RBA using international human rights law as a source of norms capable of addressing the spectrum of issues tied to the subordinate status of student athletes within the hierarchy of authority in universities.

In doing so, however, the purpose of discussion was only to indicate the possible utility of RBA. A more detailed implementation of a human rights framework into a formal code of conduct requires successive study that delves deeper to discern the complexities within universities regarding student athletes and to articulate them in corresponding prescriptive language for university sports programs. Further, it calls for universities to see the connections between human rights and their operations, as well as a willingness by universities to undertake the work to apply human rights as a means for directing their relationships with student athletes.

REFERENCES

Adams, Andrew & Emma Kavanaugh. (2020) The Capabilities and Human Rights of Performance Athletes. *International Review for the Sociology of Sport* 55(2): 147–168.

Bale, John & Mette Christensen (eds.). (2004) *Post-Olympism: Questioning Sport in the Twenty-First Century.* Berg.

Barnes, John. (1996) *Sports and the Law in Canada* (3rd ed.). Butterworths.

Bowles, Richard & Anne O'Dwyer. (2020) Athlete-Centred Coaching: Perspectives from the Sideline. *Sports Coaching Review* 9(3): 231–252.

Burke, Michael & Chris Hallinan. (2006) Women's Leadership in Junior Girls' Basketball in Victoria: Foucault, Feminism, and Disciplining Women Coaches. *Sport in Society* 9(1): 19–31.

Case of P. G. and J. H. v. The United Kingdom. (2001) *Case of P. G. and J. H. v. The United Kingdom, Application No. 44787/98, Judgment 25, September 2001.* European Court of Human Rights (ECHR). Available at: http://hudoc .echr.coe.int/eng?i=001-59665

Cho, Christie. (2015) Protecting Johnny Football: Trademark Registration for Collegiate Athletes. *Northwestern Journal of Technology and Intellectual Property* 13(1): 65–85.

Clayton, Ashley, et al. (2015) Winning Is Everything: The Intersection of Academic and Athletics at Prestige University. *Journal of Cases in Educational Leadership* 18(2): 144–156.

Clift, Bryan & Ronald Mower. (2013) Transitioning to an Athletic Subjectivity: First-Semester Experiences at a Corporate (Sporting) University. *Sport, Education, and Society* 18(3): 349–369.

Convention on the Elimination of All Forms of Discrimination Against Women (CEDAW). (1979) Office of the High Commissioner for Human Rights. Available at: www.ohchr.org/EN/ProfessionalInterest/Pages/ CEDAW.aspx

Cooper, Emily. (2010) Gender Testing in Athletic Competitions—Human Rights Violations: Why Michael Phelps Is Praised and Caster Semenya Is Chastised. *Journal of Gender, Race, and Justice* 14(2010): 233–264.

Court of Arbitration for Sport (CAS). (2021) *Sport and Human Rights: Overview from a CAS Perspective.* Available at: www.tas-cas.org/fileadmin/ user_upload/Human_Rights_in_sport__CAS_report_updated_16.04.2021 _.pdf

Czarnota, Paul. (2012) Athlete Privacy Rights and Endorsement Contracts: An Analysis of US, UK, and Australian Law. *Virginia Sports and Entertainment Law* 11(2): 460–506.

Davis, Louise & Sophia Jowett. (2014) Coach-Athlete Attachment and the Quality of the Coach-Athlete Relationship: Implications for the Athlete's Well-being. *Journal of Sports Sciences* 32(15): 1454–1464.

De Haan, Donna & Leanne Norman. (2020) Mind the Gap: The Presence of Capital and Power in the Female Athlete–Male-Coach Relationship within Elite Rowing. *Sports Coaching Review* 9(1): 95–118.

Denison, Jim & Joseph Mills. (2014) Planning for Distance Running: Coaching with Foucault. *Sports Coaching Review* 3(1): 1–16.

Denison, Jim, Joseph Mills, & Timothy Konoval. (2017) Sports' Disciplinary Legacy and the Challenge of "Coaching Differently." *Sport, Education, and Society* 22(6): 772–783.

De Souza, Adriano & Judith Oslin. (2008) A Player-Centered Approach to Coaching. *Journal of Physical Education, Recreation, and Dance* 79(6): 24–30.

Donnelly, Peter. (2008) Sport and Human Rights. *Sport in Society* 11(4): 381–394.

Drake Group. (2019) *The NCAA and Member Institutions Must Prohibit Physical Punishment of College Athletes.* Available at: www.thedrakegroup.org/2019/11/05/the-ncaa-and-member-institutions-must-prohibit-physical-punishment-of-college-athletes/

Federation Internationale de Football Association (FIFA). (2021) *Social Impact: Human Rights and Anti-Discrimination.* Available at: www.fifa.com/social-impact/human-rights

Findlay, Hilary. (2016) Accountability in the Global Regulation of Sport: What Does the Future Hold?, in Yves Vanden Auweede et al. (eds.), *Ethics and Governance in Sport: The Future of Sports Imagined.* Routledge.

Foster, Ken. (2003) Is There a Global Sports Law? *Entertainment and Sports Law Journal* 2(1).

Foster, Kevin. (2003) Panopticonics: The Control and Surveillance of Black Female Athletes in Collegiate Athletic Program. *Anthropology and Education Quarterly* 34(3): 300–323.

Garlewicz, Adam. (2020) Athlete Biometric Data in Soccer: Athlete Protection or Athlete Exploitation? *DePaul Journal of Sports Law* 16(1): ii–34.

Gervis, Misia, Daniel Rhind, & Amber Luzar. (2016) Perceptions of Emotional Abuse in the Coach-Athlete Relationship in Youth Sport: The Influence of Competitive Level and Outcome. *International Journal of Sports Science and Coaching* 11(6): 772–779.

Giulianotti, Richard & David McArdle (eds.). (2006) *Sport, Civil Liberties, and Human Rights.* Routledge.

Grenardo, David. (2016) The Continued Exploitation of the College Athlete: Confessions of a Former College Athlete Turned Law Professor. *Oregon Law Review* 95(1): 223–286.

Hansen, Per Oystein & Svein Andersen. (2014) Coaching Elite Athletes: How Coaches Stimulate Elite Athletes' Reflection. *Sports Coaching Review* 3(1): 17–32.

Hardman, Alun, Carwyn Jones, & Robyn Jones. (2010) Sports Coaching, Virtue Ethics, and Emulation. *Physical Education and Sport Pedagogy* 15(4): 345–359.

Human Rights Council (HRC). (2020) *Intersection of Race and Gender Discrimination in Sport, A/HRC/44/26.* Office of the High Commissioner for Human Rights. Available at: https://ap.ohchr.org/Documents/dpage_e.aspx?si=A/HRC/44/26

Ingersoll, Mike. (2015) Amateurism and the Modern College Athlete. *Elon Law Review* 7(2): 607–636.

International Covenant on Civil and Political Rights (ICCPR). (1966) Office of the High Commissioner for Human Rights. Available at: www.ohchr.org/en/professionalinterest/pages/ccpr.aspx

International Covenant on Economic, Social, and Cultural Rights (ICESCR). (1966) Office of the High Commissioner for Human Rights. Available at: www.ohchr.org/en/professionalinterest/pages/cescr.aspx

International Covenant on the Elimination of All Forms of Discrimination (ICERD). (1965). Office of the High Commissioner for Human Rights. Available at: www.ohchr.org/en/professionalinterest/pages/cerd.aspx

International Olympic Committee (IOC). (2020) *Olympic Charter*. International Olympic Committee. Available at: https://stillmed.olympics.com/media/Document%20Library/OlympicOrg/General/EN-Olympic-Charter.pdf?_ga=2.63823212.2130033476.1632534383-503096825.1632534383

International Olympic Committee (IOC). (2021) *Protection and Respect of Human Rights*. International Olympic Committee. Available at: https://olympics.com/ioc/human-rights

International Olympic Committee (IOC). (2022a) *Code of Ethics*. International Olympic Commitee. Available at: https://stillmedab.olympic.org/media/Document%20Library/OlympicOrg/Documents/Code-of-Ethics/Code-of-Ethics-ENG.pdf#page=14&_ga=2.159102330.1177896064.1618845860-971153820.1601050134

International Olympic Committee (IOC). (2022b) *Introduction to the Key Principles of the IOC Human Rights Strategic Framework*. International Olympic Committee. Available at: https://stillmed.olympics.com/media/Documents/Beyond-the-Games/Human-Rights/Introduction-IOC-Human-Rights-Strategic Framework.pdf#_ga=2.236036929.1165446930.1656556106-235042604.1656556106

Isidori, Emanuele & Mirca Benetton. (2015) Sports as Education: Between Dignity and Human Rights. *Procedia-Social and Behavioral Sciences* 197(2015): 686–693.

Jolly, J. Christopher. (2008) Raising the Question #9: Is the Student-Athlete Population Unique? And why should we care? *Communication Education* 57(1): 145–151.

Karcher, Richard. (2012) Broadcast Rights, Unjust Enrichment, and the Student-Athlete. *Cardozo Law Review* 34(1): 107–172.

Kassing, Jeffrey & Dominic Infante. (1999) Aggressive Communication in the Coach-Athlete Relationship. *Communication Research Reports* 16(2): 110–120.

Kavanagh, Emma, Lorraine Brown, & Ian Jones. (2017) Elite Athletes' Experience of Coping with Emotional Abuse in the Coach-Athlete Relationship. *Journal of Applied Sport Psychology* 29(4): 402–417.

Kidd, Bruce & Peter Donnelly. (2000) Human Rights in Sports. *International Review for the Sociology of Sport* 35(2): 131–148.

Kimball, Aimee. (2007) "You Signed the Line": Collegiate Student-Athletes' Perceptions of Autonomy. *Psychology of Sport & Exercise* 8(5): 818–835.

Kosiewicz, Jerzy & Kazimierz Obodynski. (2003) *Sport in the Mirror of the Values*. Podkarpackie Society of Science.

Kreft, Lev. (2014) Sport, Education, and Peace, in Emanuele Isidori, F. J. Lopez Frias, & A. Muller (eds.), *Philosophy, Sport, and Education: International Perspectives.* Sette Citta.

Lee, Sae-Mi, et al. (2018) Student-Athletes' Experiences with Racial Micro-aggressions in Sport: A Foucauldian Discourse Analysis. *The Qualitative Report* 23(5): 1016–1043.

Lee v. Louisiana Board of Trustees. (2017) *Lee v. Louisiana Board of Trustees for State Colleges, and Grambling State University, So. 3d 176 (La. Ct. App. 2019).* State of Louisiana Court of Appeal, First Circuit. Available at: https://law.justia.com/cases/louisiana/first-circuit-court-of-appeal/2019/2017ca1432.html

Light, Richard & Stephen Harvey. (2017) Positive Pedagogy for Sport Coaching. *Sport, Education, and Society* 22(2): 271–287.

Lorimer, Ross. (2013) The Development of Empathic Accuracy in Sports Coaches. *Journal of Sport Psychology in Action* 4(1): 26–33.

Lubaale, Emma. (2019) Confronting Stereotypes as an Entry Point to Realigning IAAF Regulations with Human Rights and Developments in Science. *Gender and Behaviour* 17(4): 14413–14432.

MacGregor, Wendy. (2021) The Silenced Athlete Voice: Responding to Athlete Maltreatment through Empowerment and Education. *Education and Law Journal* 30(1): 77–117.

Madrigal, Leilani & Jamie Robbins. (2020) Student-Athlete Stress: An Examination in United States Collegiate Athletics. *Journal for the Study of Sports and Athletes in Education* 14(2): 123–139.

Mageau, Genevieve & Robert Vallerand. (2003) The Coach-Athlete Relationship: A Motivational Model. *Journal of Sports Science* 21(11): 883–904.

Mathieson, Anna. (2006) The World Anti-Doping Agency and the World Anti-Doping Code: Can the Right of an Athlete to Compete Freely and the Right of Sport to Regulate Competition. *ANZSLA Commentator* 66(2006): 24–32.

McCormick, Robert & Amy Christian McCormick. (2006) The Myth of the Student-Athlete: The College Athlete as Employee. *Washington Law Review* 81(1): 71–157.

McDonald, Brent & Michael Burke. (2019) Coaching Pedagogy and Athlete Autonomy with Japanese University Rowers. *Sport in Society* 22(8): 1433–1448.

Miller, Patricia & Gretchen Kerr. (2002) The Athletic, Academic, & Social Experiences of Intercollegiate Student Athletes. *Journal of Sport Behavior* 25(4): 346–367.

Mills, Joseph & Jim Denison. (2013) Coach Foucault: Problematizing Endurance Running Coaches' Practices. *Sports Coaching Review* 2(2): 136–150.

Mitten, Matthew. (2017) Why and How the Supreme Court Should Have Decided *O'Bannon v. NCAA. The Antitrust Bulletin* 62(1): 62–90.

Nam, Benjamin, et al. (2018) Rethinking Social Activism Regarding Human Rights for Student-Athletes in South Korea. *Sport in Society* 21(11): 1831–1849.

National Collegiate Athletic Association (NCAA). (2021) *NCAA Adopts Interim Name, Image, and Likeness Policy, June 30, 2021.* Available at: www.ncaa.org/about/resources/media-center/news/ncaa-adopts-interim -name-image-and-likeness-policy

National Collegiate Athletic Association v. Alston *(NCAA v. Alston).* (2021) United States Supreme Court. Available at: www.supremecourt.gov/ opinions/20pdf/20-512_gfbh.pdf

National Labor Relations Act (NLRA). (1935) Available at: www.nlrb.gov/ guidance/key-reference-materials/ley-de-relaciones-obrero-patronales

National Labor Relations Board (NLRB). (2021) *NLRB General Counsel Jennifer Abruzzo Issues Memo on Employee Status of Players at Academic Institutions, September 29, 2021.* Available at: www.nlrb.gov/news-outreach/news-story/ nlrb-general-counsel-jennifer-abruzzo-issues-memo-on-employee-status-of

Nelson, Lee, et al. (2014) Carl Rogers, Learning and Educational Practice: Critical Considerations and Applications in Sports Coaching. *Sport, Education, and Society* 19(5): 513–531.

Office of the High Commissioner for Human Rights (OHCHR). (2021) *What Are Human Rights?* Available at: www.ohchr.org/en/issues/pages/whatare humanrights.aspx

Ojala, Anna-Liisa. (2018) Being an Athlete and Being a Young Person: Technologies of the Self in Managing an Athletic Career in Youth Ice Hockey in Finland. *International Review for the Sociology of Sport* 55(3): 310–326.

Oly, Mary Harvey. (2020) Why Athlete Rights Should Be at the Core of Sport. *Human Rights Defender* 29(2): 9–11.

Osborne, Barbara. (2006) No Drinking, No Drugs, No Lesbians: Sexual Orientation Discrimination in Intercollegiate Athletics. *Marquette Sports Law Review* 17(2): 481–502.

Porvaznik, Paul. (1995) When Drug Testing Violates the Student Athlete's Right to Privacy. *DePaul-LCA Journal of Art and Entertainment Law* 5 (1994–1995): 173–182.

Priest, Robert, et al. (1999) Four-Year Changes in College Athletes' Ethical Value Choices in Sports Situations. *Research Quarterly for Exercise and Sport* 70(2): 170–178.

Redeker, R. (2002) *Le Sport Contre Les Peuples.* Berg International Editeurs.

Rhind, Daniel & Sophia Jowett. (2010) Relationship Maintenance Strategies in the Coach-Athlete Relationship: The Development of the COMPASS Model. *Journal of Applied Sport Psychology* 22(2010): 106–121.

Roper, Larry. (2017) The Ethics of the Collegiate Locker Room. *Journal of College and Character* 18(1): 70–73.

Ruggie, John. (2016) *"For the Game. For the World." FIFA and Human Rights.* Harvard Kennedy School. Available at: www.hks.harvard.edu/sites/default/ files/centers/mrcbg/programs/cri/files/Ruggie_humanrightsFIFA_report April2016.pdf

Schneider, Angela. (2004) Privacy, Confidentiality, and Human Rights in Sport. *Sport in Society* 7(3): 438–456.

Schurmann, V. (2012) Sports and Human Rights. *Journal of the Philosophy of Sport and Physical Education* 34(2): 143–150.

Schwab, Brendan. (2018) Celebrate Humanity: Reconciling Sport and Human Rights through Athlete Activism. *Journal of Legal Aspects of Sport* 28(1): 170–207.

Shahlaei, Faraz. (2017) When Sports Stand Against Human Rights: Regulating Restrictions on Athletes; Speech in the Global Sports Arena. *Loyola of Los Angeles Entertainment Law Review* 38(1): 99–120.

Sinden, Jane Lee. (2012) The Sociology of Emotion in Elite Sport: Examining the Role of Normalization and Technologies. *International Review for the Sociology of Sport* 48(5): 613–628.

Standen, Jeffrey. (2009) The Manly Sports: The Problematic Use of Criminal Law to Regulate Sports Violence. *Journal of Criminal Law and Criminology* 99(3): 619–642.

Stephens, Dawn & Basil Kavanagh. (2003) Aggression in Canadian Youth Ice Hockey: The Role of Moral Atmosphere. *International Sports Journal* 7(2003): 109–119.

Stirling, Ashley & Gretchen Kerr. (2008) Defining and Categorizing Emotional Abuse in Sport. *European Journal of Sport Science* 8(4): 173–181.

Stirling, Ashley & Gretchen Kerr. (2009) Abused Athletes' Perceptions of the Coach-Athlete Relationship. *Sport in Society* 12(2): 227–239.

Stirling, Ashley & Gretchen Kerr. (2013) The Perceived Effects of Elite Athletes' Experiences of Emotional Abuse in the Coach-Athlete Relationship. *Sport and Exercise Psychology* 11(1): 87–100.

Stirling, Ashley & Gretchen Kerr. (2014) "Safeguarding Athletes from Emotional Abuse," in Melanie Lang & Mike Hartill (eds.), *Safeguarding Child Protection and Abuse in Sport*. Routledge.

Teetzel, Sarah & Charlene Weaving. (2014) From Silence to Surveillance: Examining the Aftermath of a Canadian University Doping Scandal. *Surveillance and Society* 11(4): 481–493.

Timpka, Toomas, et al. (2019) Lifetime History of Sexual and Physical Abuse among Competitive Athletics (Track and Field) Athletes: Cross-Sectional Study of Associations with Sports and Non-sports Injury. *British Journal of Sports Medicine* 53(22): 1412–1417.

Truscan, Ivona. (2012) Child Athletes Find Support in Human Rights Law for Tackling Punitive Forms of Training. *Human Rights and International Legal Discourse* 6(2): 302–328.

United Nations Education, Scientific, Cultural Organization (UNESCO). (2015) *International Charter of Physical Education, Physical Activity, & Sport*, SHS/2015/PI/H/14 REV. Available at:https://unesdoc.unesco.org/ark:/48223/pf0000235409

Universal Declaration of Human Rights (UDHR). (1948) United Nations. Available at: www.un.org/en/about-us/universal-declaration-of-human-rights

World Athletics Council. (2021) *222nd World Athletics Council Meeting*. Available at: https://www.worldathletics.org/about-iaaf/documents/council

Campus Policing

What Authority and Limits Are Appropriate?

Rita Manning

ABSTRACT

Campus police are a powerful force at most public universities and many private ones. At public universities they are almost all armed, and many public universities are the recipients of military equipment given to them by the Pentagon.

Given the risks of having police on a university campus, it is time to think very carefully about other alternatives. In this chapter, I will address these alternatives by looking at a number of questions: Given the appropriate role of campus police in supporting the mission of the university, what authority should the campus police have, and what kind of limits are appropriate? Should the campus police have the power to arrest? Should their authority extend beyond campus constituents to the larger community? Should they be armed? If they should be armed, should they accept and use military equipment that they can acquire at minimal cost through the Pentagon's 1033 program? Should the campus police have the qualified immunity that most police forces enjoy?

Keywords: alcohol, armed police, campus policing, Clery Act, gentrification, power to arrest, qualified immunity, sexual assault, student conduct, sworn police officer, Title IX, Violence Against Women Act

In the wake of the worldwide protests that followed the police killing of George Floyd, the entire country has been engaged in a searching exploration of policing. As the country rethinks the role of the police, colleges and universities must carry out a similar investigation of their own policing institutions and practices.

Campus policing has had its own widely publicized examples of the ways that policing can go seriously astray. In 2011, a University of California Davis police officer pepper-sprayed passive, seated students participating in an Occupy Wall Street protest. The violence inflicted by campus police was not only devastating for the victims and their families, but it came with substantial liability for the university (Martinez and Chan 2012). A surveillance video shows the fatal shooting of eighteen-year-old Gil Collar by campus police at the University of South Alabama (*Daily Mail* 2012). Collar was naked, unarmed, and obviously under the influence of drugs when he was killed.

In 2013, Tyrone West, an African American man, died after a struggle during a traffic stop with Baltimore and Morgan State University police officers. His family reportedly settled for $1 million in a wrongful death suit against the city and the college (McLeod 2017). The Texas Supreme Court recently held for the family of Cameron Redus in a wrongful death suit in his 2013 death by campus police of the University of the Incarnate Word (KSAT News 2020). We will return to this case when we look at the issue of police immunity. The 2014 killing of Antonio Guzman Lopez by San José State campus police is still being litigated, but the video of the shooting was released in 2019 in response to a new California law (Green 2019).

In 2015, Sam DuBose, an unarmed black man, was shot and killed by a University of Cincinnati police officer. The university's $4.85 million civil settlement with DuBose's family included a role for the family in campus police reform (*Harvard Law Review* 2016). A wrongful death lawsuit was filed by the family of Scout Schultz, a Georgia Tech student killed by campus police during a mental health crisis in 2017 (Selk, Shapiro, and Lowery 2017). A widely publicized example of racial profiling happened at Columbia University, where Alexander McNab, a black senior, was stopped by Barnard police officers, who asked him for his student ID as he was heading into a Barnard library (Columbia and Barnard students have access to facilities at both campuses) (Otterman 2019). When McNab refused to provide his ID, the officers pinned him down against a counter. Charges were recently dropped against Charles Thomas, who was shot by University of Chicago campus police in 2018 when he was most likely suffering from a mental crisis. His family is continuing their lawsuit against the university (Hendrickson 2021). A Yale University campus police officer was one of two officers who fired sixteen rounds at Stephanie

Washington, an unarmed black woman, during a 2019 traffic stop in New Haven (Suansing 2021). Washington's lawsuit is pending.

None of us want our campuses to reproduce these shocking incidents, but we can only protect our communities against policing excess if we look very closely at a number of issues. The first question to ask is whether we want to have a campus policing function and, if so, how we should structure this practice. There are basically three structural models of campus policing. First, a college or university may simply have no campus policing function. This is not to say that they do not protect the campus and surrounding community but that they do not do so with a formal campus policing function. Second, a university might contract out these formal policing functions using local police agencies. Third, universities may have their own police forces. Each of these models has its own risks. If a university has no campus police function, it will need to develop other nonpolicing models to provide the safety and order that the university community desires.

The university must also be sensitive to the practices of local police agencies, as these agencies extend their authority over the university students, faculty, and staff. If a university contracts out these functions with a local police force, the university must interrogate every clause of these contracts. If they choose to have their own police forces, they must think very hard about the authority they grant and the limits they set for the campus police.

As universities reflect on what model of policing is appropriate, there are fundamental questions that must also be raised. Since the role of the police should be compatible with the basic function of a university, the first question concerns the basic function of a university and how this function shapes the university's relationship with its constituents: students, faculty and staff, and the larger community. Given the basic function of a university, how should campus policing support that function?

The next question is, Given the appropriate role of campus police in supporting the mission of the university, what authority should the campus police have, and what kind of limits are appropriate? I will address these specific questions: How much authority should the campus police have? Should the campus police have the power to arrest? Should their authority extend beyond campus constituents to the larger community? Should they be armed? If they should be armed, should they accept and use military equipment that they can acquire at minimal cost through the Pentagon's 1033 program? Should the campus police have the qualified immunity that most police forces enjoy?

In this chapter, I begin by looking at the basic functions of a university and the way this function shapes the authority and limits of campus policing. I then turn to the questions above as we rethink what campus policing should look like. I will return to the three structural models of campus policing as we focus on the questions above and consider how campus policing can be restructured to respond to these issues.

THE BASIC FUNCTION OF A UNIVERSITY
AND THE ROLE OF POLICING

Rather than engage in a discussion of the basic mission of a university, we can look at what is shared among universities worldwide. One source for this is a study that examined the mission statements of the highest-ranked universities around the globe (Bayrak 2020). Unsurprisingly, "higher education institutions in every region call attention to the importance of serving community. . . . Moreover, as expected, across the five regions, there is a commitment to generating and disseminating knowledge and focusing on teaching excellence. . . . North American universities speak of maintaining and serving a diverse body of faculty, students, and community" (Bayrak 2020). The proper role of campus policing in the US, then, is to support the mission of institutions dedicated to knowledge and learning while nurturing and sustaining a diverse community of faculty, students, and community. The question is what kind of policing would best support this mission.

First, we need to look at what policing is and can be. *Policing* is usually defined as "organized forms of order maintenance, peacekeeping, rule or law enforcement, crime investigation and prevention and other forms of investigation and information brokering" (Jones and Newburn 1998, 18). We needn't accept this as the only possible description of the activities of campus policing. Instead, we can decide what kind of model we want to see on our campuses. The history of policing provides two very different models of policing.

One model sees the function of policing as protecting the community, where this protection is seen as the responsibility of all adult members of the community. One example is the British model, which began with the 1215 Statute of Winchester, which required that every man play a role in defending his own community by working as a night watchman who patrolled the streets and gates at night to guard against threats from and against the community (Mulone 2019). If a watchman perceived a threat, he would set up a hue and cry that would bring his fellow citizens out to help him respond to the threat. This role was shared with other men in the community and was seen as a responsibility owed to the community. There are two themes that we find in the night watchman model of policing. First, everyone is committed to protecting everyone else, and second, the threats to be protected against include threats of community members against fellow members and threats from those outside.

The current university parallel to the night watchman model is the honor code model. William and Mary University had the first honor code in a US university, and its students still take the pledge: "As a member of the William and Mary community, I pledge on my honor not to lie, cheat, or steal, either in my academic or personal life. I understand that such acts violate the honor code and undermine the community of trust, of which we are all stewards." While the honor code at William and Mary has shrunk to focus primarily on academic honesty, there is no reason in principle why an honor code cannot be the foundation of policing on college campuses.

The contrasting model of policing is protecting the interests of the elite. The Lieutenance Générale de Paris that was created in 1667 during the reign of Louis XIV is an early example of this model (Mulone 2019). The primary purpose of this police force was to protect the king and keep a close watch on any challenges to his power. The only role the community played was as a place to hunt down threats to the king. Many contemporary adherents of the defund the police movement see the Paris model as the primary model of policing in the US. Critics of the University of Chicago campus police see this police force following the Paris model. The University of Chicago police force is the second-largest private police force in the world. Situated on a college campus with seventeen thousand students, the campus police force exercises its enormous power against the sixty-five thousand community members outside the college campus for the primary purpose of protecting the university's interests (Baptiste 2015).

HISTORY OF CAMPUS POLICING

To understand the different choices that universities have made with respect to campus policing, it is instructive to look at its history (Anderson 2015). Campus policing began when universities reacted to the policing of Vietnam War protests on their campuses. They thought that their own police would respond more compassionately to student protests in the wake of tragedies like the killing of students by the National Guard at Kent State and the police at Jackson State.

Federal law required universities to report crimes and cases of discrimination. Title IX requires that sexual assault be documented and addressed as part of the Education Amendments of 1972's focus on sex discrimination.The federal requirement that universities prevent and respond to sexual violence began with an instruction on the implementation of Title IX of the Education Amendments of 1972 (20 U.S.C. §§ 1681 et seq., 2011 Dear Colleague Letter, available at www2.ed.gov/about/offices/list/ocr/letters/colleague-201104.pdf). For a summary of the most current regulations on Title IX, see www2.ed.gov/about/offices/list/ocr/docs/titleix-summary.pdf. This version was a revision by the Trump administration of the changes made by the Obama administration. The Biden administration is currently reviewing these regulations.

The federal Clery Act of 1990 requires colleges and universities to track crimes that occur both on and near their campuses. They are also required to notify students, families, and the public of threats to safety and criminal activities. The Violence Against Women Act reauthorization of 2013 added sexual assault, dating violence, domestic violence, and stalking to the list of Clery crimes that colleges must report. Finally, the massacre at Virginia Tech in 2007 left thirty-three dead and at least fifteen injured. Most of the victims were students (Hauser and O'Connor 2007). This inspired campus police to focus more on protecting students.

Another trend is the gentrification of neighborhoods surrounding universities often spurred by universities buying up cheap property and adopting various market-based strategies to gentrify surrounding neighborhoods (Carpenter, Goldblatt, and Hanson 2016). This often resulted in the destruction of traditional African American neighborhoods and their transition into convenient spaces for faculty and students. The extension of campus policing into these neighborhoods is part of this gentrification. Duke University, once referred to as "the plantation" by the black service workers who were employed there, is currently one of the sources of Durham's gentrification but has also provided much of the academic theorizing about it (White 2016).

The history illustrates three forces that explain the growth in campus policing since the 1960s: a concern for the safety of students, a response to federal mandates to address and report on various crimes in and around university campuses, and the gentrification of neighborhoods surrounding universities.

The next fundamental question we must answer is, What threats should the campus police protect against? We can assume that the university will expect the campus police to protect the university's buildings and property, and the property and physical persons of students, faculty, and staff, and in some cases the larger community.

Academic Honesty

Since the central mission of a university is teaching and learning, academic dishonesty is a threat both to students and to the university. Universities take this on as a separate threat and do not designate campus police as enforcers of their academic honesty policies.

Instead, they address this problem by using student conduct services. One university campus divides the entire world of student misconduct into two spheres—academic dishonesty and everything else: "Social misconduct is any misconduct that does not involve a student's academic coursework" (University of California at Riverside). At some universities many student conduct issues, including ones involving crimes, are addressed by university student conduct offices (University of Maryland, Academic Calendar).

Drug and Alcohol Abuse

Aside from academic dishonesty, a common threat to students is their own excessive use of alcohol, and campus police departments are very involved in policing this threat. Excessive use of alcohol is seen as a problem because of its involvement in other harms: death, assault, sexual assault, and academic problems (National Institute on Alcohol Abuse and Alcoholism). Excessive use of alcohol is also involved in suicide attempts, varied health problems and injuries, unsafe sex, driving under the influence, vandalism, and property damage (National Institute on Alcohol Abuse and Alcoholism). It is not surprising that arrest records parallel this concern with alcohol violations.

According to one consulting group report, campus police departments "made over 65,000 total arrests in the most recent year of data. The median CPD made 44 arrests: 12 for liquor laws, 8 for marijuana possession, 6 for driving under the influence (DUI), 5 for drunkenness, and 4 or fewer for each of the following: larceny, assault, disorderly conduct, vandalism, and drug possession" (Knowles 2020). Alcohol and drug misuse are also usually handled by campus police, which explains this pattern of arrest.

Sex Offenses

While the arrest records above suggest that drug and alcohol misuse and related activities are by far the most common problems addressed by campus police, when we look at other reporting sources, we see a very different story. There we see forcible sex offenses comprising a very large percentage of crimes. "Among the various types of on-campus crimes reported in 2018, there were 12,300 forcible sex offenses, which constituted 43 percent of all criminal incidents"(Irwin et al. 2021). These crimes were reported and compiled using a number of statistical data sources supported by the federal government and reported under a requirement of the Clery Act, so the arrest statistics of the campus police and the crimes reported in this data are not necessarily incompatible.

One explanation is that sexual assault crimes are not often reported to campus police. This explanation is evidenced by a 2019 study of sexual offenses reporting (Richards 2019). This study found that reports of rape and nonconsensual sexual contact were reported to campus Title IX administrators at twice the rate indicated by the annual security reports required by the Clery Act.

Related sexual offenses (e.g., partner violence, stalking) were reported to Title IX coordinators at three times the rate indicated by the annual security reports required by the Clery Act. Clery annual security reports are based on reports to campus law enforcement officers, campus safety officers, and local law enforcement officers, while Title IX reports are based on reports from any "employee who has the authority to take action to redress sexual violence, who has been given the duty to report to appropriate school officials about incidents of sexual violence or any other misconduct by students, or who a student could reasonably believe has this authority or responsibility." (This document was created by the White House Task Force to Protect Students from Sexual Assault, April 2014. The Biden administration is currently reviewing the changes that were made by the previous administration.)

In spite of the seriousness of these offenses, sexual misconduct, ranging from sexual harassment to rape, is almost always handled by campus administrative offices. While campus and local police are sometimes involved, this is uncommon. Universities are increasingly proactive in responding to sexual offenses because this problem has become a very visible concern of students, faculty, administrators, parents, and alumni. In addition, federal law requires that every university have a policy to prevent and respond to sexual assault. The federal requirement that universities prevent and respond to sexual violence began with an instruction on the implementation Title IX of the Education Amendments of 1972 (20 U.S.C. §§ 1681 et seq., 2011 Dear Colleague Letter; see US Department of Education 2011).

The definition of *sexual assault* as it is used for Violence Against Women Act programs is "any nonconsensual sexual act proscribed by federal, tribal, or state law, including when the victim lacks capacity to consent" (34 U.S.C. § 12291(a) (29)). In 2014, the Clery Act began to require universities to report two categories of forcible sexual assault: forcible rape and forcible fondling (Irwin et al. 2021, note 1). Not only is sexual assault a serious physical and emotional harm to victims, it provides a unique challenge as universities confront the questions of whether, how, and under what circumstances they should restructure their campus policing. It is a unique problem because sexual assault is both underreported by victims and requires extensive disclosure by universities.

I begin with the data about the prevalence of sexual assault and the rates of reporting it. While men are also victims of sexual assault, women are far more likely to be sexually assaulted. According to a widely cited source, 19 percent of undergraduate women have experienced attempted or completed sexual assault since entering college (Krebs et al. 2009). A National Crime Victimization Survey of data from 2005–2013 noted that only 20 percent of rape and sexual assaults of college students were reported to authorities, compared to 32 percent of nonstudent victims between the ages of eighteen and twenty-four (Langton and Sinozich 2014). The reporting was even lower among victims who were assaulted while under the influence of drugs or alcohol (DeMatteo et al. 2015). At the same time, 70 percent of campus sexual assault victims reported disclosing details of the sexual assault to a family member, friend, or roommate (Krebs et al. 2009). Only 22 percent of the reported perpetrators were strangers, and the reasons for not reporting include personal reasons (26 percent), fear of getting the perpetrator in trouble (10 percent), fear of reprisals (20 percent), and the feeling that the incident was not important enough to the respondent to report (12 percent) (Langton and Sinozich 2014).

The federal laws that govern the response of universities to various sexual offenses includes the Clery Act, the Violence Against Women Act, and Title IX of the 1972 Education Amendments. The Clery Act requires annual disclosures of a wide range of crimes committed on campus. It was amended in 1992 with the Campus Sexual Assault Victims' Bill of Rights, which requires that academic institutions develop prevention policies and respond directly to victims of sexual assault. The Violence Against Women Act (2013) expanded requirements for the disclosure of campus incidents of violent sex crimes, outlined the disciplinary proceedings following rape allegations, and established procedures for the protection of the rights of the accused and accusers.

Title IX of the 1972 Education Amendments prohibits sex discrimination in education: "No person in the United States shall, on the basis of sex, be excluded from participation in, be denied the benefits of, or be subjected to discrimination under any education program or activity receiving Federal financial assistance" (Title IX 2006). Universities have good reason to take Title IX seriously because violations can be punished by the termination or denial of federal funding. The US Supreme Court held in *Franklin v. Gwinnet County Public Schools* 503 U.S. 60 (1992) that individual plaintiffs can recover monetary damages from universities under Title IX. The Department of Education Office of Civil Rights investigates all federal civil rights violations and investigates sex discrimination under Title IX.

Under Title IX, the Office of Civil Rights can initiate an investigation or complaints can be brought by "anyone who believes that an education institution that receives Federal financial assistance has discriminated against someone on the basis of race, color, national origin, sex, disability, or age." The person or organization filing the complaint need not be a victim of the alleged discrimination but may complain on behalf of another person or group (US Department of Education 2020). The Office of Civil Rights is currently investigating almost four hundred complaints of sexual discrimination in institutes of higher education (US Department of Education 2020). This is a slow process, as evidenced by the fact that some of the open investigations were filed in 2012.

We return again to the central question of whether a university should have its own campus police, contract with a local police department, or control its campus using nonpolice functions. Here, we can apply these different strategies to address sexual offenses that occur at or adjacent to the university.

If we choose to respond to sexual offenses by having our own campus police, we should note that campus police must be duly sworn if they are to have the power to arrest. If we decide that sworn campus police with the power to arrest is the appropriate response to a pervasive climate of sexual offenses, we are choosing to address at least some sexual offenses as crimes. When we treat sexual assault as a crime, we will need the power of police to stop, investigate, and, if warranted, arrest. After the arrest, the power to subpoena or compel the production of evidence will be the province of the district attorney.

If the complaint results in a criminal charge, criminal punishment may follow if the defendant is found guilty beyond a reasonable doubt. As of 2009, of the sexual assault cases reported, whether to the campus administration or campus police, less than 1 percent of perpetrators receive any disciplinary action from the school and only 6 percent were arrested, prosecuted, or convicted in the criminal justice system

(Krebs et al. 2009). Thus, while a referral to the criminal justice system could result in more severe punishment than an administrative referral, the percentage receiving any disciplinary action in either case is very small.

The administrative path will not result in a criminal investigation or arrest because other administrative offices, like student conduct or counseling, have no power to arrest, subpoena, or compel the production of evidence. An investigation through university administrative functions will have to use the current department standard for a university's adjudication of a sexual assault complaint, a preponderance of evidence. This is a lower standard than the "beyond a reasonable doubt" standard that would be required if the complaint were handled in the criminal courts.

On the other hand, many survivors and their defenders argue that mandatory referral to the criminal justice system is a very bad idea for a number of reasons (National Women's Law Center 2017). Prosecutors rarely bring charges, especially when the victim is acquainted with the perpetrator; and among some communities of color and LGTBQ communities, there is a strong distrust of the criminal justice system. More importantly, the administrative remedy provides women with the support and counseling that the criminal justice system lacks. The campus administration can provide the victim with a housing and even class transfer to protect the victim from the perpetrator, emotional and psychological counseling, and accommodations for classwork.

Sexual assault in a university setting, when it is reported at all, is usually handled by various administrative offices. In addition to the support the administration can give the victim, another advantage to avoiding using campus policing to handle sexual offenses concerns the belief that one of the primary causes of sexual offense is rape culture. If that is the case, then prevention will be a significant part of the solution, and that is best done by a wide range of nonpolice functions. "Our findings indicate that . . . universities, need cultural shifts to encourage more comprehensive reporting of campus crimes, to stop ignoring VAW [violence against women], or to halt cover-ups that seem to occur at some universities. When perpetrators receive encouragement, or no punishment, from peers and campus administrators, then the lack of effective guardianship leads to a rape-supportive culture, whereby men are not only motivated to be violent, but women are also willing to take blame and never report sexual assault. . . . Thus, the student culture on college campuses needs to change" (Wiersma-Mosley et al. 2020, 636–658).

Janet Napolitano, the former president of the University of California, worries about the confusing scene that ensues when offices other than campus police departments attempt to address sexual assault: "Many institutions are hiring employees or outside consultants with legal and law enforcement backgrounds to ensure that investigations are being performed with appropriate expertise. . . . A cottage industry is being created where law and consulting firms are selling these services so that institutions can attempt to meet ambiguous legal requirements" (Napolitano 2015, 400).

Because of her concerns about using just the university's nonpolice function, she advocates using law enforcement as well because it has "the tools to effectively investigate these crimes. The criminal justice process has the authority to impose serious punishments on offenders, including incarceration. The most serious sanction that a college can impose is dismissal, which is wholly inadequate where a crime has been committed. Having law enforcement conduct investigations ensures, if properly done, that effective investigations will be conducted and that there will be appropriate punishments that have a strong deterrent effect, all to the ultimate benefit of the survivors and the safety of the university community as a whole" (Napolitano 2015, 400).

Notice that using law enforcement does not assume that the university has its own campus police. A university can have various arrangements with a local police department, one of which might include responding to sexual assault.

To sum up the discussion so far, we first looked at two contrasting models of policing. The first understands policing as something that the community engages in as a way to protect all the members of the community. The second understands policing as a way to protect the interests of powerful institutions. Presumably no university wants a policing devoted to subordinating the communities in which we live and work, but given the prevalence of universities doing just that, we must be vigilant about how our university operates in the larger community.

We then asked from what threats our university community should be protected. We looked at the patterns of what kinds of issues are likely to be addressed by campus police and what kinds of issues are addressed by other administrative university structures. Academic dishonesty is widely handled by student conduct offices. Alcohol and drug offenses and personal and property crimes were mostly handled by campus police. Sexual assault and related sexual offenses were either unreported or handled by other administrative structures.

Of course, universities may choose to deal with many types of misconduct by using things like a conduct code or by viewing much of this conduct as a public health issue or as a failure of our university to nurture a protective and inclusive culture. But on the assumption that many of you are now considering having some kind of policing at our universities, we move on to examining the kind of authority campus policing structures might and should have and how we could set limits on these structures.

AUTHORITY AND LIMITS OF CAMPUS POLICING

All state and local police officers must be duly sworn under the relevant statutes in the state in which they serve. Police officers who are directly employed by the universities where they serve must be duly sworn as police officers by the states in which they serve if they want to have authority that includes arrest. In California, the campuses of the University of California, California State University, and the community college system are authorized to employ police officers with the power and designation of "peace officers" under California law.

Penal Code § 830.2(b) authorizes campus police officers from the University of California to serve as peace officers. Under Education Code § 92600, their authority extends to the area within one mile of the exterior boundaries of the campus to which they are assigned. Penal Code § 830.2(b) and Education Code § 89560 provide the same authority to California State University police officers. Community college police officers are authorized under § 72330 of the education code. Officers at a private university are authorized only under a memorandum of understanding with the local police department under § 830.7 of the penal code. All these officers have the authority to arrest. Private higher education institutions in California and many other states have to enter into contractual arrangements with the local police department (Penal Code § 837 (b)).

It is useful to look at what other universities are doing as each university reflects on whether and how to restructure its own campus policing function. The most recent research on the prevalence and practice of campus policing is from the Bureau of Justice Statistics in 2012 (Reaves 2015). More than two-thirds of the over nine hundred four-year colleges and universities in the US with twenty-five hundred or more students use sworn police officers, and more than nine in ten public colleges and universities have sworn officers. Whereas 91 percent of public universities used armed officers, only 36 percent of private universities allowed their police to be armed; 86 percent of sworn campus police officers have arrest authority, and 81 percent have jurisdictions that extend beyond campus borders.

Should Campus Police Have the Power to Arrest?

States will have varying descriptions of who it may arrest, but a legal arrest must comply with the requirements spelled out in various US Supreme Court decisions. California law specifies who and under what circumstances peace officers may arrest in the jurisdiction to which their authority extends. This peace officer may arrest anyone if they have a warrant to do so. If they do not have a warrant, they may arrest anyone who commits any public offense, including a misdemeanor, in the officer's presence. They may also arrest a person if they have cause to believe that the person has committed a felony, though it needn't be in the officer's presence (Penal Code § 836).

Generally, a university will not have the authority to exclude a sworn police officer employed by local, state, or federal jurisdictions from arresting someone on their campus if the conditions above are met, but, if their states allow, they can choose whether to have their own campus police with the power to arrest. They may also have an agreement with the local police department to have this department proactively policing the campus.

If your campus decides not to have its own campus police department, it may simply rely on local police (and state and federal when appropriate) to investigate and arrest people when crimes are committed on campus. If your campus decides to have its own campus police, it still will not have the power to exclude other police forces, but in practice the local police departments will not aggressively police on campus, and the campus police force has the discretion, as do local police, to focus its investigatory and arrest powers only on certain offenses.

This way the university can have more control over how its campus will be policed. If the university chooses to enter into an agreement with a local police department, as with all contractual agreements, both parties will be able to negotiate how this agreement would work. This gives the university more control than simply relying completely on local police but not quite as much as they would with their own police force.

Assuming that the university has its own police force, would the university want its officers to have arrest authority? The US Supreme Court sets the law on what constrains the police in most of their activities, including when and under what conditions they can arrest someone. *Atwater v. City of Lago Vista* 532 U.S. 318 (2001) held that the police could arrest someone for a simple seatbelt violation: "If officer has probable cause to believe that an individual has committed even a very minor criminal offense in his presence, he may, without violating the Fourth Amendment, arrest the offender." After any arrest, even for a minor traffic offense, the police may search the person and, if it is a traffic violation, their car, including any containers within it.

If you authorize your campus police to arrest, you will have to live with the possibility that they will arrest students, faculty, and staff for very trivial matters. At San José State University, I was arrested for a traffic violation, and when I had the audacity to complain in writing about the inappropriateness of this particular traffic violation, the police department retaliated by adding felony disobedience of an officer to the charges. My fellow faculty raised the money to cover my $1,500 lawyer's bill, but it took six months of turmoil before the nightmare was over. Even before the arrest, police officers have the authority to stop someone if they have a reasonable belief that a crime is afoot. This is called a Terry stop, based on the US Supreme Court case *Terry v. Ohio* 392 U.S. 1 (1968).

Suppose you are the parent of a student who is stopped by the police. Suppose that the police officer has a reasonable belief that this student might be armed and dangerous. The officer then has the authority to pat the student down. This is a Terry frisk, which is also constitutional if the officer has a reasonable belief that the person stopped may be armed and dangerous. Suppose your black or brown son has never followed your advice and continues to dress in a way that you fear will make him look like a gangster. Let's also suppose his university is in a state that criminalizes the marijuana he enjoys, and the object that the officer finds in a pat down turns out to be the marijuana he planned to bring to the party he was heading to. You and your son might be able to get this evidence excluded in the criminal process that might be right around the corner, but do you want him to live on a university campus where arrests can occur in the building in which he lives and the room in which he sleeps?

Should Campus Police Authority Extend beyond Campus Constituents to the Larger Community?

If you decide to have or keep your campus police force, do you want them to have authority beyond the borders of the campus? In

California, all the University of California and California State University campus police officers have this authority in a one-mile area extending beyond the borders of the campus. If you are associated with one of these campuses, this is a matter of state law, and you do not have the power to limit the borders or deactivate your campus police force.

The argument for allowing campus police to police surrounding communities is that the universities increasingly own property in these communities, and their faculty and students often live there. Given the pressure of gentrification on rents and the low salaries of many of the service workers at universities, the staff often cannot afford to live in the communities that border universities. The downside of university involvement in local communities outside their borders, including campus policing, is the long and disturbing history of universities gentrifying their surrounding communities.

Ira Harkavy, associate vice president and founding director of the Netter Center for Community Partnerships at UPenn, describes current realities: "I believe firmly that overall universities are not yet part of the solution to the tragic and inexcusable conditions in the poorer communities that are near them. . . . They contribute more to privilege and to sustaining the current situation than they do to change it" (as noted in Baldwin 2021, 39). Duke and its history with Durham and the University of Virginia and its history with Charlottesville provide examples of the complex relationship a university may have with the neighboring community (Ustundag 2015; Carpenter et al. 2016).

Should Campus Police Be Armed?

Defenders of arming campus police point out that virtually all sworn police officers in this country are armed, as are the "criminals" that threaten the campus community. The tragic stories that open this chapter provide a central reason for not allowing campus police to be armed: they have used these weapons to kill and maim. In addition, the atmosphere that armed police create, especially for marginalized students, faculty, and staff, is a reason for not arming campus police. Miriam Lam, University of California Riverside's vice chancellor for diversity, points out that armed campus police exist in a culture and practice that prioritizes security, discipline, and punishment and that is frightening to black and brown and other marginalized students and therefore "is one that appears antithetical to the UC academic mission" (Watanabe 2021).

Should Campus Police Use Military Equipment?

If you are willing to allow armed campus police, would you be comfortable with the campus police obtaining military weapons? The Pentagon provides military equipment through its 1033 program. Local police departments have been the recipients of much of this equipment, but 124 campus police departments have also received military equipment through this program (Anguiano 2020). Ohio State obtained a mine-resistant ambush vehicle, and Central Florida acquired a grenade launcher. M-16 rifles were given to sixty-six universities. How comfortable do you feel about your campus being similarly armed?

Should Campus Police Have the Rights and Qualified Immunity that Most Police Forces Enjoy?

The wrongful death suit filed by student Cameron Redus's mother was challenged under the qualified immunity defense. Qualified immunity is a defense that is available for government agencies in lawsuits seeking damages for the constitutional violations of the person bringing the suit (the plaintiff). Qualified immunity is sovereign immunity that has some limits, unlike absolute immunity. Sovereign immunity traces its history back to the protection that the king would have, and today it refers to the immunity that governments have. Many police officers are reimbursed for monetary damages in a civil suit by their own employment contracts, but the police departments are liable and must generally argue for qualified immunity.

The theory behind qualified immunity is that we must protect government agencies from monetary damages because otherwise they could be tied up in litigation that would distract them from their mission and could undermine their willingness to do their jobs. Most police departments have qualified immunity because they are government agencies. Qualified immunity is not automatic, even for government agencies. To overcome qualified immunity, a plaintiff must show that the defendant's conduct "violate[d] clearly established statutory or constitutional rights of which a reasonable person would have known."

Lest the reader feel assured that qualified immunity for police will only be supported in rare circumstances where the police are behaving decently, it is instructive to look at the Supreme Court's decision in the 2018 case of *Kisela v. Hughes.* Officer Kisela shot and seriously injured Amy Hughes when she was standing six feet away from a neighbor holding a kitchen knife at her side with the blade turned away from her neighbor. The police arrived at the scene as a welfare check after someone reported that Hughes was behaving erratically, using the knife to carve a tree.

When the police arrived, both Hughes and the neighbor were conversing calmly. The other officers wanted to converse with Hughes, but Kisela decided that deadly force was warranted. The Supreme Court held that Kisela's response justified qualified immunity for him. Justice Sonia Sotomayor, in a powerful dissent, disagreed with the court's assessment of Kisela's conduct: "If this account of Kisela's conduct sounds unreasonable, that is because it was." She went on to describe the majority's holding of qualified immunity for Kisela as transforming "the doctrine into an absolute shield for law enforcement officers . . . [that] sends an alarming signal to law enforcement officers and the public. It tells officers that they can shoot first and think later, and it tells the public that palpably unreasonable conduct will go unpunished."

Unfortunately, Justice Sotomayor's eminently reasonable opinion is the dissent. The majority opinion on Kisela's conduct sets the bar frighteningly low for police officers. Now that we have some idea about what qualified immunity for the police involves, would you want police officers at your university to have qualified immunity, keeping in mind that they will likely be protected even if they behave as unreasonably as Kisela? If yours is a public university and your state licenses campus police officers as government officials, you cannot restrict their access to the qualified immunity defense.

The only way you can avoid qualified immunity for campus police is to not have a campus police force. If yours is a private university, your campus police may not have qualified immunity. In the state of Texas, for example, campus police at private universities do not have qualified immunity. Individual states can have statutes that grant, or withhold, the qualified immunity defense from police departments at private universities.

Cameron Redus's family was able to circumvent qualified immunity because the campus police officer who killed Cameron was employed by a private university, the University of the Incarnate Word. The University of the Incarnate Word argued that their police department was licensed by the government, but the Supreme Court of Texas did not accept this argument. They found for Redus's family on the issue of qualified immunity.

CONCLUSION

Campus police are a powerful force at most public universities and many private ones. At public universities, they are almost all armed, and many public universities are the recipients of military equipment given to them by the Pentagon. Virtually all universities use their student conduct office to manage academic honesty and many other student conduct issues. Most universities will probably be able to manage drug and alcohol conduct using the campus administration, and they are likely already very heavily invested in drug and alcohol prevention programs using staff other than police officers. Most universities are probably already preventing and responding to sexual assault using the offices on their campus that are managing Title IX, the Violence Against Women Act, and the Clery Act. Given the risks of having police on a university campus, it is time to think very carefully about other alternatives.

The first other alternative is to simply not have a campus police department or function on campus. The US Military Academy at West Point is a unique university since all of its students are enlistees in the US Army. Still, much of the policing is done by the cadets using the honor code. "A cadet will not lie, cheat, steal, or tolerate those who do." The academy's code is part of its educational mission and also the way that the academy is policed.

The University of Maryland model is a hybrid of campus police and the student honor code. Its honor code enlists students to police many issues that would not be regarded on other campuses as student conduct issues. Its students manage academic honesty issues and many other issues, including "acts of violence, intimidation, disruption, or rioting; substantial theft or vandalism; fraud or forgery; use or distribution of illegal drugs" (University of Maryland). The university also has a campus police department, but it has only around one hundred officers who patrol its statewide campuses with a student population of over forty thousand (University of Maryland Police Department). By comparison, the University of Chicago has approximately one hundred officers on a campus of about seventeen thousand. The University of Chicago officers have a large jurisdiction that extends well beyond the campus borders and stretches its control over sixty-five thousand persons not on campus. Their often-heavy footprint has inspired substantial community pushback (Kartik-Narayan 2018).

The next alternative is to have an agreement with a local police department. If your university has or would like to have such an arrangement, negotiate very hard to see that the protections you want for your campus and campus community are included in this contract.

Next, if you currently have a campus police department, investigate how much flexibility you have in imposing limits on what your campus police department is authorized to do. Within these constraints, negotiate whatever limits you think will protect your campus community from the tragic excesses we have discussed in this chapter.

Finally, do not simply accept any of the constraints that are imposed by your state, by the inertia on your campus, or by the economic interests that may have infected your university. The issues we discussed are moral, legal, economic, and political. Think long and hard about what needs to be changed. Then organize, communicate, litigate, demonstrate, and vote.

WORKS CITED

Anderson, Melinda D. (2015). "The Rise of Law Enforcement on College Campuses." *Atlantic*, September 28, 2015. https://www.theatlantic.com/education/archive/2015/09/college-campus-policing/407659/

Anguiano, Viviann. (2020). "4 Actions Colleges Can Take to Address Police Brutality." Center for American Progress, July 15, 2020. https://www.americanprogress.org/issues/education-postsecondary/news/2020/07/15/487647/4-actions-colleges-can-take-address-police-brutality/

Baldwin, Davarian L. (2021). *In the Shadow of the Ivory Tower: How Universities Are Plundering Our Cities*. Bold Type Books.

Baptiste, Nathalie. (2015). "Campus Cops: Authority without Accountability." *American Prospect*, November 2, 2015. https://prospect.org/civil-rights/campus-cops-authority-without-accountability/

Bayrak, Tuncay. (2020). "A Content Analysis of Top-Ranked Universities' Mission Statements from Five Global Regions." *International Journal of Educational Development* 72. https://doi.org/10.1016/j.ijedudev.2019.102130

Carpenter, Bennett, Laura Goldblatt, and Lenora Hanson. (2016). "The University Must Be Defended! Safe Spaces, Campus Policing, and University-Driven Gentrification." *English Language Notes* 54, no. 2: 191–198.

Daily Mail. (2012). "Surveillance Video Shows Naked Alabama Student 'High on LSD' Moments Before He Was Shot Dead as He Chased Campus Police Officer." *Daily Mail*, October 12, 2012. www.dailymail.co.uk/news/article-2216612/Gil-Collar-shooting-Surveillance-video-shows-naked-Alabama-student-high-LSD.html

DeMatteo, David, Meghann Galloway, Shelby Arnold, and Unnati Patel. (2015). "Sexual Assault on College Campuses: A 50-State Survey of Criminal Sexual Assault Statutes and Their Relevance to Campus Sexual Assault." *Psychology, Public Policy, and Law* 21, no. 3: 227–238.

Green, Jason. (2019). "San Jose State Releases Footage of Fatal Officer-Involved Shooting." *Mercury News*, March 10, 2019. www.mercurynews .com/2019/03/09/san-jose-state-releases-footage-of-fatal-officer-involved -shooting/

Harvard Law Review. (2016). "The Shooting of Samuel DuBose." *Harvard Law Review* 129, no. 1168. https://harvardlawreview.org/2016/02/the -shooting-of-samuel-dubose/

Hauser, Christine and Anahad O'Connor. (2007). "Virginia Tech Shooting Leaves 33 Dead." *New York Times*, April 16, 2007. www.nytimes.com/ 2007/04/16/us/16cnd-shooting.html

Hendrickson, Matthew. (2021). "Charges Dropped Against U of C Student Shot by Campus Police." *Chicago Sun Times*, May 21, 2021. https://chicago.sun times.com/2021/5/21/22447380/charges-dropped-against-u-of-c-student -shot-campus-police

Irwin, Véronique, Ke Wang, Jiashan Cui, Jizhi Zhang, and Alexandra Thompson. (2021). "Postsecondary Campus Safety and Security: 2020 July 2021," NCES 2021-092 U.S. Department of Education; NCJ 300772 U.S. Department of Justice, Office of Justice Programs. https://bjs.ojp.gov/sites/g/files/ xyckuh236/files/media/document/iscs20.pdf

Jones, Trevor, and Tim Newburn. (1998). *Private Security and Public Policing.* Oxford: Clarendon.

Kartik-Narayan, Ashvini. (2018). "The Fight Over Chicago's Largest Private Police Force." *South Side Weekly*, July 18, 2018. https://southsideweekly .com/the-fight-over-chicagos-largest-private-police-force-university-of -chicago-ucpd/

Knowles, Jared E. (2020). *Policing the American University.* Watertown, MA: Civilytics Consulting.

Krebs, Christopher P., Christine H. Lindquist, Tara D. Warner, Bonnie S. Fisher, and Sandra L. Martin. (2009). "College Women's Experiences with Physically Forced, Alcohol- or Other Drug-Enabled, and Drug-Facilitated Sexual Assault Before and Since Entering College." *Journal of American College Health* 57, no. 6.

KSAT News. (2020). "Texas Supreme Court Rules in Favor of Cameron Redus' Family to Allow Wrongful Death Lawsuit." *KSAT News*, May 22, 2020. https://www.ksat.com/news/local/2020/05/22/texas-supreme-court-rules -in-favor-of-cameron-redus-family-to-allow-wrongful-death-lawsuit/

Langton, Lynn, and Sofi Sinozich. (December 2014). "Rape and Sexual Assault Victimization Among College-Age Females, 1995–2013." *Special Report Department of Justice*, NCJ 248471.

Martinez, Michael, and Stella Chan. (2012). "University of California Offers $30,000 Each to Pepper-Sprayed Students." CNN, September 28, 2012. www .cnn.com/2012/09/26/us/california-occupy-pepper-spray/index.html

McLeod, Ethan. (2017). "State, City Agree to Pay Combined Settlement of $1 Million to Family of Tyrone West." *Baltimore Fishbowl*, July 26, 2017. https://baltimorefishbowl.com/stories/state-city-agree-to-pay-combined -settlement-of-1-million-to-family-of-tyrone-west/

Mulone, Massimiliano. (2019). "History of Policing," in *The Handbook of Social Control*, Mathieu Deflem and Charles F. Wellford, eds., 212–213. Wiley.

Napolitano, Janet. (2015). "Only Yes Means Yes: An Essay on University Policies Regarding Sexual Violence and Sexual Assault." *Yale Law and Policy Review* 33, no. 387: 400.

National Institute on Alcohol Abuse and Alcoholism. "College Drinking." www .niaaa.nih.gov/publications/brochures-and-fact-sheets/college-drinking

National Women's Law Center. (2017). "Forcing Students to Report Sexual Assault to the Police Makes Them Less Safe: What You Should Know about Mandatory Police Referral Bills." National Women's Law Center, Fact Sheet. https://nwlc.org/wp-content/uploads/2017/04/Forcing-Students-to -Report-Sexual-Assault-to-the-Police-Makes-Them-Less-Safe.pdf

Otterman, Sharon. (2019). "Black Columbia Student's Confrontation with Security Becomes Flashpoint over Racism on Campus." *New York Times*, April 18, 2019. www.nytimes.com/2019/04/18/nyregion/black-columbia -student-alexander-mcnab.html

Reaves, Brian A. (2015). "Survey of Campus Law Enforcement Agencies, 2011–2012." United States Department of Justice, Office of Justice Programs, Bureau of Justice Statistics. https://doi.org/10.3886/ICPSR36217.v1

Richards, Tara N. (2019). "No Evidence of 'Weaponized Title IX' Here: An Empirical Assessment of Sexual Misconduct Reporting, Case Processing, and Outcomes." *Law and Human Behavior* 43, no. 2: 180–192.

Selk, Avi, T. Rees Shapiro, and Wesley Lowery. (2017). "Call about Suspicious Man Was Made by Georgia Tech Student Killed by Police, Investigators Say." *Washington Post*, September 18, 2017. www.washingtonpost .com/news/grade-point/wp/2017/09/17/knife-wielding-campus-pride-leader -killed-by-police-at-georgia-tech

Suansing, Razel. (2021). "Shooting of Stephanie Washington and Paul Witherspoon Sparks Further Scrutiny of New Haven, Yale, Hamden Police Departments." *Yale News*, May 23, 2021. https://yaledailynews.com/ blog/2021/05/23/shooting-of-stephanie-washington-and-paul-witherspoon -sparks-further-scrutiny-of-new-haven-yale-hamden-police-departments/

University of California at Riverside. "Conduct." https://conduct.ucr.edu/for -faculty-and-staff/reporting-social-misconduct

University of Maryland. "Academic Integrity and Student Conduct Codes." www.studentconduct.umd.edu

University of Maryland Police Department. "About." www.umpd.umd.edu/ about/

US Department of Education. (2011). "Dear Colleague Letter," April 4, 2011. www2.ed.gov/about/offices/list/ocr/letters/colleague-201104.pdf. (This document has been formally rescinded.)

US Department of Education. (2020). "A Summary of the Most Current Regulations on Title IX." www2.ed.gov/about/offices/list/ocr/docs/titleix -summary.pdf

Ustundag, Ezqi. (2015). "Gentrification and Human Rights in Durham." *Duke Today*, October 1, 2015. https://humanrights.fhi.duke.edu/gentrification-and-human-rights-in-durham/

Watanabe, Teresa. (2021). "Defund or Reform UC Campus Police? Sharp Disagreement Surfaces." *Los Angeles Times*, February 3, 2021. www.latimes.com/california/story/2021-02-03/defund-campus-police-or-reform-them-sharp-disagreement-surfaces-at-uc

White, Gillian B. "The Downside of Durham's Rebirth." *Atlantic*, March 31, 2016. www.theatlantic.com/business/archive/2016/03/the-downside-of-durhams-rebirth/476277/.

White House Task Force. (2014). "Intersection of Title IX and the Clery Act."

Wiersma-Mosley, Jacquelyn D., Malachi Willis, Kristen N. Jozkowski, and Michael J. Cleveland. (2020). "Do Party Schools Report Higher Rates of Violence Against Women in Their Clery Data? A Latent Class Analysis." *Violence Against Women* 26, no. 6–7: 636–658.

Part III

CHALLENGES

9

The Role of the Humanities in Trauma-Informed Pedagogy

Zenon Culverhouse

ABSTRACT

At many institutions of higher education, there is a chronic shortage of mental health resources, particularly in the number of counselors available to students. While faculty often serve as first responders for students' psychological well-being, the shortage of counselors means faculty are sometimes the only responders. To make matters worse, there is increasing criticism concerning how educational institutions address students' psychological needs. Take, for instance, the perception that the dominant response to mental health needs is to coddle students with trigger warnings and safe spaces that only shield them from the slightest discomfort. While this perception is largely distorted, there is still a need for clearly defined best practices for faculty without expert training in psychological counseling in responding effectively to the mental health needs of their students.

To this end I consider current, prominent work on creating a "trauma-informed" classroom, particularly in courses where traumatic material is read and discussed. I identify some limitations of current work and some ways in which a humanities-based approach can make up for those limitations. The peril of a humanities course is that its subject matter often depicts trauma, violence, and adversity and therefore risks traumatizing or retraumatizing students if not handled carefully. But the promise of humanities disciplines is that they offer insight into the human condition and shape our responses to adversity. A trauma-informed, humanities-based approach, therefore, is especially well-suited to weave mental health care into the fabric of its curriculum.

Keywords: humanities, mental health care, post-traumatic stress disorder, trauma-informed pedagogy, trigger warnings, undergraduate curriculum

Before the start of the new semester, a student came to my office to introduce themselves, as they were enrolled in a new course I was offering that term, titled *Philosophy and Trauma*. The student explained that they were a combat veteran facing many mental health struggles as a result of trauma and told me in a matter-of-fact way that "looking forward to this class kept me from committing suicide." I was stunned at this, and panicked, for this made very real what was until then an abstract concern in the planning of this course: Is it irresponsible of me—a teacher of philosophy, wholly lacking any clinical training—to teach about trauma, given that the stakes are so high for many of my students?

The fact is, those of us who teach the humanities already teach materials that depict or discuss violent human interaction, though not typically under the name *trauma*. But these are events that can broadly be described as traumatic or, specifically, as events that can result in post-traumatic stress disorder (PTSD), the psychiatric designation found in the *Diagnostic and Statistical Manual of Mental Disorders (DSM)*. Religious texts, Greek mythology, literature, art, history, and many other subjects that are regularly taught in humanities courses are replete with depictions of such events and can have a deep, sometimes negative, impact on students. This negative impact can range from temporary emotional distress to symptoms of PTSD, in both students with no history of personal trauma as well as those with such history. Carello and Butler (2014, 155) identify some preliminary studies on this effect but note that there is no empirical research on this outside of the effect of exposure in clinical work.

These texts are often necessary, for they invite us to confront and contemplate the more distressing aspects of our humanity. This fact led some of us humanities faculty at my institution to secure a grant from the National Endowment for the Humanities, titled "Trauma: Conflict and Aftermath." The ultimate aim of the grant was to develop new and existing humanities courses that emphasize the role of the humanities in understanding psychological trauma, particularly trauma resulting from violent human interaction, such as war and sexual violence. To aid our effort, we researched, read, and discussed a variety of works on trauma and consulted with many who had been down this path already, both within and outside the humanities. My course, *Philosophy and Trauma*, is one of several new courses that resulted from this grant. The grant focused not only on content but also on how best to serve our students. Research shows that many adults have experienced trauma in their lives, and university students are no exception. See Carello and Butler in "Perilous Pedagogies"(2014) and "Practicing What We Teach" (2015).

The topic was timely when we began in 2015, and unfortunately it has only become more prominent over the years, with the ongoing wars in Iraq and Afghanistan, the #MeToo movement, the protests over police brutality, the Black Lives Matter movement, increasing political divisiveness, and the COVID-19 pandemic, just to name a few. Our university is a Hispanic-serving institution in San Antonio, Texas, whose student body consists of many directly impacted by traumatic events. For example, San Antonio is also known as "Military City," and many of our students and staff are combat veterans. Looking at our teaching through the lens of trauma gave newfound urgency to long-standing pedagogical questions about what we teach and how we teach it, questions about the value of reading literary depictions of violence, where to draw the line between instructor and therapist, and many others.

WHAT IS TRAUMA-INFORMED PEDAGOGY?: ITS ORIGIN AND PRINCIPLES

Over the last two decades, recognition of the ubiquity of trauma in society led teachers in higher education to incorporate instruction on trauma and its effects into the undergraduate curriculum. Early efforts in this area were specific to programs such as psychology and sociology, whose students will likely work with traumatized populations. Out of this emerged what is generally called trauma-informed care, a mode of care (e.g., as practiced by clinical psychologists and social workers) that avoids retraumatizing persons "by thoroughly incorporating . . . an understanding of the prevalence and impact of trauma and the complex paths of healing and recovery" (Fallot and Harris 2009).

Given the prevalence of trauma in all populations, researchers and educators turned their focus on the student population. While trauma impacts learning in all disciplines, courses that expose students to works that depict violence and its effects, and invite them to reflect on it in class discussion and written assignments, can especially put students at risk of a mental health crisis, resulting in incomplete assignments, absences, lack of engagement, and even intervention from mental health services. Carello and Butler (2015) cite statistics on this.

More recently, therefore, trauma-informed pedagogy has become prominent, with many of the lessons of trauma-informed care tailored to teaching in higher education. There is currently little empirical research available that can identify effective ways to teach traumatic topics (Carello and Butler 2014, 163). In the meantime, then, the principles of trauma-informed pedagogy aim to minimize the risk of retraumatizing students through educating faculty on trauma and prioritizing student safety, support, and empowerment (2014, 163).

Before identifying the basis of the principles of trauma-informed pedagogy as well as their limitations, what follows is an outline of the most recent version of the principles themselves (All the following principles are quoted from Carello at https://traumainformedteachingblog .files .wordpress .com/2020/03/titl-self-assessment-for-educators-3.20-1.pdf):

1. Safety: Efforts are made to create an atmosphere that is respectful of the need for safety, respect, and acceptance for all class members in both individual and group interactions, including feeling safe to make and learn from mistakes.

The instructor should ensure, first and foremost, that students feel safe in the classroom, physically, emotionally, and academically. This means that the instructor should be alert to potential signs of distress in students and take appropriate action, such as checking in with the student. This can also mean that students are not required to read, view, or discuss traumatic events.

If, for example, reading about such topics is part of the course, the faculty should let the students know ahead of time that the course contains distressing material and allow them to opt out or do an alternate assignment. There is some research that disputes the value of content or trigger warnings, with data indicating that content warnings, by themselves, do not help students prepare for exposure to material that could potentially trigger symptoms of past trauma and may even "reinforce survivors' view of their trauma as central to their identity" (Jones et al. 2020).

Though Carello and Butler do not say so explicitly in their publications, it seems that content warnings could still work effectively when complemented by some additional trauma-informed measures that can help students cope with negative reactions to disturbing material. Carello and Butler recommend, for example, checking in with students by discussing or using written responses to difficult material, which "allows students to process, reorient, and regain emotional distance" (Carello and Butler 2015, 270). They also recommend educating students on trauma and what those who experience trauma go through in an effort to normalize discussion about it (2015, 270). This effort to normalize discussion of trauma could especially address the ways in which trauma need not be central to one's identity.

2. Trustworthiness and transparency: Trust and transparency are enhanced by making course expectations clear, ensuring consistency in practice, maintaining appropriate boundaries, and minimizing disappointment.

One way to ensure a feeling of safety is for the instructor to be clear not just about potentially disturbing material but also about all course expectations, such as assignments and their due dates and late or makeup policies.

3. Support and connection: All class members are connected with appropriate peer and professional resources to help them succeed academically, personally, and professionally.

Students should be made aware of the resources available to them, for both academic and personal needs. For instance, the syllabus may include contact information for peer and professional tutoring services as well as for the campus counseling center and various crisis hotlines. The instructor should also make clear their own availability.

4. Collaboration and mutuality: All class members act as allies rather than as adversaries to help ensure each other's success. Opportunities exist for all class members to provide input, share power, and make decisions.

Students ought to have some agency in the course, not just providing input regarding course content but also regarding assignments and course policies. This is especially important if a course contains trauma-related content. Students should have a choice as to whether and how they engage with such content. Students should not be required to disclose personal experiences of trauma, but such an option should be available to those who want to, assuming it is appropriate to the assignment.

5. Empowerment, voice, and choice: All class members emphasize strengths and resilience over deficiencies and pathology; they

empower each other to make choices and to develop confidence and competence.

As an extension of collaboration and mutuality, students should be afforded many and different ways of sharing their ideas, thoughts, and feelings.

6. Social justice: All class members strive to be aware of and responsive to forms of privilege and oppression and to respect each other's diverse experiences and identities.

This applies to classroom activities and course policies. The instructor should be aware of any biases, whether their own or the students', and be able to address them appropriately. This principle is potentially controversial, with Texas and other states passing legislation that effectively bans teaching about racism (historical and systemic), white privilege, and other aspects of what is thought to be critical race theory. For now this legislation is restricted to K–12 schools, but there are efforts in Texas to extend it to higher education (www.kxan.com/news/texas-politics/lt-gov-dan-patrick-proposes-ending-tenure-over-critical-race-theory-battle/).

7. Resilience, growth, and change: All class members recognize each other's strengths and resilience, and they provide feedback to help each other grow and change.

The American Psychiatric Association defines *resiliency* as "the process of adapting well in the face of adversity, trauma, tragedy, threats, or significant sources of stress" (www.apa.org/topics/resilience). In a classroom, this can involve students providing each other critical, but helpful, feedback on their written and other assignments.

What makes these principles trauma-informed? Aside from content warnings and informing the students about what trauma is in the first place, it would not be obvious to someone who only read these principles by themselves why they are effective in preventing retraumatization or minimizing negative, counterproductive reactions in students. Rather, they seem mainly to offer general ways in which to foster a supportive learning environment for all students, regardless of whether they have been affected by trauma.

To be fair, these principles need to be general enough to apply in all courses, not just those that address trauma. But in those courses that do address trauma, one might still wonder, for example, how to conduct a discussion about difficult topics in a way that best ensures safety. My question, therefore, is more specifically this: What is it about trauma that especially informs or points to the need for safety, empowerment, mutuality, and so on? To answer this, it is first necessary to identify the concept of trauma that is the basis of the trauma-informed principles outlined above.

One of the recommendations of proponents of trauma-informed pedagogy is that faculty should be expected to understand what trauma is and how it impacts learning (Carello and Butler 2014, 163–164). But the term *trauma* in popular usage is vague and therefore can be used to describe almost any negative experience. Trauma-informed pedagogy emerged from psychology and the social sciences, and therefore the concept of trauma that informs teaching is based on the psychiatric designation of PTSD in the *DSM-5*. The literature on trauma-informed pedagogy does not explicitly make this connection, but it is clearly implied. For instance, Carello and Butler (2014, 157) describe the prevalence of traumatic experiences among college-age students by citing studies that define trauma in terms of PTSD.

In other words, trauma-informed pedagogy is really PTSD-informed pedagogy. As such, trauma-informed pedagogy essentially asks educators to defer to experts in clinical psychology. The initial set of recommendations that Carello and Butler offer, for example, urges faculty to "become familiar with scientific research on" trauma and to inform students of available counseling, suicide hotlines, and other resources should the student need it (2014, 164). This basis for trauma is certainly informative, but it also has limits.

The *DSM* entry is primarily a diagnostic tool for clinicians, but it is also the basis for understanding what trauma is. According to the most recent edition, the *DSM-5*, a necessary condition of PTSD is exposure to a traumatic event, in which a person experiences, witnesses, or is otherwise exposed to death, the threat of death, serious injury, or sexual violence. A person can be diagnosed with PTSD when such exposure results in persistent, intrusive memories, dreams, or reliving of the traumatic event(s); avoidance of things that could remind one of trauma (often resulting in social isolation); being in a constant state of high alert (e.g., hypervigilance, difficulty concentrating, difficulty sleeping); and negative thoughts and feelings about oneself and society (e.g., feeling shame, thinking that no one can be trusted) (DSM-5, 271–272).

The term *trauma* originated from the ancient Greek term *troma/ trauma*, which refers exclusively to a physical wound or injury (*Greek-English Lexicon, by H. G. Liddell & R. Scott, Oxford 1843*). Only with the work of Sigmund Freud, Pierre Janet, and others in the nineteenth century did the term come to describe psychological injury resulting from violence and other disturbing events. It was not until 1980, with the publication of the third edition of the *DSM*, that trauma received official designation as PTSD. The criteria for PTSD have changed somewhat over the various editions of the *DSM*, but its general features have remained, and PTSD is the dominant way of thinking about trauma today. For an excellent history of trauma, see Judith Herman, *Trauma and Recovery*.

This conception of trauma offers some insight into the principles of trauma-informed pedagogy. An instructor may recognize that a student's absence could be avoidance rather than lack of interest. A student's difficulty concentrating or need to sit at the back of the classroom could be due to trauma and not simply a lack of interest. Giving students the benefit of the doubt in these instances will be especially important if the class does cover traumatic material. It also specifies when to provide content warnings, such as when reading about or discussing sexual violence.

The fact that those afflicted with PTSD experience intrusive, unwanted, and distressing memories of these events explains why depictions or discussions of trauma can trigger intrusive memories and, therefore, why such content warnings are necessary. If one of the main reactions to intrusive memories is to avoid such reminders, it is likely that a student in this position will shut down in class rather than engage with the course material.

While the *DSM* designation of PTSD serves as a common basis for understanding trauma and can inform some of the principles of trauma-informed pedagogy, when it comes to teaching trauma, it should not be relied on exclusively for becoming trauma-informed, because the *DSM* is a classification of symptoms only. In his work on values in the *DSM*, John Sadler identifies this particular feature as "hyponarrativity": "To diagnose a person under the *DSM* is to reveal little of the person's biography: what is important to them, how they came to be as they are, what people or events had an important impact on them . . . and, most importantly, how the illness experience interacts with these narrative aspects" (Sadler 2005, 176–177). More importantly, the hyponarrative character of PTSD in the *DSM* does not (and is not intended to) offer an etiology of trauma or any other mental disorder, nor does it recommend any course of treatment. An additional consequence of this is that it is impossible for instructors to anticipate all potential reminders of trauma, since many reminders of trauma can be very specific to a person's experience. Content warnings, therefore, are restricted to the more overt examples of trauma, such as war, sexual assault, death, and so on.

Exposure to a traumatic event is only a necessary condition for PTSD, because not all who experience such exposure develop persistent symptoms of PTSD. Without an etiology, it is less apparent what trauma tells us about us as human beings, particularly why we react to extreme stress in these ways and how we cope with it. Without an etiology, it is less apparent how some of the principles of trauma-informed pedagogy, such as safety and empowerment, can be implemented. If avoidance, for example, is a symptom of exposure to or reminder of trauma, the instructor cannot assume that the student is ready to confront trauma. Indeed, neuroscientific research on trauma shows that sometimes no amount of talk or cognitive stimulation will calm a person who has shut down or is on high alert. In *The Body Keeps the Score* (2014, 72), Bessel van der Kolk explains that the part of the nervous system responsible for alerting one to danger is rewired in trauma victims such that the part of the brain that reasons, reflects, and interprets experiences is not engaged: "Conventional talk therapy, in those circumstances, is virtually useless" (72). In such instances, van der Kolk recommends a "bottom-up approach to therapy," which calms the mind through the body by, for example, taking a break to exercise, do yoga, or stretch. This, too, could be an effective pedagogical practice. For instance, I invite a yoga teacher who works with traumatized persons to visit my classes just before final exams to explain her work and give students some techniques for handling stress.

But at the same time, no one is suggesting that the instructor should avoid teaching trauma entirely if doing so is valuable to the students. It remains an open question as to what extent it is valuable and how to teach it effectively when it is depicted in, say, literature and art.

As I mentioned above, research suggests that content warnings are not effective by themselves. Some of the recommendations of trauma-informed pedagogy could help provide a context for such warnings, particularly a classroom culture that has already normalized talk of trauma, what it is, and how it impacts people. But what does such normalizing talk consist of, besides outlining PTSD in the *DSM?* Additional scientific literature, such as the neuroscientific account of trauma I mention above, can be valuable for showing that responses to trauma are normal and are not always in a person's control. This can go some way toward dispelling a common myth about many mental disorders—namely, that it is all in the mind and so the afflicted need to just "get over it."

But scientific literature on trauma may not be sufficient by itself. Judith Herman writes that "the conflict between the will to deny horrible events and the will to proclaim them aloud is the central dialectic of psychological trauma" (1992, 1). She explains that in trauma—especially that which results from human violence—this conflict not only exists within the traumatized individual but is also between the victim, who wishes to proclaim; the perpetrator, who wants to deny; and society, who is caught in the middle but historically tends to side with the perpetrator. In both senses, the will to deny is what makes trauma "unspeakable" and to some even incomprehensible (Herman 1992, 1.). The notion of trauma's incomprehensibility comes from Freud but is central to the psychoanalytic view of trauma found in, for example, Cathy Caruth's *Unclaimed Experience*.

Understanding the social forces that inform our view of trauma and our experience of it can be empowering too. If we can identify institutions in society that perpetuate trauma, we perhaps can move toward preventing it or at least toward speaking about it in less shame-inducing ways. But for this we need to study the humanities—history, religion, literature, and philosophy—not just science.

PERILOUS PEDAGOGIES: CRITIQUES OF TEACHING TRAUMA IN THE HUMANITIES

The most prominent advocates of trauma-informed pedagogy, Carello and Butler, identify what they term "potentially perilous pedagogies" in writing and humanities courses that teach trauma. Their criticisms of these practices gave rise to some of the aforementioned trauma-informed principles for teaching used in higher education today. The most recent version is from Carello (2020). These principles in various iterations appear on university websites that advocate for trauma-informed pedagogy.

Carello and Butler identify several questionable pedagogical assumptions underlying the teaching of traumatic materials. Foremost among these is the assumption that "pain [from reading or writing about trauma] can be a precursor to health . . . and that [faculty] can determine how much pain students should express and can withstand" (Carello and Butler 2014, 160).

They cite two works by writing faculty who describe their students' reactions to writing assignments that, in some cases, require students to write about personal trauma, suicidal tendencies, depression, and similar experiences (Carello and Butler 2014, 158–159). These faculty report that some of their students' reactions were severe enough to require clinical intervention, but instead of revising or dropping the assignment, they took such reactions as evidence of the assignments' value for growth and learning (Carello and Butler 2014, 160).

Another unwarranted assumption that Carello and Butler identify is that the boundary between instructor and therapist can and should be blurred in the classroom. Though writing as a form of therapy has had some success in clinical settings, Carello and Butler argue that it does not necessarily translate to success in the classroom. Some of the people they criticize cite, for example, psychologist James Pennebaker's work on the healing power of writing as justification for their course writing assignments. The problem is that Pennebaker's findings result from controlled experiments under specific conditions (e.g., anonymity) not found in the classroom. At minimum, the student is disclosing to the instructor and, given the power instructors can wield, the student's disclosure may not be entirely voluntary (Carello and Butler 2014, 161–162).

This sort of "misappropriation" of clinical work in the classroom blurs the boundary between instructor and therapist. In noting one instructor's claim to be "'writing teacher as healer . . . [and] political agent,'" Carello and Butler remark that "unfortunately it appears that 'writing teacher as writing teacher' remains a devalued role" (2014, 161). Carello and Butler's remark here also applies to their observations about courses that expose students to others' narratives about trauma—for example, from Holocaust survivors. Here, too, teaching literature and history is sometimes thought to have therapeutic benefits despite its negative effects on students. Carello and Butler especially single out the work on testimony and witnessing by Shoshana Felman. In her essay "Education and Crisis, or the Vicissitudes of Teaching," Felman recounts how her students were deeply affected by watching Holocaust testimonies: "There was a sort of panic that consisted in both emotional and intellectual disorientation, loss of direction" (Felman 1992, 49).

One student described watching the testimonies as "a shattering experience" (Felman 1992, 49). Felman sees the act of witnessing as a way for those who did not experience the event directly to feel what the victim felt and thereby recognize the universality of human experience. Carello and Butler point out that evoking these feelings does not in itself count as learning even if the students are able to process these feelings effectively. Without trauma-informed practices, it seems, the students' success was incidental to the lesson.

Generally speaking, these criticisms are fair. It is risky if not reckless to provoke negative emotions in students without understanding how doing so affects their ability to learn, especially those who have experienced past traumas. But Carello and Butler overlook some of the context that Felman provides for her own students before and after watching Holocaust testimonies, and overlooking this context makes their criticism somewhat of a straw man argument. This is instructive to consider, because it is an example of the larger point I want to make about the role of the humanities in trauma-informed pedagogy—namely, that humanities texts often do not simply depict trauma and suffering; they can also inform us about trauma in productive and insightful ways.

First, Felman does not leave the students to their own devices in working through their emotions. She writes that she consulted with Dori Laub, a psychiatrist who was present for the screenings, spoke with students individually, and discussed the testimonies with students as a class, connecting it to their ongoing lesson about the effect and value of testimony and witnessing (1992, 48–52). Second, she did not simply expose the students to pain and suffering. Rather, she selected testimony that shows how the survivor uses her pain and suffering to survive. She writes of one survivor's testimony, "The woman's story is the story of a catastrophic loss which leads, however, to an insight into the mystery of *life* and of the need for *testimony*" (Felman 1992, 49).

This insight is trauma-informed in the sense that Felman is operating on the psychoanalytic theory about the etiology of trauma, a view that stems from Freud and is shared by Judith Herman in *Trauma and Recovery*. Felman introduced students to this view early on in her class. Freud was the first to recognize that traumatic experiences so overwhelm a person that they are not able to process it and thereby repress or push the memory of the experience into the unconscious. Herman agrees: "The ordinary response to atrocities is to banish them from consciousness" (1992, 1).

Despite mainstream psychiatry's turn away from Freudian psychoanalysis, contemporary psychiatric conceptions of trauma retain the general features identified first by Freud. From the psychoanalytic view drawn from Freud, a traumatic event is overwhelming enough that the person exposed to it is unable to process the event in the way that experiences of nontraumatic events are processed. As a result, memory of the event is repressed or fragmented. Herman writes that traumatic memories are fragmented in that they "are not encoded like the ordinary memories . . . in a verbal linear narrative that is assimilated into an ongoing life story" and that they "lack a verbal narrative and context; rather they are encoded in the form of vivid sensations and images" (Herman 1992, 37–38).

This makes it very difficult for the survivor to describe trauma in a coherent way and, therefore, is why traumatic experiences are described as unspeakable or incomprehensible. In presenting students with testimonies in the context of this understanding of trauma, Felman's teaching is trauma-informed, but in ways that give narrative to the *DSM*'s hyponarrative catalog of symptoms. Another important feature of the psychoanalytic view is that events themselves are traumatic, and the effects are universal to all times and places. Traumatic memory is an unvarnished engraving of the event in the psyche. Testimony, therefore, is a "means of accessing reality," as Felman puts it, and witnessing reveals something about our shared humanity, because it "give[s] reality to one's own vulnerability" (Felman 1992, 29). As such, witnessing can produce empathy in those who have not been traumatized as well as comfort those who have experienced trauma with the knowledge that they are not alone.

COMFORT THE AFFLICTED AND AFFLICT THE COMFORTABLE: TOWARD A HUMANITIES-BASED APPROACH TO TEACHING TRAUMA

Trauma-informed pedagogy is not only teaching texts with a sensitivity to trauma. The text (written, visual, etc.) can inform us about trauma in ways that support the current principles of trauma-informed pedagogy. So regardless of whether the psychoanalytic view is correct, such a view informs how students engage with representations of trauma in literature and other media. It draws from psychology but is not limited to it. For a critique of this and other views, see Alexander (2012, 6–15).

By the same token, there is not always a clear separation of psychology-based from humanities-based views of trauma. There are also close affinities between the findings of neuroscientific studies of trauma and the psychoanalytic view. For example, Caruth cites van der Kolk's work on the neurobiology of trauma in support of the view that traumatic memories are unspeakable, given how they are encoded in the brain (1996, 160 n.6).

After all, Freud's thinking about trauma was deeply influenced by literature. Another proponent of the psychoanalytic view, Cathy Caruth, observes, "If Freud turns to literature to describe traumatic experience, it is because literature, like psychoanalysis, is interested in the complex relationship between knowing and not knowing" (Caruth 1996, 3). Jonathan Shay, a former psychiatrist for Veterans Affairs, saw in his patients the warrior Achilles, the central figure of Homer's epic *The Iliad*. What Homer taught him, and what he came to see in his patients, was more than PTSD. He saw moral injury, a betrayal of shared values that leads to rage and social withdrawal (Shay 1994). The main point, which is overlooked or undervalued in current literature on trauma-informed pedagogy, is that literature, history, art, and philosophy not only depict trauma but can also contain insight on how to understand and respond to it.

Not only do the humanities offer insights into trauma, but engagement with the texts and other media of the humanities can be central to establishing a safe, collaborative classroom environment. Because trauma can result in isolation, reestablishing social trust and connection is vital to recovery (Herman 1992, chapters 3 and 7). The creator and author of *Theater of War*, Brian Doerries, relates a remark made by a high-ranking military officer upon viewing a staging of Sophocles's *Ajax*, a play about a decorated veteran of the Trojan War who is betrayed by his own leadership and commits suicide. The officer said, "I think [Sophocles] writes these plays to comfort the afflicted and afflict the comfortable" (Doerries 2015, 116). This phrase traces back to journalist Finley Peter Dunne, who has a fictional character use it to describe what a newspaper is supposed to do (*Observations by Mr. Dooley*, 1902).

This is what the play itself does, performed live in a theater of people. Doerries writes that the staging and audience discussion of ancient Greek plays about war gave combat veterans "voice to their secret struggles and convey[ed] to them that they were not alone" (2015, 4). The play also provides those who have not experienced war firsthand a glimpse into the psychological toll of war. In this way, Doerries and others see Greek theater—staged in ancient Athens, with nearly all of the city in attendance—as a means of "communalizing trauma" (2015, 57; see also, Shay 1994, 39–40. For an excellent example of communalization in a writing-intensive course, see Hamilton 2016, 205–226.).

It is such communalization that inspired my own efforts in my course *Philosophy and Trauma*. The principles of trauma-informed pedagogy were helpful guides in planning the course. For example, I invited guest speakers from areas outside of my expertise, including a member of the campus counseling office to talk about resources and PTSD and the campus Title IX coordinator to talk about how trauma informs their handling of cases. But the focus was on exposing students to a variety of texts from psychology, philosophy, history, and literature, all of which analyze or depict trauma as part of human experience.

Here is one example from literature, in which the texts themselves actively engage the reader in resisting society's effort to ignore trauma—namely, Heller's war satire *Catch-22* and Nabokov's story of sexual abuse, *Lolita*. These two stories try to lull us into accepting a world in which the horrible acts appear normal when they go unnoticed in a nihilistic world. *Catch-22* gets us to laugh at the absurd, and we are at risk of allowing the horrors in the novel to go unnoticed because of that. *Lolita* does the same: even though we are told upfront, and told again and again, that the character H.H. is a monster and that Lolita is a child, we are at risk of getting carried away by H.H.'s charm and the eroticization of Lolita. Using what we understood about trauma and these author's methods, as a class we were enabled as agents to resist what Herman describes as the "will to deny."

There is, of course, much more to say about the role of the humanities in understanding trauma. For now, the main point is to suggest that trauma-informed pedagogy in the humanities is not simply a set of strategies for content delivery and course management. With the instructor facilitating students' engagement with the text, trauma-informed pedagogy can also include how the content itself teaches us about trauma, how people experience it, and how they cope with it. Further research on the effects of teaching trauma should consider this too.

WORKS CITED

Alexander, J. *Trauma: A Social Theory*. Cambridge: Polity Press, 2012.

American Psychiatric Association. *Diagnostic and Statistical Manual of Mental Disorders*, 5th edition. Washington, DC: American Psychiatric Association, 2013.

Carello, J. "Examples of Trauma-Informed Teaching and Learning in College Classrooms." March 2020. https://traumainformedteachingblog.files.word press.com/2020/03/examples-of-titl-in-college-classrooms-3.2020-color-3 .pdf

Carello, J. & Butler, L. D. "Potentially Perilous Pedagogies: Teaching Trauma Is Not the Same as Trauma-Informed Teaching." *Journal of Trauma and Dissociation* 15 (2014): 153–168.

Carello, J. & Butler, L. D. "Practicing What We Teach: Trauma-Informed Educational Practice." *Journal of Teaching in Social Work* 35 (2015): 262–278.

Caruth, C. *Unclaimed Experience.* Baltimore: Johns Hopkins, 1996.

Doerries, B. *Theater of War.* New York: Alfred A. Knopf, 2015.

Fallot, R. & Harris, M. *Creating Cultures of Trauma-Informed Care.* 2009. www.theannainstitute.org/CCTICSELFASSPP.pdf

Felman, S. "Education and Crisis, or the Vicissitudes of Teaching," in *Testimony: Crises of Witnessing in Literature, Psychoanalysis, and History,* edited by S. Felman and D. Laub, 1–56. New York: Routledge, 1992.

Hamilton, A. H. "First Responders: A Pedagogy for Writing and Reading Trauma," in *Critical Trauma Studies,* edited by M. Casper and E. Wertheimer, 205–226. New York: New York University Press, 2016.

Herman, J. *Trauma and Recovery.* New York: Basic Books, 1992.

Jones, P. J., et al. "Helping or Harming? The Effect of Trigger Warnings on Individuals with Trauma Histories." *Clinical Psychological Science* 8 (June 2020): 905–917.

Liddell, H. G. & Scott, R. Greek-English Lexicon. Oxford: Clarendon Press, 1843.

Sadler, J. Z. *Values and Psychiatric Diagnosis.* Oxford: Oxford University Press, 2005.

Shay, J. *Achilles in Vietnam.* New York: Scribner, 1994.

Van der Kolk, B. *The Body Keeps the Score.* New York: Penguin Books, 2014.

Pedagogical Issues

The General Education Challenge

Laura Nader

ABSTRACT

This chapter focuses on developing effective pedagogy in general education classes using a case from this author's own experience. I started as a new professor at University of California Berkeley with an Anthropology of Law class that used "complaint diaries" to become familiar with the student audience but soon realized that was not enough. Thus came the next step—to introduce more critical thinking into the class. This was done by having the students look at the dynamics of power. What followed was the creation of a new class, one centered on controlling processes. The course was open to all and had no prerequisites. It also allowed considerable freedom on the part of the students in defining their subject matter. The creativity and quality work had life-changing results, as the many examples made clear at the time and make clear now. As I argue here, there are important lessons to learn from this.

Keywords: complaint diaries, controlling processes, critical thinking, dynamics of power, general education, mechanisms of indirect control, pedagogy

This chapter discusses a pedagogy that has been evolving and about the standards of right behavior of an anthropology professor who changed her pedagogy over a sixty-year period of teaching undergraduates at University of California (UC) Berkeley.

When I was a young professor at UC, my distinguished colleague Sherry Washburn advised me that my courses had too much reading and that the grading was too tough. He said, "This isn't Harvard. These kids work as well as go to school." In other words, I had to understand my students. Washburn himself was a popular teacher with hundreds of students in the introductory classes. He was right, and I was wrong. I began to change my teaching.

First, in my Anthropology of Law class, I asked students to keep complaint diaries, and before turning them in they had to analyze the patterns of complaints. Some students complained about messy room-mates, others about being unable to share with parents their sexual partners' physical abuse, others about sports coaches, and others about American politics. And they were all in one class! All this taught me a good deal about my student audience, and the assignment was bor-rowed by a colleague at Stanford University.

However, knowing my student audience was not enough. My goal moved to the next level—teaching critical thinking. For example, while it was clear that students understood power—who has it and who does not (e.g., power over money, politics)—they also needed to understand the dynamics of power. This was not achieved by the complaint diary assignment. So I invented a new course, a general education course like the ones that I had participated in at Harvard. It became Anthropology 139: Controlling Processes, a course open to all with no prerequisites.

Controlling Processes quickly became a popular course. Even parents and townspeople dropped in to see for themselves what they had heard from students. Each year I had three hundred students over twenty five years. However, some of my colleagues, mainly archaeolo-gists, did not support the course with teaching assistants, only with exam graders. I myself had to read hundreds of papers each year with no graduate assistance. Why such support was not forthcoming is not yet clear. However, one guess has to do with the syllabus.

General education courses are not strictly disciplinary in terms of readings—not even interdisciplinary, rather transdisciplinary. General education readings might include novels, journalistic pieces, and rel-evant films, along with academic writings from anthropology in this case. More demerits might have been linked to my class style, which was more conversational, not reading lectures, and students could interrupt me whenever they had questions. In other words, the class was not the usual anthropology course as was my Anthropology of Law class. The point was to encourage critical thinking, or thinking outside the box. Central to the critical thinking mission, of themselves in the world, was the paper assignment: "Find a controlling process in your life and tell me how it works and use class assignments where helpful." The assignment often changed their lives as they understood their self in contemporary culture.

Students themselves had to identify their subject matter, not the professor. Decades afterward, I still receive letters from students telling me what that paper assignment meant in "changing their lives." Recently I received a letter from a student who took the course in 1991. He wanted to tell me how it changed his life and what he was doing in his nonprofit on learning in different countries. Another, a single father whose daughter was about to go to college, wrote about citizen work on voting issues. And another who was working on water issues in the Amazon wrote about how the course led to her work there.

CONTROLLING PROCESSES: THE COURSE

I introduce the course with the following statement: This course deals with the means by which people's behavior, actions, and at times thoughts are controlled by social and cultural mechanisms, and the means by which people avoid, resist, or invent countercontrols. These mechanisms are called controlling processes. The study of controlling processes is of increasing interest to scholars and laypeople alike because of the intensification of centralized control in the world and the efficiency of that control by means of technology. The New World Order is today post-1984, and some believe a contemporary period of deepening Brave New Worlds.

Anthropologists working in "traditional" societies describe cultural and social mechanisms of indirect control. Recently, they are attentive to indirect controlling processes operating in globalized industrialized nation-states. Political theorists tend to focus on overt forms of domination, such as force and intimidation, but increasingly social scientists are examining the important role of cultural forms like language, ritual, symbols, and ideology in securing people's consent to their own domination.

This course will primarily examine indirect mechanisms of control, paying special attention to cultural forms, as well as direct ones, and the processes by which control may gradually become more hidden, voluntary, and unconscious in Western industrialized societies.

Students interested in the fields of language, science and technology, law, violence, politics, religion, medicine, development, sex and gender, marketing, and the media will be able to explore mechanisms of indirect control operating in spheres of social life through the course readings and in lectures and films. And, finally, people are frequently unaware of control, especially cultural control, during periods when gullibility is commonplace. The class is an introduction to methods for studying control and will enable students to discover and analyze patterns of control in their own lives in relation to historical developments and cross-cultural processes. The implications of controlling processes are discovered by a method of thinking that emphasizes connections rather than disciplinary boundaries.

The readings start with two novels: *1984* by George Orwell and *Brave New World* by Aldous Huxley. Although most students had already read one or both of these novels prior to college, directions for reading included asking students to list the controls used in each book. This first assignment is critical to understanding what is to follow, while comparing direct with indirect controls, silent controls, and the interpersonal realm.

What follows are readings about corporate industrialization with a primary reading of David Noble's *America by Design*, a powerful book about the conscious-making of corporate America. Then we have an example of control in science best illustrated by the making of the bomb in the film *The Day After Trinity*. Many of the students did not realize that the US had ever dropped a nuclear bomb. This is followed by readings on control through the professions—best illustrated by Mary Furner's book *Advocacy and Objectivity* (or its absence). Business and state controls are illuminated by Frances Piven and Richard Cloward's book *Regulating the Poor*.

The third part of the course deals with processes of control in law, language, war, power and trade, cults, gender, sex and family control, and control in everyday life through advertising. Two documentary films are shown: *Rosie the Riveter* and *Marketing Cool*. Thus, by the time we move to part 4, Future Directions and Debate, students have a broad range of materials from which to choose a controlling process in their lives and an understanding of how controlling processes work in their lives.

Indeed, the paper topics were wide-ranging. Many of the papers were selected for publication in the *Kroeber Anthropological Society Papers*. They dealt with law, the workplace, university dormitories, museums, Native American reservations, and various forms of resistance. As the papers indicated, culture easily impacts on a fragile or vulnerable mind, and hegemonic influence often limits our imagination. Institutions of power are well aware of the power of complex cultural codes—for example, inducing women to undergo body-altering surgery under the illusion of free choice or in reconstructing science work.

In particular, such accounts illustrate how control through normalization works to control "First World" citizens. The beauty of a controlling process approach to power, which has roots in the theories of Gramsci, Foucault, Bourdieu, and others, is that it allows us to look at old questions in new and provocative ways that point to the potential of reconfiguring the mundane or "normal" in a way that is not bereft of human agency. For example, the redefinition of previously normal moods and behaviors as medical disorders is a case in point, one that goes far beyond the widespread use of Prozac and Ritalin. The final colonization is the colonization of the mind, and not surprisingly, anthropologists themselves are not immune to such processes, a challenge for us all.

As noted earlier, the papers ranged far and wide: the practice of AIDS education, the privatization of justice, the moral economy of gambling, silicone breast implants in the US, storage plants for nuclear waste on Native American reservations, the science and antiscience debates at the Smithsonian Institution, the construction of the corporation as a legal person, the media's role in presenting the Gulf War as virtual violence and the resistances to such manipulations, and finally an examination of the inevitability syndrome as it operates in the House of Representatives, our media, and our workplace. From the outset, it is clear that students are attempting to understand how control works, realizing of course that it works unevenly and thus is not total. But let me give more detail from the specific papers that were published in the *Kroeber Anthropological Society Papers*.

For example, in Michael Zara's paper, the story is about how the corporation came to be a legal "person" with the legal rights of human beings. His research further explains how the fictitious person of the corporation came to be legally considered a psychological person as well. He traces the evolution of this legal-political concept from the 1807 US Supreme Court case *Bank of the United States v. Deveaux*, through several other cases over two hundred years that incrementally increased the economic and political rights of the corporation. The cumulative drift is antithetical to Sir Henry Maine's historical evolutionism. Zara spotlights how the private and business-oriented individualism of American industrialism gets legitimated through law, which over time threatens to displace the natural individual in favor of fictitious corporate persons.

In the ethnographic study of pharmaceutical sales practices, Michael Oldani explores the workings of double loyalty. Pharmaceuticals contribute through research for the good of humankind. At the same time, they contribute to a bottom-line mentality for shareholders through aggressive promotion of their products. Salespeople are caught in a double bind between profit and health care. As a true participant observer—that is, as a former salesperson—Oldani was apparently also caught in this sales dilemma.

As it turns out, it was not a necessary dilemma but a manufactured one, resulting from ideological moorings created in opposition to the Food and Drug Administration. Sometimes such corporate tactics erupt in scandals, followed by a cracking down within the industry on "spinselling." He describes the sales indoctrination, the sales process itself, as well as rituals of the trickster salesperson being caught. In the end, he labels his subject "the culture of cheating" in the context of "the culture of winning." He concludes by pointing to the gap in the literature on the "rep and the doctor," while at the same time pointing out how pharmaceutical corporations and he, as a salesperson, use the authority of science and knowledge of anthropology to "spinsell."

In the course of harmony, the use of harmony verdicts (not adversarial) is used as a technique of pacification (Nader 2005a). I trace the harmony law model from its use by Spanish colonialists in Mexico to its use in the United States and then as a tool of modern imperialism.

Linda Coco's paper "Silicon Breast Implants in America: A Choice of the 'Official Breast'?" brings us full circle (Nader 2005b). She writes about the internalized imperative that makes most women feel that "they are making the decision for breast implants on their own and for themselves." As she explains, however, this choice can often be distilled to economic survival. She concludes that women in America, in fact, do not choose implantation because the women she interviewed were neither freely situated nor critically informed. Coco probes the mechanisms of power, asking to what end has flat-chestedness for women become a disease and why do millions of women accept such medical diagnosis as authoritative to the point of risking their lives through invasive surgery in order to achieve "perfect" standardized breast dimensions.

Marianne McCune questions how it has come to be that the revolt against parental authority by adolescent girls delivers such youngsters into the hands of unseen authorities with such efficiency.

The essay "Brave New Workplace" compares the techniques of the new industrial relations with those of thought reform programs. Roberto Gonzalez uses as material experience in work teams and quality circles in a General Motors automotive assembly plant. He asks, "Are quality circles coercive, and if so, how—that is, through what mechanisms are workers coerced?"

Jay Ou's paper on the political economy of nuclear waste storage projects in the United States focuses on negotiations among the federal government, Native American tribes, and the nuclear industry in searching for potential sites for nuclear waste disposal. Exploring the new radioactive colonialism highlights the problematic nature of industrial interests on Indian land of which the Navajo case is probably the most well-documented. Tribal sovereignty and economic development of cultural capital are at issue.

Kathleen Wilusz's essay is about the media and the Persian Gulf War. Her work is based on survey materials on how the war was presented as a virtual event. She posits that having learned from public protests during the Vietnam era, the media repeatedly presented sanitized images of the Gulf War without death or destruction. These antiseptic presentations allowed for the continued bombing of Iraq after the declaration of the ceasefire, without media coverage. And the censorship plan worked; dissent disappeared, and war without protest was the way the Gulf War was billed in the media. What protesters there were got depicted as negative or dangerous as compared to other Americans. Stories were systematically comparing Iraq as dangerous with its opposite the American way of life. The media portrayed "expert" testimony as "strategic ritual," increasing its credibility and authority.

Unique to this war was the absence of reports detailing human destruction or even counts of the dead. The Iraqis were portrayed as destroyers of civilian populations, while Americans employed advanced technologies (e.g., "smart bombs") that avoid unnecessary destruction. The stage was set for prime time media events. Names of operations resembled video war games. Following the war, the sanctions allowed for a new type of aggressive war: the economic embargoes. The silence continued, and the author claims that the absence of a formal declaration of war by the United States Congress allows escape from legal redress.

In the final paper, Peter Shorett focuses on the irreversibility of "the inevitability syndrome" and shows how "inevitability thinking" works in practice in three contexts: (1) in United States House of Representatives hearings on the World Trade Organization, (2) in the media presentations of neoliberal globalization as a natural and inevitable process, and (3) as a manipulative device for managing armed forces. Such inevitability exercises result in a "strategic form of non-recognition," a prelude to passivity, acquiescence, and helplessness because there appear to be no other options. In addition, he describes the most extraordinary use of attaining, more specifically, the knowledge of group processes.

In summary, these last essays from *Kroeber Anthropological Society Papers*, No. 92/93, discover how control works and with what consequences: what slow corporate takeover case-by-case for over a century has meant. All of my work on controlling processes was for my part a response to challenging times, not just to a pandemic but to a disease of technology, for example. Google, Apple, and Facebook, with so-called smartphones, are penetrating the lives of people worldwide. And, as one of my students said, "At least I know what I'm up against." We need pedagogies in higher education that develop critical thinking, not just preparation for jobs, now more than ever, especially for those who cherish the principles of our democratic society.

The general education challenge goes beyond the classroom to the culture writ large.

WORKS CITED

Furner, Mary. 1976. *Advocacy and Objectivity: A Crisis in the Professionalization of American Social Science, 1865–1905.* Lexington: University of Kentucky Press.

Nader, Laura. 2005a. "Introduction: Essays in Controlling Processes." *Kroeber Anthropological Society Papers*, no. 92/93.

Nader, Laura, ed. 2005b. "Controlling Processes: Selected Essays 1994–2005." *Kroeber Anthropological Society Papers*, no. 92/93.

Noble, David F. 1977. *America by Design: Science, Technology and the Rise of Corporate Capitalism.* New York: Knopf.

Piven, Frances Fox and Richard A. Cloward. 1991. *Regulating the Poor: The Functions of Public Welfare.* New York: Vintage Books.

⚊

Is Your Grading Scale Unfair?

Paul Renteln

ABSTRACT

By utilizing one of the more popular grading scales, some instructors may be inadvertently penalizing the poorer students in their classes. In this chapter, I discuss the relative merits of various grading schemes and consider ways in which instructors might more closely align their grading practices with their own ethical principles.

Keywords: fairness, grading, grading scales, scoring practices

When teachers congregate, the conversation frequently turns to the subject of grading. There usually follows a dirge for the demise of real standards and a lament over the precipitous decline in the quality of students (as compared, say, with the cohort to which they themselves belonged). Although I must confess to having voiced similar opinions, it is not my intention here to repeat them. Rather, I would like to point out that the purported decline may, in some instances, be attributed in part to an inequitable grading scheme. Given the hundreds of years the academic community has had to come to terms with this problem, one might think this subject could safely be proclaimed dead. Yet recent experience suggests otherwise.

In the last several years, I have had occasion to speak with many college professors in different disciplines concerning their grading and scoring practices. I was shocked to learn that some of them use a grading scheme that I consider to be manifestly unfair to the poorer students. Although the better students are mostly unaffected, the poorer students tend to receive worse grades than they deserve. In this way,

Scale 1

Grade	Number
A	4.0
B	3.0
C	2.0
D	1.0
F	0.0

it seems, the grades of students realize the expectations of their professors concerning diminishing student performance.

I wish to emphasize that what follows is, for the most part, a matter of personal preference; it is an argument against one type of grading scheme in favor of a different one. Some instructors will not see a problem with the scheme I shall discuss. But some instructors may be using this scheme without realizing that it contravenes their own sense of fairness. For this reason, I thought I would disinter the problem again, in the hope of informing those instructors who may be unwittingly perpetuating a practice that, were they to consider it in the following light, they would see to be unjust.

The problem arises when one wishes to convert from letter grades to number grades and *vice versa*. We are all familiar with the usual table (see scale 1). There is some controversy surrounding this scheme. For example, where does one put the cutoff for half-grades? Some put a B+ at 3.2, some at 3.3, and some at 3.5.

Many instructors avoid this ambiguity by adopting some sort of scale that makes half-grades explicit. It is popular to use a scale based on 100 points, presumably because this corresponds to 100 percent. Such a scale also allows the assignation of whole point totals rather than fractional point totals to students' work. The problem is that a scale of 100 points is not naturally adapted to the twelve grades (and half-grades) from F to A. By forcing the scale to 100 points, some instructors distort the relative proportions of each grade, with unfortunate consequences. I have in mind the scheme (or some variant thereof) shown in scale 2. *Prima facie*, this scale appears no more reasonable or unreasonable than any other. But it has the potential for serious misuse.

To illustrate, consider the following example. Suppose there are two questions on an exam, each weighted 50 percent. Suppose that Alice gets a B on both questions. Naturally, we expect her to end up with a B on the exam. In this special case in which the score is the same on each question, scale 2 (or any other scale for that matter) is

Scale 2

Grade	Number	Grade	Number
A	95–100	C	65–69
A-	90–94	C-	60–64
B+	85–89	D+	55–59
B	80–84	D	50–54
B-	75–79	D-	45–49
C+	70–74	F	0–44

perfectly adequate. This is because, whatever point value x is assigned to the letter B, the algorithm for computing the final grade is to multiply the score from the first question by 0.50, multiply the score from the second question by 0.50, and add the two numbers together. Starting with any number x for a B, the above algorithm yields x again, which is to say a B. Indeed, this will be true no matter what the relative weights of the questions, provided the weights add to 100 percent and the two questions receive the same letter grade.

But now suppose Bob gets an A for the first question and an F for the second. Suppose we assign 98 to the A. Suppose Bob put no answer down for the question to which we assigned the F. What number do we assign to it? The natural response is usually 0—after all, it makes no sense to assign some points for no answer. Yet if we do this, and we use scale 2, we commit a grievous error, because, although we would naively expect the grade to be a C (midway between an A and an F), Bob actually receives a D-! ($98 \times 0.50 + 0 \times 0.50 = 49 = $ D-.)

What has gone wrong? The answer, of course, is that the scale does not evenly weight the grades. Far too much weight is assigned to the F, by a ratio of 3:1. As a consequence, the poorer students get poorer grades relative to the better students. Although such a scheme may appeal to some, it does not conform to my sense of justice. I believe many students have suffered unfairly from inequitable schemes such as this one.

Some instructors realize intuitively that the scale gives unfair results, and so they fiddle with the grades *ex post facto* to try to restore some sort of balance. Other instructors, when confronted with this observation, deny that they use the scale in this way. That is, they assert that they give all numerical grades until, at the very end, they take the weighted average of everything and assign a letter. They claim that, by so doing, everything is internally consistent. Of course, this does not obviate the problem. The reason is that the scale is implicitly used every time a grade is assigned. In particular, failing work

Scale 3

Grade	Number	Grade	Number
A	93–100	C	73–76
A-	90–92	C-	70–72
B+	87–89	D+	67–69
B	83–86	D	63–66
B-	80–82	D-	60–62
C+	77–79	F	53–59

is usually assigned a 0 and not, say, a 22 or a 44, whence the above problem recurs.

Some instructors feel the scale is fair. That is, they feel that a student who, say, fails to complete an assignment ought to receive a 0 (and therefore a D- in Bob's case), because this reflects his effort. I cannot help feeling that this is overly harsh—it is effectively penalizing someone disproportionately—but as I have been careful to emphasize, this is a matter of personal opinion.

Scale 3 is an attempt to avoid this problem by assigning a nonzero score to an F grade. Typically, the instructor using this scale assigns 55 points for an F grade. At first sight, this seems a little odd to those not acquainted with it. Yet it is more equitable. It treats the F as if it were the next lower grade on the scale A, B, C, D (skipping the non-existent F+). One problem with scale 11.3 is that the grades are still weighted disproportionately: the half-grades get only 3 points while the full grades get 4. This difference, although slight, can have an effect. For example, the average of the highest C (76) and the highest D+ (69) is, after rounding up, a C (72.5 = 73) rather than a C- as we would expect.

Scale 3 has another interesting feature. It allots 8 points for an A, making it easier for the student to receive an A using scale 3 instead of, say, scale 1. In effect, scale 3 distinguishes two sorts of A grades: a low A (93–96) and a high A (97–100). The latter category could be called A+. Although the A+ grade is not used in some places, there are times when I feel it is called for.

Any scale that assigns the letter grades uniform numerical intervals will avoid the drawbacks associated with those that do not. My personal favorite is scale 4. This scale assigns 0 to an F, as one's intuition suggests, and also has a gap for the nonexistent F+. It avoids the ambiguity of scale 1 by explicitly assigning numbers to half-grades: after computations are carried out, one can round off to the nearest integer to assign the corresponding letter. The relative weighting of

Scale 4

Grade	Number	Grade	Number
A+	13	C	6
A	12	C-	5
A-	11	D+	4
B+	10	D	3
B	9	D-	2
B-	8	F	0
C+	7		

the F to other grades is 1.5:3 (or 1:2), which is certainly generous. It displays a pleasing economy, using only as many numbers as are needed. Also, with this scale, Bob gets the C I feel he deserves. Finally, it allows for an A+ grade, giving the instructor the option to distinguish between A (excellent) and A+ (outstanding).

For those unwilling to abandon percentages altogether, and for whom scale 3 seems strange, there is always scale 5, which is obtained from scale 4 by computing simple proportions and rounding. Although scale 5 is fairer than scale 2, it is not very aesthetic. Moreover, considering that most instructors already have intuitions regarding the assignment of percentages to grades, scale 5 has the potential to introduce even more confusion into the process. For this reason, scale 3 might be a better alternative for some.

Implicit in the above discussion is the controversy that surrounds the F grade. In our supposedly egalitarian society, instructors feel somewhat ambivalent about giving out F grades. Such a grade makes obvious the differences among students that we know are there but that we are unwilling, for political reasons, to admit. Certainly, one way to avoid the difficulties associated with scale 2 is to avoid giving F grades altogether. Some instructors are famous for this. In a sense, adopting scale 3 would make it easier to give out F grades without feeling quite so guilty about it.

Scale 5

Grade	Percent	Grade	Percent
A+	100	C	46
A	92	C-	38
A-	85	D+	31
B+	77	D	23
B	69	D-	15
B-	62	F	0
C+	54		

Another difficulty with the F grade is that there are two sorts of circumstances in which such grades are usually assigned. The first is when a student fails to put down any sort of answer, and the second is when the student puts down an entirely inadequate answer. We have some sort of intuition that the former should be treated more severely than the latter, but a fixed grading scheme requires us to treat both sorts of F in a like manner. One solution to this problem would be to give an F in the first case and a D in the second. Better yet, one should explicitly state on an examination that blank answers are penalized more than inadequate ones.

Grades are the modern-day equivalent of runes: graduate and professional schools as well as other employers pore over them to deduce which student is more or less worthy of admission or hiring. Therefore, they deserve the highest scrutiny. Nothing will ever change the subjective nature of grading, but at least we can allow everyone to compete on an even footing, even the students who sometimes fail.

⑫

Do Aging Academics Have a Moral Obligation to Retire?

Rosemarie Tong

ABSTRACT

In 1986, an amendment to the Age Discrimination Employment Act forbade discrimination on the basis of age alone. Among the exceptions to this amendment were college and university professors. They would have to retire at age seventy. In 1994, the exception to a mandatory retirement age for tenured professors was nullified. Henceforward they could be dismissed only for cause (e.g., extremely poor performance, blatant plagiarism, or gross sexual misconduct). Many tenured professors started to teach into their seventies, eighties, and even nineties. Fewer tenure-track positions are available for newly minted PhDs, and colleges and universities are hiring an increasing number of part-time faculty. A result is fewer fresh and diverse perspectives in the academy.

In this chapter, I will discuss a number of strategies universities and colleges are using to solve the problem I just described: what I term haphazard attrition, buyouts *(sometimes termed* voluntary separation incentive agreements), *phased retirement programs, and "detenuring" faculty after a certain age. Then I will discuss pro and con arguments for whether faculty members have a moral obligation to retire at a certain age, concluding that they do. Here I refer to some arguments of John Hardwig and Ezekiel J. Emanuel. Finally, I will ask whether my arguments for a moral obligation to retire at age seventy-five can withstand Martha Nussbaum's arguments that no such moral obligation exists.*

Keywords: Age Discrimination Employment Act, ageism, buyouts or voluntary separation incentive agreements, detenuring faculty at a certain age, haphazard attrition, meaning post-retirement years, moral obligation to retire after a certain age, phased retirement programs

Before ageism joined the ranks of racism and sexism, policies that required academics to retire at seventy years old were legally permissible. Employers could dismiss, retire, or fire employees "at will" for reasons having to do with their age alone. This way of handling aging employees ended with the 1986 amendment to the Age Discrimination Employment Act (Legal Information Institute 1986) forbidding discrimination on age per se (Legal Information Institute). Employers would have to refer to low performance or some such criterion to force employees to retire.

Exceptions to this new legal requirement were "pilots, law enforcement personnel, state court judges, law firm and investment bank partners, and Catholic bishops" (Nussbaum and Levmore 2018). To this list provided by Saul Levmore, the William B. Graham Distinguished Service Professor of Law at the University of Chicago, we may add tenured college and university professors. All these employees remained subject to mandatory retirement at a specific age, no matter how great they were at their jobs. In the halls of the academy, the mandatory retirement age was seventy.

In 1994, the exception to a mandatory retirement age for tenured professors was nullified. Henceforward, they could not be retired because of their age alone, although they could be forced out of their jobs "for cause," such as extremely poor performance, blatant plagiarism, and gross sexual misconduct (Nussbaum and Levmore, 2018). A victory for the forces of antiageism was declared. But the applause grew faint as tenured college and university professors started to live longer but not necessarily healthier lives. According to Ezekiel Emanuel, the good news was that "life expectancy for American males born in 2011 [was] 76.3, and for females it [was] 81.1" (2014). But the bad news was that "over recent decades, increases in longevity seem to have been accompanied by increases in disability" (Emanuel 2014).

For example, according to Professor Eileen Crimmins, "In 1998, about 28 percent of American men 80 and older had a functional limitation; by 2006, that figure was nearly 42 percent. And for women, the result was even worse; more than half of women 80 and older had a functional limitation" (as noted by Emanuel 2014). Other bad news was that even if we aren't among the one-third of American people who succumb to Alzheimer's disease after the age of eighty-five, "age-associated declines in mental-processing speed, working and long-term memory, and problem-solving are well established . . . distractibility increases."

According to Emanuel (2014), "We cannot focus and stay with a project as well as we could when we were young. As we move slower with age, we also think slower." Moreover, Dean Keith Simmons, an expert on the relationship between aging and creativity, points out that "creativity rises rapidly as a career commences, peaks about 20 years into the career at about age 40 or 45, and then enters a slow, age-related decline" (as noted by Emanuel 2014). To be sure, there are exceptions to these dire forecasts, and academics, on the average, seem to think they are among them, but the fact remains that the body and mind of a seventy-year-old cannot be compared favorably to the body and mind of a thirty-five-year-old.

Robert Zaretsky cites a study by TIAA-CREF, the financial services company many academics use, that "revealed that the number of professors who are 65 or older nearly doubled between 2000 and 2010. Nothing suggests this trend has slackened." Why would it? Another study, by Fidelity Investments, showed that of these faculty boomers delaying retirement because of professional reasons, 89 percent "want to stay busy and productive," while 64 percent "love the work too much to give it up" (Zaretsky 2019).

In addition to baby boomer academics' disinclination to retire because of their love of the job are important financial considerations. The 2008 financial recession in the United States flattened the portfolios of many college and university professors over the age of sixty (Farr 2014). This financial hit was felt most intensely by those aging academics who considered themselves members of the so-called sandwich generation (Farr 2014), squeezed on one side by college-aged children with large tuition bills and by parents and other family members with large nursing home bills on the other (Farr 2014). Not surprisingly, many of these faculty members felt they had to work as long as possible to plump up their savings for their not very "golden" retirement years. For them, it didn't matter so much that they were no longer stellar teachers, productive researchers, and/or effective service workers.

As they saw it, their tenure was a protective shield insulating them from criticism for all but the most egregious shortcomings. And, to be sure, dislodging a tenured professor "for cause" is notoriously difficult. It is an emotionally arduous, politically unpopular, financially costly endeavor (Levmore 2018), not to be undertaken by a college or university unless it has compelling evidence that a tenured professor is indeed the deadest of "dead wood" or entirely morally bankrupt (Nussbaum and Levmore, 2018).

But all this being said, as more and more tenured faculty work until they are seventy, seventy-five, or even eighty years old, departments become top-heavy with little room for adding young, eager, and talented tenure-track faculty. According to TIAA-CREF, "While 36 percent of all workers plan to put off their retirements beyond the age of 65, the proportion of university and college faculty who intend to delay stepping down is more than double that [72 percent]" (Marcus 2015). In addition to this study, Jon Marcus (2015) identified another study that "found that 60 percent of faculty planned to work past 70, and 15 percent to stay until they're 80."

Compounding this situation is the fact that the number of students in some disciplines, especially the humanities, is not growing (Marcus 2015) and that many students seem satisfied with distance learning since COVID-19. Close contact with a professor in a small group setting may not seem all that important to them. Why get up, get dressed, drive to the university in awful traffic, and pay an exorbitant parking fee when one can instead get up, make a cup of coffee, click on the computer, and listen to Professor X's action-packed PowerPoint without getting out of one's pajamas? Rather than adding an up-and-coming tenure-track individual to an already heavily tenured department, college and university administrators are easily tempted to replace any tenured member who does retire with low-cost instructors, adjunct faculty, and/or graduate students with year-by-year or even semester-by-semester contracts (Marcus 2015, referring to research done by John Barnshaw at the American Association of University Professors).

According to Marcus (2015), the Association of Governing Boards of Universities and Colleges reported in 2015 that the proportion of part-time faculty had climbed from 22 percent in 1969 to 67 percent in 2015. Among these low-cost professors were many men and women willing to work for peanuts in hope of proving themselves tenure-track-worthy. Unfortunately, if or when a college or university does finally decide to give a heavily tenured and aging department one or two new tenure-track lines, chances are that the year-by-year or semester-by-semester faculty will not find themselves among the finalists for these much-desired jobs, and this, despite the fact that they may have been teaching ungodly course loads, trying to be productive scholars, and/or doing more than their fair share of unrecognized service work like website creation and maintenance, student advising, extra study sessions, and so forth. My evidence for this statement is based on thirty-five years of experience in the academy plus the anecdotes of personal friends in the academy.

Realizing that a successful college or university needs a faculty well balanced between wise sages with years of experience and impressive teaching, research, and service records on one side and newly minted PhDs familiar with the latest developments in their respective disciplines on the other, college and university administrators have struggled to develop policies that honor the achievements of their senior faculty while simultaneously recognizing the potentialities of their would-be junior faculty waiting in the wings. Among these policies are so-called buyouts, phased retirement programs, the abolition of tenure at a certain age or after a certain number of years of service to the institution or academy, the wholesale abandonment of tenure in any shape or form, and haphazard attrition. Each of these policies is worth examining in turn because of the rapid "graying" of the faculty.

Let's begin with the policy that isn't so much a policy as a reaction: haphazard attrition. According to Alexia Fernández Campbell, a 2016 report from the American Association of University Professors showed that "in the past 40 years, the percentage of professors in full-time, tenured positions dropped by 26 percent and tenure-track positions dropped by 50 percent. Meanwhile, academia has seen a 62 percent jump in full-time, non-tenure-track positions and a 70 percent jump in part-time teaching positions. Today, the majority of academic positions are part-time jobs" (Campbell 2016). This troubling situation is likely to be exacerbated by the spillover effects of the 2020–2021 COVID-19 pandemic.

As mentioned above, students have grown accustomed to virtual learning. College and university administrators might be tempted to teach the "masses" via a bare-bones staff who are savvy enough to create information-packed, lively online courses that are easy to grade or, for that matter, easy to listen to, as one rests comfortably on their couch. Indeed, Richard Vedder, Distinguished Professor of Economics Emeritus at Ohio University, has opined that financial exigencies may inspire colleges and universities to have some classes—maybe a lot of classes—"taught online very cheaply by foreign academics working for a fraction of American academic pay" (Vedder 2020).

In all fairness, most colleges and universities in the United States do not want to use the pandemic as an excuse to seek foreign nationals to teach their students online for cheap. But many of them are willing to consider buyouts, euphemistically referred to as "voluntary separation incentive" agreements (Campbell 2016). According to Campbell, one such institution was Oberlin College, a prestigious liberal arts college in Ohio. In 2016, 90 percent of Oberlin's faculty was tenured, many of them over the age of sixty-five and earning top dollar. Because of financial considerations, Oberlin offered about one-third of its employees a buyout. Those eligible for the buyout had to be at least fifty-two years old and employed by Oberlin for at least ten years. Employees accepting the buyout would receive one year of their salaries subsequent to resigning from Oberlin. Oberlin made this offer to staff as well as faculty.

Initially, about eighty-five employees, sixteen of them tenured full professors, accepted the deal. Oberlin's president stressed that his goal was not to replace tenured professors with non-tenure-track academics but only to save $3 million, depending on how many positions he replaced (Campbell 2016). Implicit in the president's remarks was the possibility of making another buyout offer in future years. But how many times can a college or a university offer employees large buyouts before they no longer make fiscal sense?

The same question can be asked about so-called phased retirement programs, the purpose of which is to encourage tenured faculty members over a certain age to retire so as to make room for younger tenure-track faculty, especially women, racial and ethnic minorities, and people who identify themselves as members of the LGBTQ community. Nowadays most colleges and universities wish to diversify both their student bodies and their faculties. One of the reasons that it is harder to diversify a faculty than a student body is that a disproportionate number of tenured faculty members, especially tenured full professors, are white men who see no reason to retire from their financially secure and still enjoyable/meaningful jobs unless they are given an incentive they cannot refuse.

For example, as a result of the University of California Voluntary Early Retirement Incentive Program (VERIP), a program established in 1990 and concluded in 1994, the number of tenured faculty over the age of sixty-five dropped from 125 to 31 at Berkeley. But according to Karie Frasch, Marc Goulden, Angelica Stacey, and Janet Broughton (2019), as soon as the VERIP program ended, the number of tenured faculty over sixty-five at Berkeley grew from 31 in 1994 to 143 in 2002, "even higher than the pre-VERIP total of 125." Although Karie Frasch et al. do not provide information about how much money the University of California, Berkeley, saved between 1990 and 1994 or how much it lost between 1994 and 2002, as a matter of conjecture, it may have lost more money than it saved. Also as a matter of conjecture, but on the happier side, the composition of the tenured faculty in 2002 was probably more diverse than it was in 1994.

Another phased retirement program is the one Harvard's Faculty of Arts and Sciences established as a permanent fixture in 2010. According to Madeleine R. Nakada and Luke W. Xu, this program

> allows tenured faculty over the age of 65 who have worked at least 10 years at the University to work half-time for either two years or four years before retiring. Under the two-year plan, faculty are paid two years of full salary while they work half-time. Alternatively, they may take two semesters of paid sabbatical and work two semesters full-time. Under this four-year plan, professors are paid their full salary for the first year and half their salary for the remaining three years. Faculty over the age of 73 only have the option of a two-year track to retirement, under which they are paid half their salary for both years. (Nakada and Xu 2018)

Although some members of the Faculty of Arts and Sciences at Harvard found this phased retirement plan attractive, it was not attractive enough to tempt the majority of tenured professors to retire sooner rather than later. The salary of tenured professors, especially if they are full professors, is large enough to encourage them to keep on working full time between the ages of sixty-five and seventy-five, especially if they enjoy their work and if their health, both mental and physical, is good.

More ambitious than buyouts and phased retirement plans are proposals to terminate tenure, not employment, at age seventy, at which point "everyone's contract [would] automatically convert to a lecturer contract, renewable annually [or every two or three years] at the option of the university" (Earle and Kulow 2015, 419). Beverly Earle and Marianne Delpo Kulow espoused this policy because they speculated that colleges and universities would find it easier to terminate formerly tenured as opposed to tenured professors for any one or more of the following conditions:

- Are not as qualified or as good a current fit with the department's current needs as other candidates
- Do not meet the current standard of qualifications
- Have not published anything or very little of quality for some time
- Are not research active in an institution where [this] is or has become a faculty requirement
- Demonstrate relative poor teaching by lack of enrollments in classes, inadequate syllabi and materials by current standards, failure to use requisite technologies, or student and peer teaching evaluations that are significantly below the average, indicating a gross disconnect with the students (Earle and Kulow 2015, 416–417)

As Earle and Delpo Kulow saw it, at present, tenure protects inadequate over-seventy faculty because it is very difficult to show cause for firing *tenured* faculty. But is this really the case? Most colleges and universities have post-tenure review policies, some of them with real teeth. Rather than failing to prove their worth, many tenured faculty members prefer to resign if they know there is no way they can markedly improve their teaching, research, and service before their next post-tenure review. Thus, it is not clear that tenure must be abolished to get over-seventy faculty members to put forth their best effort. Shame is a remarkably effective tool to achieve this goal.

Moreover, getting rid of tenure and its free speech protection is, according to some, more necessary than ever. College and university policies meant to protect students from the use of trigger words, acts of microaggression, and so forth can be abused or misused in this day and age when social media can ruin a person's reputation overnight. Professors who say "outrageous" things, support the "wrong" political party, espouse "socialist" programs like universal health care insurance, and so forth may need the protective shield of tenure well into their seventies and eighties (Vedder 2020).

Another weakness of Earle and Delpo Kulow's otherwise well-argued position is that not much money will be saved by a college or university if it gives over-seventy professors multiyear, annual, or semester by semester contracts. It is one thing to reduce a full professor to the status of a nontenured lecturer, at age seventy, and quite another to reduce their salary to that of a lecturer and/or to increase their workload to that of a lecturer. An over-seventy faculty member would really need to love teaching, research, and service work to accept such a deal. This being said, it seems that Earle and Delpo Kulow are amenable to the suggestion that over-seventy, formerly tenured professors could bargain for a yearly, multiyearly, or semester contract that paid them as much as they were paid at age sixty-nine with the same reduced course load. But permitting such arrangements might not yield sufficient funds to pay for one or two new tenure-track professors (Earle and Kulow 2015, 420).

Although buyouts, phased retirement programs, and "detenuring" deals that also reduce one's salary and increase one's course load may permit a department to ease out faculty over seventy so that it can hire one or two new tenure-track professors, they may also permit a dean to deny a department new tenure-track lines, ordering it to hire several inexpensive part-time lecturers instead. But such a course of action might prevent a department from building a strong department for the future, one in which its newest tenure-track professors are drawn from a diverse applicant pool that includes a substantial number of women, racial and ethnic minorities, and LGBTQ persons (Nakada and Xu 2018).

Some of these candidates, especially women, may be older than other tenure-track candidates as a result of taking time out from the academy to care for young children or elderly relatives. For this reason, detenuring all tenured faculty members at age seventy would not seem fair to those academics who got a late start on their careers or had to interrupt them (Nakada and Xu 2018). Better to detenure all tenured faculty after a number of years of service to the profession gained at one or more universities or colleges. That number might be thirty. So, if John got tenure at age thirty-five, he would be detenured at age sixty-five. In contrast, if Mary got tenure at age forty-five, she would not be detenured until age seventy-five. The "fairness" of such a system is, of course, debatable, but the basic idea is that each person would get to be a tenured professor for a total of thirty years.

So far I have been nibbling at the ethical edges of the problem I really wish to discuss—namely, Do professors have a *moral* obligation to retire at age seventy or after X number of years of teaching, researching, and service at one or more institutions of higher learning? According to Brian Leiter, a philosopher at the University of Chicago and a controversial blogger, one of his commentators asked, "Since keeping one's position and not retiring is likely to directly cause the unemployment/underemployment of young philosophers, is it wrong to postpone one's retirement past a certain age? If so, at what age should one retire?" (Fister 2008).

Arguments against this moral obligation were fourfold:

- To whom would senior faculty members owe such an obligation? Young graduates? "That suggests life owes them a career."
- "Retiring when economic times are bad with the idea that it will provide a position for younger philosophers rests on the assumption that the department will retain lines" (for up-and-coming, new tenure-track candidates). But this is not necessarily the case. The result could be no replacements.
- "Suppose it is granted that unproductive senior faculty have a special unmet obligation to would-be faculty or the profession as a whole. Do they have to retire to meet this obligation?" After all, if they are replaced by a horde of inexpensive instructors, adjuncts, post-docs, the tenure system could be weakened. There are very few protections for academe's underclass. Why not let old-timers stay around? After all, they are "in a wonderful position to be politically active on behalf of the profession" because they have little to lose by getting up on a bully pulpit.

- It takes a long time to get to be a well-paid, tenured full professor. Is it fair to ask these academics to retire earlier than their pocketbook permits? They may still have house mortgages, children's college bills, and so forth (Fister 2008).

Arguments for a moral obligation to retire were also fourfold:

- Some professors are pursuing the easy life. Their productivity is virtually nil. If a university or college cannot get rid of them because of tenure, just increase their course load; that might make retirement seem like a good course of action.
- Getting old-timers to retire is "about reducing the huge inequality between an age cohort that's had it extremely good (those hired in the 1960s)" and an age cohort that are finding it very hard to get a tenure-track job.
- There is "something ethically suspect about holding onto a professorship just out of self-serving economic concerns."
- "Older people don't have a right to keep their jobs indefinitely. Remember, tenure is designed to ensure academic freedom, it is not designed to prevent the influx of new blood into the profession" (Fister 2008).

In many ways, these standard arguments for and against a moral obligation to retire weigh about the same on the scales of justice. But, for what it is worth, I wish to add a few pounds to the arguments in favor of retiring. As odd as it may seem to some readers, I wish to draw on the controversial ideas of two bioethicists: John Hardwig, PhD, and Ezekiel J. Emanuel, MD.

About thirty years ago, bioethicist Hardwig published an article titled "Is There a Duty to Die?" As Hardwig saw it, our technological ability to prolong life already permits some of us to live too long in a debilitated state, draining those we claim to love of their vital energies and material resources. Therefore, in the very near future, probably when the baby boomers hit the skilled nursing homes, we may all be compelled to acknowledge that "there can be a duty to die before one's illnesses would cause death, even if treated only with palliative measures. In fact, there may be a fairly common responsibility to end one's life in the absence of any terminal illness at all. Finally, there can be a duty to die even when one would prefer to live" (Hardwig 1990, 34).

Clearly, Hardwig took the purported duty to die seriously. He implied that a relatively happy fifty-five-year-old man who is beginning the descent into the depths of Alzheimer's, Huntington's, or Parkinson's may well have a duty to request medical aid in dying from his physicians before his condition gets the best of him, and certainly at the point his continuing existence threatens to seriously harm other individuals, particularly those individuals to whom he is most closely related (Hardwig 1990, 39–40). Hardwig then claimed that bioethicists typically reject a duty to die because their thought processes are held captive to what he terms "the individualistic fantasy" according to which our lives are separate, unconnected, and our own to rule (1990, 39–40). From my point of view, Hardwig rightly concludes that in the real world such selves do not actually exist, for "we are not a race of hermits" (Hardwig 1990, 39–40). At all times, but especially when we are most vulnerable in body, mind, and/or spirt, we are dependent on others, usually our family members, and it is probably our dependency on others that is the source not only of others' obligations to us but ours to them. At some point in a functioning relational network, the receivers are required to become the givers or vice versa (Hardwig 1990, 36).

Seeking support for his claim that among our strongest obligations to others is a duty to die for our loved ones' sake, Hardwig stressed that most people report they do not want to drain their friends and families of their physical, emotional, and financial resources. The fact that most people express such feelings does not surprise Hardwig, for as he saw it, "Those of us with families and loved ones always have a duty not to make selfish or self-centered decisions about our lives" (Hardwig 1990, 36). In words that would make utilitarians beam, Hardwig announced that individuals blessed with friends and families should always "choose in light of what is best for all considered" (Hardwig 1990, 36).

And so, if my intimates view caring for my disintegrating self as a tremendous benefit rather than an enormous burden to them, then "I have no duty to die based on burdens to them" (Hardwig 1990, 37). But if my intimates view caring for me as depriving them of a normal lifestyle, then I probably do owe them a duty to die. To be sure, conceded Hardwig, families and friends owe me a certain level of caregiving—they should not expect me to die for them for trivial reasons—but I must always remember that the cross I bear is fundamentally mine (it is meant for me) and that in determining whether I owe it to others to die, my interests and preferences are no more important than theirs. I do not have a right to live at all costs.

Convinced that the only real argument against a purported duty to die is the negative effects one's dying might conceivably have on others, Hardwig readily dismissed three other arguments against this duty. Observing that we live in a fundamentally secular society, he immediately rejected the argument that it is God's prerogative to determine the moment of an individual's death. Next, Hardwig discounted the view that in deciding to die to ease others' lives, an individual "disrespects" his or her own life, implying that it is not worth as much as other persons' lives. On the contrary, insisted Hardwig, an individual disrespects himself or herself by cowardly clinging to life instead of courageously ending it for the sake of others. Finally, Hardwig countered the point that it is cruel to impose a duty to die on already vulnerable, dying people with the counterpoint that it is equally cruel to impose a duty to care on living and loving people stretched to their limits (Hardwig 1990, 37).

Repeatedly, Hardwig stressed that death is not the worst event that can befall a human being, a point that Socrates made centuries ago when he chose to drink poison hemlock rather than to stop teaching Athenian youth to live an "examined" life—that is, a meaningful life truly worth living. There is, said Hardwig, something noble about the duty to die, a duty that he then qualified as neither universally applicable nor unilaterally determined by oneself. Whether one has such a duty or not will, he said, depend on a host of very particular and contextual circumstances, but especially on the degree to which one's continuing existence is, objectively considered as well as subjectively experienced, very burdensome on one's caregivers (Hardwig 1990, 37).

Related to Hardwig's views, but more self-regarding than other-regarding, is Ezekiel Emanuel's 2014 article "Why I Hope to Die at 75." Emanuel, who is sixty-three at the time of writing, hopes to die at age seventy-five before the infirmities of old age beset him. An opponent of physician-assisted suicide and euthanasia, Emanuel (2014) said that if he is alive at age seventy-five, he will no longer do anything to lengthen his life: no screenings, no testings, no annual physicals, no healthy eating, no pacemakers, no chemotherapy, and so forth—just palliative care if he is in pain: no resuscitation, no respirators, no feeding tubes, no antibiotics, and so on. Why? Not because of a need to ration health care, save resources that could be directed to his survivors, or address public policy issues like the problems arising from more and more people living into their eighties and nineties. For every eighty-five-year-old grandma running a marathon, there are thousands of grandmas too tired to do much more than see the grandchildren, watch television, surf the internet, eat, and sleep.

Thus, Emanuel said that he wants to "delineate [his] views for a good life and make [his] friends and others think about how they want to live as they grow older" (2014). That is, he wants people "to think of an alternative to succumbing to that slow constriction of activities and aspirations imperceptibly imposed by aging" (2014). Rather than trying to live as long as possible, one should try to live as well as possible for a reasonable number of years. Although Emanuel's reasons for "calling it quits" are more self-interested than Hardwig's more other-directed reasons, they amount, in large measure, to the same thing—namely, the realization that at some point our "consumption" is not worth our "contribution" (2014).

So what do Hardwig and Emanuel have to say to most professors age seventy or seventy-five? Simply this: Be introspective. Remember that there was room for you in some "inn" or another because colleges and universities had trouble supplying the demand for professors in the early 1960s, or because there was no mandatory retirement age after 1994, or because there were generous buyouts or phased retirement programs beginning in the late 1990s that one could accept or reject. Then ask yourself if you have had a fair share of a really good thing.

Your answer may be no if you are a woman, a person of color, an LGBTQ person, or a poor white man who, for a variety of reasons, had to be an adjunct, lecturer, or part-timer for many years, got started on graduate studies late in the game, or had to take time out of work because of heavy caregiving responsibilities. But if your climb to the top has been relatively smooth, then maybe you do owe it to your profession, your colleagues, and, yes, yourself to pass the torch on to another generation of academics with bold ideas, advanced technological skills, social media savvy, abundant energy, and so on. I know that this view is not likely to be met by applause from all over-seventy academics. For example, philosopher Martha Nussbaum, whose views I generally find congenial as well as rigorously and elegantly presented, refuses to accept any age-related law, program, or initiative to dislodge over-seventy tenured faculty members from their seats.

In an excerpt from her coauthored book *Aging Thoughtfully: Conversations about Retirement, Romance, Wrinkles, and Regret* (Nussbaum and Levmore 2017). Nussbaum states, "Like all American academics of my generation, I have been rescued from a *horrible* fate by the sheer accident of time. At sixty-nine [seventy-two at time of writing] I am still happily teaching and writing with no plan for retirement, because the United States has done away with compulsory retirement. Luckily for me, too, the law changed long enough ago that I never had to anticipate compulsory retirement or to think of myself as a person who would be on the shelf at sixty-five, whether I liked it or not" (Nussbaum 2018). Nussbaum went on to pity her counterparts in Asia or Europe who are forced to retire at the age of sixty-five. Specifically, she focused on "the best case of compulsory retirement [she has] encountered" (2018)—namely, the one in Finland, where retirement is compulsory at age sixty-five in all walks of life, including the academy.

According to Nussbaum, "finish norms" require retired academics not to complain because they can no longer teach or even have an office on university grounds. This rule against whining, said Nussbaum, is softened by two facts: (1) Finland's generous, universal health care insurance scheme, and (2) no Finnish professor needs to feel ashamed about retiring at age sixty-five because everyone age sixty-five is treated alike. But, asked Nussbaum, why would "any rational person think it is good 'equality' when all aging people are treated equally *badly*?" (Nussbaum 2018). What worried her about Finland is "that when you are told from the cradle that productive work ends at sixty-five, you will believe it, and you will define your possibilities and projects around this. You will expect to go on the shelf and others will expect you to be on the shelf" (Nussbaum 2018). Gradually, people will stop inviting you to events and asking you to participate in projects. Nussbaum gave the example of one of her retired Finnish friends who, after two years of retirement, felt too "ashamed" to come to a dinner after a talk by Nussbaum because she felt she didn't belong. Nussbaum then undercut her own position by suggesting that "the emeritus status might conceivably be redesigned to be less stigmatizing as when in [her] law school, retired professors keep an office, are welcome at workshops and roundtable lunches, and teach if they want to. But nobody has thought this through in a convincing way across the wide span of the professions" (Nussbaum 2018).

Nussbaum's (2018) point is well taken. But why should American academics feel that if they don't have an official job at their college or university because of their age, they are "useless"? There are still many opportunities for them to write articles and even a book. Moreover, they can volunteer their free services at civic, political, charitable, or church organizations. Speaking for myself, I "phased" retired at the age of sixty-seven. Six years later, I still have office space, computer assistance, invitations for professional events, requests to teach the occasional class, letters from former students requesting a recommendation, and, if you can believe it, free parking. In addition, I work when I please for as long as I please. No longer do I feel the pressure to publish the right kind of material, to update my technological skills, to attend boring administrative meetings, to write reports, and so on. Most importantly, I have plenty of time for family and friends and am even considering becoming a "pet parent."

Please do not think that I'm an ageist. Far from it; I think ageism is wrong, if ageism means devaluing, demeaning, and or discrediting "old" academics. Moreover, I favor buyouts, phased retirement programs, post-tenure reviews, creative ways to include emeritus professors in the life of the academy, and some carefully constructed detenuring schemes provided they protect provocative professors and professors who because of their sex, race, ethnicity, and/or sexual preference got tenure late in the game.

Some combination of such initiatives may help faculty members in their seventies and eighties discharge their "duty" to step aside so that a diverse group of younger academics can experience the privileges and responsibilities they have enjoyed for many years. Just because we decide to retire does not mean, as Nussbaum suggested, that we no longer view ourselves as "worthy" and capable of leading a "productive" and "respected" life (Nussbaum 2018). On the contrary, it may be in retirement that we discover our true worth and our ability to lead meaningful lives outside of the confines of the academy.

WORKS CITED

Campbell, Alexia Fernandez. "The Workforce That Won't Retire." June 17, 2016, Atlantic, www.theatlantic.com/business/archive/2016/06/colleges -offer-retirement-buyouts-to- professors/487400/.

De Cruz, Helen. "Do Professors Have a Moral Duty to Retire?" November 17, 2014, Philosophers' Cocoon, https://philosopherscocoon.typepad.com/blog/ 2014/11/do-html.

Eagleton, Jennifer. "Should Older Academics Be Forced to Retire?" September 10, 2014, Thesis Whisperer, https://thesiswhisperer.com/2014/09/10/older -academics-please-retire-now/.

Earle, Beverly, and Marianne Delpo Kulow. "The 'Deeply Toxic' Damage Caused by the Abolition of Mandatory Retirement and Its Collision with Tenure in Higher Education: A Proposal for Statutory Repair." Southern California Interdisciplinary Law Journal 24, no. 369 (2015): 419–420.

Emanuel, Ezekiel J. "Why I Hope to Die at 75." October 2014, Atlantic, www.the atlantic.com/magazine/archive/2014/10/why-I-hope-to-die-at-75/379329/.

Farr, Moira. "When's the Right Time to Retire?" October 20, 2014, University Affairs, www.universityaffairs.ca/features/feature-article/whens-right-time -retire/.

Fister, Mary. "A Moral Obligation to Retire?" July 21, 2008, Inside Higher Ed, www.insidehighered.com/views/2008/07/21/moral-obligation-retire.

Fitzgerald, Deborah K. "A Professor's Last Crucial Decision: When to Retire." May 30, 2018, Chronicle of Higher Education, www.chronicle.com/article/ a-professor-last-crucial-decision-when-to-retire/.

Frasch, Karie, Marc Goulden, Angelica Stacy, and Janet Broughton. "Thinking about Retirement." Spring 2019, American Association of University Professors, www.aaup.org/article/thinking-about-retirement#.YoJilujMJPY.

Friedman, Michael. B. "The Moral Obligations You Have in Old Age." December 9, 2016, *HuffPost*, www.huffpost.com/entry/moral-obligations-in-old-age_b_13378024.

Hardwig, John. "Is There a Duty to Die?" *Hastings Center Report* 27, no. 2 (1990): 34–42.

Jack, Zachary Michael. "Let's Retire Ageism in Academe." June 24, 2019, Higher Education, https://diverseeducation.com/article/148195/.

Jaschik, Scott. "When and Why Professors Retire." November 13, 2007, Inside Higher Ed, www.insidehighered.com/news/2007/11/13/when-and-why-professors-retire.

Legal Information Institute. "Age Discrimination in Employment Amendments of 1986," Pub. I, no. 99–592, 100 Stat. 3342 (1986). www.law.cornell.edu/topn/age_discrimination_in_employment_amendments_of_1986.

Marcus, Jon. "On Campus, Older Faculty Keep on Keepin' On." October 9, 2015, NPR ed, www.npr.org/sections/ed/2015/10/09/446568519/on-campus-older-faculty-keep-on-keeping-on.

McChesney, Jasper, and Jacqueline Bichsel. "The Aging of Tenure-Track Faculty in Higher Education." January 2020, College and University Professional Association for Human Resources.

Morris, Nancy. Comment on "No Room for New Blood: Harvard's Aging Faculty." May 23, 2018, *Harvard Crimson*, www.the crimson.com/article/2018/5/23/yir-aging-faculty/.

Nakada, Madeleine R., and Luke W. Xu. "No Room for New Blood: Harvard's Aging Faculty." May 23, 2018, *Harvard Crimson*, www.thecrimson.com/article/2018/5/23/yir-aging-faculty/.

Nash, Robert J. "Why I Have Not Yet Retired." June 12, 2019, Inside Higher Ed, www.insidehighered.com/advise/2019/06/12/professor-who-has-taught-more-half-century-explains-why-he-hasent-been-willing-to-retire.

Nussbaum, Martha. "No End in Sight." April 10, 2018, University of Chicago Law School, www.law.uchicago.edu/news/honest-talk-aging-and-retirement.

Nussbaum, Martha C., and Saul Levmore. *Aging Thoughtfully: Conversations about Retirement, Romance, Wrinkles and Regrets*. Oxford: Oxford University Press, 2017.

Nussbaum, Martha C., and Saul Levmore. "Honest Talk on Aging and Retirement." April 10, 2018, University of Chicago Law School, www.law.uchicago.edu/news/honest-talk-aging-and-retirement.

Tenner, Edward. "When Should Academics Retire?" July 14, 2011, *Atlantic*, www.theatlantic.com/national/archive/2011/07/when-should-academics-retire/241817/.

Vedder, Richard. "Tenure Is Dying." April 13, 2020, *Forbes*, www.forbes.com/sites/richardvedder/2020/04/13/academic-tenure-rip/?sh=227983b315cf.

Wansink, Brian. "Trying to Retire from Academia." June 30, 2019, Solve & Share, www.brianwansink.com/academics-only/trying-to-retire-from-academia.

Zaretsky, Robert. "We Need a Mandatory Retirement Age for Professors." June 28, 2019, *Washington Post*, www.washingtonpost.com/opinions/we -need-a-mandatory-retirement-age-for-professors/2019/06/28/322dd9fa-982f -11e9-830a-21b9b36b64ad_story.html.

⓵⓷

Human Rights of International Students in Higher Education

Theory and Practice

Cher Weixia Chen

ABSTRACT

This chapter intends to examine the human rights issues related to international students in higher education with a focus on identifying main theories and policy practices. It first explores the existing literature on the human rights of international students and discerns the major theories that have been provided, followed by an examination of the relevant policies proposed to protect and promote the human rights of international students, such as the Principles to Promote and Protect the Human Rights of International Studies adopted by the Australian Human Rights Commission in 2012. Finally, suggestions on the direction for future research and policies regarding the human rights of international students are offered.

Keywords: human rights, international students, racism, university ethics, xenophobia

In 2019 , there were over six million international students (UNESCO, 2022). More than half of these were enrolled in educational programs in six countries: the United States, the United Kingdom, Australia, France, Germany, and the Russian Federation. As their status is vulnerable and uncertain, they have been subject to unique human rights abuses (Marginson, 2012). This chapter explores the human rights issues of international students in higher education. First, it reviews the literature on the human rights of international students, in an attempt to identify key theories. It then examines the relevant policies that have been proposed and instituted to protect and promote the rights of international students. Lastly, the chapter discusses future directions for research and policies concerning the human rights of international students.

HUMAN RIGHTS OF INTERNATIONAL STUDENTS: RACISM AND XENOPHOBIA

With the rise in the number of international students in higher education, we have witnessed a limited but growing body of research addressing "the international sojourn," defined as temporary between-culture contact within higher education (Ward, Bochner & Furnham, 2001). Within this contact, racism, xenophobia, and the associated violence and discrimination against international students, a hidden problem (Pai, 2006), have attracted increasing attention.

For international students, racism remains a major concern (Baas, 2006; Collins, 2006). As Marginson et al. (2010) warned, racism and discrimination represent the "dark side of international education," which has played a significant role in the lives of many international students (Boyer & Sedlacek, 1989). In contrast to people who have settled in the host country and experienced racism, international students tend to encounter racism in a sudden and immediate manner, which has impacted their sense of being and belonging (Marginson et al., 2010). Moreover, it has affected their academic success and constituted a serious barrier to their life and well-being.

The scholarship on racism concerning international students is primarily country-focused. In the context of the United States, racism against international students has been well documented (Constantine et al., 2005; Fries-Britt, George Mwangi & Peralta, 2014; George et al., 2016; Hanassab, 2006; Lee & Rice, 2007). Nevertheless, "not all international students are subject to the same hardships" (Lee & Rice, 2007). A number of studies revealed that international students of color (such as those from Asia, the Middle East, Latin America, and Africa) observed more discrimination from domestic students and faculty than did white international students (Boafo-Arthur, 2014; Bonazzo & Wong, 2007; Hanassab, 2006; Lee, 2010; Lee & Opio, 2011; Lee & Rice, 2007; Lobnibe, 2013; Poyrazli & Grahame, 2007; Trice, 2004; Yao et al., 2019). They typically were called racial slurs and experienced social isolation and other forms of harassment (Bordoloi, 2014; Constantine et al., 2005; Ee, 2013; Fries-Britt et al., 2014; Lee

& Opio, 2011; Lee & Rice, 2007; The Civil Rights Project, 2003; Yao, 2018; Yao et al., 2019).

Their experience with racism is not limited to the campus. As Hanassab (2006) noted, international students of color also encountered racial discrimination off campus from potential employers and local community members. The global racial hierarchy has been associated with their racialized experience in the host society (Kwon, Hernandez & Moga, 2019). For instance, international students from the Middle East and Africa have experienced more harassment and discrimination than students from other regions (Hanassab, 2006).

Research on international students in the United Kingdom shared similar findings. For example, Beoku-Betts (2004) reported instances of white male professors targeting African female students, while Brown and Jones (2013), in their survey study of 153 international postgraduate students at a university in the south of England, found that 49 experienced some form of abuse.

In Australia, an early study by Mullins, Quintrell, and Hancock (1995) unearthed that "international students were more likely than local students to experience problems and to a greater degree" (p. 210). In 2009, one stabbed student from India, Sravan Kumar Theerthala, caught public attention and became a subject of controversy at the international affair. This kind of case of physical assault against South Asians, known as "curry bashing," has also prompted a voluminous scholarly study on the issue (Marginson et al., 2010; Ramia, 2021). Graycar (2010), in his report "Racism and the Tertiary Student Experience in Australia," identified certain human rights issues regarding international students. The report went beyond the campus and documented human rights violations against international students, such as racial taints and attacks, exploitation by landlords, and sexual harassment by employers or landlords.

In particular, international students from South Asia, those of Muslim faith, and those from indigenous communities were more likely to encounter racially or culturally discriminatory and demeaning events. Off campus, partly because of their visa status, exploitation of international students by employers was widespread. Female international students evinced a greater likelihood of experiencing a physical attack and sexual harassment both on and off campus.

In 2015, the 7-Eleven wage scandal exposed the brutal reality international students in Australia faced in the workplace. The scandal revealed the extensive and systemic exploitation of those international students working at 7-Eleven stores. Exploitation manifested in many forms, including underpayment; workers being coerced to stand for long periods without sitting down, eating, or taking a bathroom break; extortion; and slavery-like work conditions (Fair Work Ombudsman, 2016). In a 2017 report, Berg and Farbenblum painted a clearer picture of the discrimination international students endured at work. They found that a quarter of international students surveyed were earning $12/hour or less and 43 percent of students earned $15/hour or less, well below the minimum wage.

In addition to racism, xenophobia is another harmful practice that has hindered the success of international students. Maseko and Maweni (2019), in their study of black international students in two universities in South Africa, revealed the prevalence of xenophobic behavior in South African higher education. It was found that xenophobia, perpetrated through discriminatory practices and name-calling, was common. Black international students had difficulty reporting such instances, because both university staff and students were complicit when such behavior occurred.

The research on international students in non-English-speaking countries is sparse compared to studies conducted in Western English-speaking countries. Piguet and Efionayi (2014), in their analysis of international students from African countries studying in Poland, constructed a pattern of transnational mobility that has received little scholarly attention both in the Polish and international education literature. Later, Omeni (2016) found that many male African students in Poland experienced racially motivated violence against them in the form of physical and verbal attacks.

Solutions

Given this, how should we address the issues of racism and xenophobia against international students? Most of the existing literature still focuses on how international students could cope and assimilate (Yao et al., 2019). At the individual level, Omeni (2016) discovered that some international students relied on other students who had the same concerns and experiences and resorted to identity resources available in the host country. Their coping strategies comprised "forms of adjustment through processes of avoidance, and acquiescence" and "the development of frameworks of interpretation, including forms of knowledge about the underlying oppression and racism, which justified and further rationalised the avoidance of potential stressors" (p. 21).

Changing the rhetoric is an important step to address this issue. Graycar (2010), while exploring the potential factors that may have contributed to this phenomenon, argued that the use of the term *foreign* suggested an inappropriate hierarchy of importance and undermined the significant contribution of international students; therefore, it should be abandoned. Rose-Redwood & Rose-Redwood (2019) shared similar sentiments. In their edited volume, they unpacked and problematized terms such as *foreign student, cosmopolitanism, foreignness,* and *international* and maintained that the extant literature on international students is haphazard albeit prolific.

Broadly speaking, international students of color and their experiences should be encompassed in the discussion of race and racism in the host countries. More specifically, their identity should be included in the university data and relevant policies such as multiculturalism and inclusive excellence; otherwise, the gap between domestic students and international students of color will widen (Diangelo, 2006; Fries-Britt, Mwangi & Peralta, 2014; Sato & Hodge, 2009; Yao et al., 2019).

Higher education institutions, ultimately, should be the ones responsible for working to protect international students. It is their ethical duty (Brown & Jones, 2013; Marginson et al., 2010). A number of studies, however, have indicated that international students experienced racism, prejudice, and discrimination during their educational journey in the host country but received little to no targeted university support (Boafo-Arthur, 2014; Bonazzo & Wong, 2007; Chapman Wadsworth, Hecht & Jung, 2008; Lee, 2007; Lee & Opio, 2011; Tamale, 1996, Yao, 2018; Yao et al., 2019). Therefore, scholars have advocated for studying it in the fields of student welfare and development (Lee & Rice, 2007).

HUMAN RIGHTS OF INTERNATIONAL STUDENTS: THEORIES

Scholars have attempted to employ various theories to untangle human rights issues such as racism and xenophobia that international students have faced and are facing. Here are some main theories utilized.

Critical Race Theory

Critical race theory (CRT) emerged in the mid-1970s in the United States, pioneered by the works of legal scholars such as Kimberle Crenshaw, Derrick Bell, and Richard Delgado (Ansell, 2008). It views race as a socially constructed identity that plays an exceedingly important role and racism as a complex institutionalized aspect of society (Gillborn & Ladson-Billings, 2019). In 1995, Ladson-Billings and Tate started the first application of this theory in the field of education. The literature utilizing CRT to analyze education policies and practices has since blossomed. Applying CRT to the experience of international students is relatively new. For instance, in one of the rare attempts, Yao et al. (2019) used CRT to interrogate the systems of oppression against international students.

For the international students in the United States, race and racism are central to their lives. As Luke (2010) argued, globalization of higher education has produced a dichotomy between domestic students ("us") and foreign students "them." "International students to the US, particularly those from non-White and non-English-speaking countries, are often othered and racialized using US-constructs of race" (Yao et al., 2019, p. 39). Furthermore, the experience of international students was permeated by whiteness and white supremacy:

1. White American values are considered as the values to be maintained. Charles-Toussaint and Crowson (2010) found that American students perceived international students "as threatening their beliefs and values, while also posing threats to their social status and economic, educational, and physical well-being" (p. 423). Such prejudiced attitudes originated "from their desires for power and superiority" (p. 423).
2. White supremacy is further solidified through "the pervasiveness of English as the dominant language" (Yao et al., 2019, p. 44). As Lefdahl-Davis and Perrone-McGovern (2015) argued, English language proficiency has an important impact on international students' experience, an indication and example of the hegemonic power of the English language.
3. White supremacy is also entrenched through the dominant assumption of the need for international students to assimilate and acculturate. The overwhelming majority of the current literature centers on the individual students' coping mechanisms instead of how institutions should adjust and adopt more inclusive policies and practices (Boafo-Arthur, 2014; Diangelo, 2006; Geary, 2016; Frey & Roysircar, 2006; Lefdahl-Davis & Perrone-McGovern, 2015; Yan & Berliner, 2011; Yao et al., 2019).

Yao et al. (2019) urged for more intersectional studies of international students' experience to examine, for example, how race/ethnicity, gender, socioeconomic status, religion, and nationality complicate their experience and life in their host countries. Furthering the early attempt by Gillborn (2006) to draw the attention of educational researchers outside the United States to CRT, Yao et al. (2019) also maintained that CRT should go beyond the borders of the United States and be integrated into the study of the experience of international students in other countries.

Racial Capitalism, Neoliberalism, and Neoracism

Some have argued that the commodification of students is a form of racial capitalism. Baas (2006) used the term "cash cows" who are "milked" by an exploitive capitalist system to describe international students. For instance, Chinese international students are typically assumed to be very wealthy and are valued for economic benefits and hence are perceived through a lens of consumption (Louie & Qin, 2018). Others have highlighted the impact of neoliberalism.

As Hil (2012) observed, "Economic rationalism, commercialization, managerialism, corporate governance and other outgrowths of neoliberal ideology . . . ushered in an entirely new way of thinking about what constitutes academic life, what universities are for, and what values these institutions represent" (p. 10). In Australia, its neoliberal approach to education export and skilled migration has "initially privileged students as the ideal neoliberal subjects, and then marginalized them as problematic intrusions into the state" (Robertson, 2011, p. 2193). This neoliberal approach to international education was vehemently rejected by international students. An example of such resistance is the 2009 Indian student protest saga catalyzed by the stabbing in the head with a screwdriver of twenty-five-year-old Indian student Sravan Kumar Theerthala, as mentioned earlier. It prompted thousands of international students to stage a wave of protests against the unjust and indifferent treatment they received in Australia (Debets, 2018).

Neoracism, a form of discrimination "attributed to skin color as well as culture, national origin, and relationship between countries" (Lee, 2007, p. 28), has also been employed as a theory to explicate the discriminatory experienced by international students. For instance, those students from the Middle East, Africa, East Asia, Latin America, and India reported more incidents of discrimination than did students from Canada and Europe (Lee, 2007). Neoracism could also take other forms, including rejection of admission, receiving less objective academic evaluations and negative comments from faculty and peers, less likelihood of obtaining financial aid, and struggles in forming relationships (Lee & Rice, 2007).

Utilizing the framework of neoracism, Lee and Opio (2011) criticized the institutions in the United States for systematically recruiting African student athletes for their athleticism in the name of international education. Neoracism has been applied to the context outside the United States. Lee, Jon, and Byun (2017) found that in South Korea international students from other Asian countries recounted greater difficulties and unfair treatment when compared to students from other regions, which suggested neoracism that implies preference for students from the West.

Human Rights

In Australia, the concept of human rights of international students has gradually gained currency. Deumert et al. (2005), in their seminal work, justly pointed out that international students' rights as consumers, workers, and human beings had been neglected, and policies about international students should engage universities, civil societies, and nongovernmental organizations. This piece shifted the narrative about international students into the larger human rights discourse.

In 2010, Jakubowicz and Monai formally proposed a human rights approach to protecting and promoting the well-being of international students. But around this period, the discussion commonly considered international students as consumers. For example, Robertson (2011) situated the study of issues surrounding international students in the education-migration nexus by exploring the interconnectedness between human rights and consumer rights. In general, the human rights rhetoric on international students of that time tended to be overshadowed by "the desire for protecting Australia's lucrative market share" of international education (Robertson, 2011, p. 2206).

According to the Australian Human Rights Commission (2012), international students have a discernible set of rights, including the right to nondiscrimination and equal treatment; access to justice, housing, and information; freedom of religion and culture; and labor rights. The core of this approach, as Marginson (2012) argued, is to ensure broader cultural, social, and economic inclusivity and international students' stable human agency.

HUMAN RIGHTS OF INTERNATIONAL STUDENTS: POLICIES

As Jakubowicz and Monai duly noted, "Many of the problems experienced individually by international students are in fact systemic and common. They, therefore, require national and trans-national responses" (2010, p. 20). Australia was among the first countries to respond to the issues international students faced at the national level. In 2009, the Australian and New Zealand Race Relations Roundtable convened policymakers, race relationship experts, international students, and their representatives. It explored various existing issues and led to a community of practice on the problems.

The following year the Australian Commission on Human Rights, partnering with the Academy of Social Sciences and Universities Australia, produced two workshops, Racism and the Student Experience Policy Research and Building an Integrated Response to Improving the Safety and Well-being of International Students in Australia. The resulting papers by Adam Graycar (2010) and Andrew Jakubowicz (2010) marked a milestone in this process. In particular, Jakubowicz and Monani called on the adoption of a human rights perspective in order to translate research into action.

In 2012, the race discrimination commissioner, Dr. Helen Szoke, launched the national-level Principles to Promote and Protect Human Rights of International Students at the Australian International Education Conference. This set of human rights–based principles has been commonly regarded as the bill of rights for international students in Australia. Translated into ten languages, this document specifically mentions the rights of international students to health care, housing, and employment. It proposes four principles:

1. Enhancing the human rights of international students;
2. Ensuring all international students have access to human rights and freedom from discrimination protections;
3. Understanding the diverse needs of international students;
4. Empowering international students during their stay in Australia (Australian Human Rights Commission, 2012)

That same year, at the European Association for International Education Conference in Dublin, Erasmus Student Network, National Union of Students in the United Kingdom, Association of International Education Administrators, and International Education Association of Australia formally adopted the International Student Mobility Charter, advocating international students' rights. In addition to the urgency to protect students' safety, the importance of intercultural competence, and the need for easy access to information vital to international students' study and life in host countries, the charter notably addresses the concern and necessity to ensure the rights of international students. It acknowledges that "there is a need to secure international students' rights and welfare. In some countries and communities, international students have suffered from discrimination on the grounds of race, religion, and culture, gender and have been confronted with circumstances on and off campuses, which pose a threat to their safety, dignity and security." The "equity of treatment" is highlighted as follows: "The civil and human rights of international students must be understood and protected, and measures taken by governments and higher education institutions to safeguard against discrimination."

The charter calls on various players to support student rights: "In order to ensure quality in the provision of services for international students and to protect their rights, an independent authority both in their home and host country should be available on a local, regional or national level to which students can turn for a resolution of their legitimate problems, disputes or concerns or, if necessary, for legal advice pertaining to their studies, status and welfare."

HUMAN RIGHTS OF INTERNATIONAL STUDENTS: LOOK TO THE FUTURE

The above review of the scholarship and policies on the rights of international students indicates that a human rights approach to protecting and promoting the well-being of international students is only a recent and developing phenomenon. This approach has its apparent advantage: integrating international students into the human rights narrative that carries a more prescriptive normative power may have a better chance of constraining the behavior of relevant stakeholders, including universities, private sectors, and governments. Nonetheless, the slow development of such an approach and the geographical area where this approach has been explored being limited to Australia also suggests its theoretical weakness. International students are a unique population, and for many, they are on the higher end of the privilege spectrum.

As a result, creating a special set of human rights just for this group may not be urgent, in the public's eyes. It could also fall into the trap of "human rights inflation" and trivialize this supposedly powerful concept. Nevertheless, even though a special set of human rights for international students may not be desirable at the moment, as Debets (2018) rightfully suggested, (1) the gaps in conventional rights protection for international students need to be addressed, (2) human rights due diligence requirements ought to be imposed on education providers, and (3) there could be bilateral treaties made between the host country and origin countries. After all, the human rights of international students were a response to failed university ethics and governments' policies (or lack of policies). Governments and universities, therefore, should do more to tend to the well-being of international students.

REFERENCES

Ansell, A. (2008). Critical race theory. In R. T. Schaefer (Ed.), *Encyclopedia of Race, Ethnicity, and Society, Volume 1* (pp. 344–346). SAGE.

Australian Human Rights Commission. (2012). *Principles to promote and protect the human rights of international students.* Australian Human Rights Commission.

Baas, M. (2006). Students of migration: Indian overseas students and the question of permanent residency. *People and Place, 14*(1), 9–24.

Barlow, R. & Brown, J. (2017, March 13). International students need to know their rights. *BU Today.* www.bu.edu/articles/2017/know-your-rights/

Beoku-Betts, J. A. (2004). *African women pursuing graduate studies in the sciences: Racism, gender bias, and third world marginality.* National Women's Studies Association Journal, 16(1), 116–135.

Berg, L. & Farbenblum, B. (2017). *Wage theft in Australia: Findings of the National Temporary Migrant Work Survey.* Accessed from https://ssrn.com/abstract=3140071.

Boafo-Arthur, S. (2014). Acculturative experiences of black-African international students. *International Journal of Advanced Counseling, 36*(1), 115–124.

Bonazzo, C. & Wong, J. W. (2007). Japanese international female students' experience of discrimination, prejudice, and stereotypes. *College Student Journal, 41*(3), 631–639.

Bonistall Postel, E. J. (2020). Violence against international students: A critical gap in the literature. *Trauma, Violence, & Abuse, 21*(1), 71–82. https://doi.org/10.1177/1524838017742385

Bordoloi, S. (2014). On being brown and foreign: The racialization of an international student within academia. *Sociological Imagination, 50*(3), 50–66.

Boyer, S. P., & Sedlacek, W. E. (1989). Noncognitive predictors of counseling center use by international students. *Journal of Counseling & Development, 67*(7), 404–407. https://doi.org/10.1002/j.1556-6676.1989.tb02101.x

Brown, L. & Jones, I. (2013). Encounters with racism and the international student experience. *Studies in Higher Education, 38*(7), 1004–1019.

Chalmers, D. & Volet, S. (1997). Common misconceptions about students from South-East Asia studying in Australia. *Higher Education Research & Development, 16*(1), 87–99.

Chapman Wadsworth, B., Hecht, M. L. & E. Jung, E. (2008). The role of identity gaps, discrimination, and acculturation in international students' educational satisfaction in American classrooms. *Communication Education, 57*(1), 64–87.

Charles-Toussaint, G. C. & Crowson, H. M. (2010). Prejudice against international students: The role of threat perceptions and authoritarian dispositions in U.S. students. *The Journal of Psychology, 144*(5), 413–428.

Chow, Y. (2013, June). Race, racism, and international students in the United State. *Academic Advising Today, 36*(2).

Collins, F. L. (2006). Making Asian students, making students Asian: The racialisation of export education in Auckland, New Zealand. *Asia Pacific Viewpoint, 47*(2), 217–234.

Constantine, M. G., Anderson, G. M., Berkel, L. A., Caldwell, D. & Utsey, S. O. (2005). Examining the cultural adjustment experiences of African international college students: A qualitative analysis. *Journal of Counseling Psychology, 52*(1), 57–66. doi:10.1037/0022-0167.52.1.57.

Debets, J. (2018). The internationalisation of Australia's higher education system: Trading away human rights. *Griffith Journal of Law & Human Dignity, 6*(1), 23–64.

Deumert, A. et al. (2005). Global migration and social protection rights: The social and economic security of cross-border students in Australia. *Global Social Policy, 5*(3), 329–352.

Diangelo, R. J. (2006). The production of whiteness in education: Asian international students in a college classroom. *Teachers College Record, 108*(10), 1983–2000.

Ee, J. (2013). "He's an idiot!" Experiences of international students in the United States. *Journal of International Students, 3*(1), 72–75. https://doi.org/10.32674/jis.v3i1.522

Efionayi D, Piguet E. (2014). Western African student migration: A response to the globalisation of knowledge. International Development Policy, 5, 174–194. doi: 10.4000/poldev.1789.

Equality and Human Rights Commission. (2019). *Tackling racial harassment: Universities challenged.* www.equalityhumanrights.com/sites/default/files/tackling-racial-harassment-universities-challenged.pdf

Fair Work Ombudsman. (2016). *A report of the Fair Work Ombudsman's inquiry into 7-Eleven.* Commonwealth of Australia.

Frey, L. L. & Roysircar., G. (2006). South Asian and East Asian international students' perceived prejudice, acculturation, and frequency of help resource utilization. *Journal of Multicultural Counseling and Development, 34*, 208–222.

Fries-Britt, S., Mwangi, C. A. G. & Peralta, A. M. (2014). Learning race in a U.S. context: An emergent framework on the perceptions of race among foreign-born students of color. *Journal of Diversity in Higher Education, 7*(1), 1–13.

Geary, D. (2016). How do we get people to interact? International students and the American experience. *Journal of International Students, 6*(2), 527–541.

George Mwangi, C. A., Fries-Britt, S., Peralta, A. M. & Daoud, A. (2016). Examining intraracial dynamics and engagement between native-born and foreign-born black collegians in STEM. *Journal of Black Studies, 47*(7), 773–794.

Gillborn, D. (2006). Critical race theory and education: Racism and anti-racism in educational theory and praxis. *Discourse Studies in the Cultural Politics of Education, 27*(1), 11–32.

Gillborn, D. & Ladson-Billings, G. (2019). Critical race theory. In P. Atkinson, S. Delamont, A. Cernat, J. W. Sakshaug & R. A. Williams (Eds.), *SAGE Research Methods Foundations.* www.doi.org/10.4135/9781526421036764 633

Graycar, A. (2010). Racism and the tertiary student experience in Australia. Occasional Paper 5/2010. The Academy of the Social Sciences in Australia. Accessed from https://humanrights.gov.au/our-work/race-discrimination/publications/racism-and-tertiary-student-experience-australia-adam.

Halder, T. (2020, August 5). International students in the US are still facing precarity. Aljazeera. www.aljazeera.com/opinions/2020/8/5/international-students-in-the-us-are-still-facing-precarity

Hanassab, S. (2006). Diversity, international students, and perceived discrimination: Implications for educators and counselors. *Journal of Studies in International Education, 10*(157), 157–172. https://doi.org/10.1177/1028315305283051

Hil, R. (2012). *Whackademia: An insider's account of the troubled university.* New South.

Jakubowicz, A. & Monani, D. (2010). International student futures in Australia: A human rights perspective on moving forward to real action. Occasional Paper 6/2010. *The Academy of the Social Sciences in Australia.* Retrieved from https://2r6hgx20i76dmmstq2nmlon1-wpengine.netdna-ssl.com/wp-content/uploads/2013/11/2010_No6_JakubowiczMonani.pdf

Jakubowicz, A. & Monani, D. (2015). Mapping progress: Human rights and international students in Australia. *Cosmopolitan Civil Societies: An Interdisciplinary Journal, 7*(3), 61–80. https://search.informit.org/doi/10.3316/aeipt.216346

Jindal-Snape, D., Rienties, B. C. & Mittelmeier, J. (2018, December 1). International students: Universities must lead fight against intolerance of migrants. *The Conversation.* https://theconversation.com/international-students-universities-must-lead-fight-against-intolerance-of-migrants-107612

Kirsch, E. (2020). *Ethical possibilities in international student recruitment.* Dissertation. University of Minnesota Digital Conservancy, https://hdl.handle.net/11299/215198.

Kwon, S. A., Hernandez., X. & Moga, J. L. (2019). Racial segregation and the limits of international undergraduate student diversity. *Race Ethnicity and Education*, 22(1), 59–72. doi:10.1080/13613324.2017.1417830.

Ladson-Billings, G. & Tate, W. (1995). Toward a critical race theory of education. *Teachers College Record*, 97(1), 47–68.

Lee, J. (2006). International student experiences: Neo-racism and discrimination. *International Higher Education*, 44, 3–5. https://doi.org/10.6017/ihe.2006.44.7916

Lee, J. (2010). International students' experiences and attitudes at a U.S. host institution: Self- reports and future recommendations. *Journal of Research in International Education*, 9(1), 66–84.

Lee, J., Jon, J.-E. & Byun, K. (2017). Neo-racism and neo-nationalism within East Asia: The experiences of international students in South Korea. *Journal of Studies in International Education*, 21(2), 136–155. https://doi.org/10.1177/1028315316669903

Lee, J. J. & Opio, T. (2011). Coming to America: Challenges and difficulties faced by African international student athletes. *Sport, Education and Society*, 16, 629–644.

Lee, J. J. & Rice, C. (2007). Welcome to America? International student perceptions of discrimination. *Higher Education*, 53(3), 381–409.

Lefdahl-Davis, E. M. & Perrone-McGovern, K. M. (2015). The cultural adjustment of Saudi women international students: A qualitative examination. *Journal of Cross-Cultural Psychology*, 46(3), 406–434.

Lobnibe, J. Y. (2013). Different worlds, mutual expectations: African graduate student mothers and the burden of U.S. higher education. *Journal of Education and Learning*, 2(2), 201–209.

Loo, B. (2019). International students and experiences with race in the United States. *World Education News + Reviews*. https://wenr.wes.org/2019/03/international-students-and-experiences-with-race-inthe-united-states

Louie, A. & Qin, D. B. (2018). "Car talk': Automobility and Chinese international students in Michigan. *Identities*, 26(2), 146–164.

Luke, A. (2010). Educating the other: Standpoint and theory in the 'internationalization' of higher education. In E. Unterhalter & V. Carpentier (Eds), *Global Inequalities and Higher Education* (pp. 43–65). Palgrave Macmillan.

Marginson, S. (2012). Including the other: Regulation of the human rights of mobile students in a nation-bound world. *Higher Education*, 63(4), 497–512.

Marginson, S., Nyland, C., Sawir, E. & Forbes-Mewett, H. (2010). *International student security*. Cambridge University Press.

Marklein, M. B. (2020, July 2). International students face intimidation, hostility. *University World News*. www.universityworldnews.com/post.php?story=20200701113329510

Maseko, N. & Maweni, V. (2019). A study on perceptions of xenophobia at institutions of higher learning in Durban, KwaZulu-Natal. *Journal of African Foreign Affairs*, 6(3), 103–124. https://doi-org.mutex.gmu.edu/10.31920/2056-5658/2019/6n3a6

Mullins, G., Quintrell, N., & Hancock, L. (1995). The experiences of international and local students at three Australian universities. *Higher Education Research*, 14, 201–231.

Omeni, E. (2016). Troubling encounters: Exclusion, racism and responses of male African students in Poland. *Cogent Social Sciences*, 2(1). doi:http://dx.doi.org.mutex.gmu.edu/10.1080/23311886.2016.1212637

Pai, H. (2006, August 29). Overseas aid. *The Guardian*. http://education.guardian.co.uk/students/ overseasstudents

Poteet, M. & Gomez, B. (2015). "It's both ways": How international students negotiate belonging in local and global contexts. *Journal of New Brunswick Studies / Revue d'études Sur Le Nouveau-Brunswick*, 6(1). https://journals.lib.unb.ca/index.php/JNBS/article/view/23061

Poyrazli, S. & Grahame, K. M. (2007). Barriers to adjustment: Needs of international students within a semi-urban campus community. *Journal of Instructional Psychology*, 34(1), 28–46.

Ramia, G. (2021). Crises in international education, and government responses: A comparative analysis of racial discrimination and violence towards international students. *Higher Education*, 82(1), 599–613.

Robertson, M., Line, M., Jones, S. & Thomas, S. (2000). International students, learning environments and perceptions: A case study using the Delphi technique. *Higher Education Research & Development*, 19(1), 89–102.

Robertson, S. (2011). Cash cows, backdoor migrants, or activist citizens? International students, citizenship, and rights in Australia. Ethnic and Racial Studies, 34 (12).

Rose-Redwood, C. A. & Rose-Redwood, R. (Eds.) (2019). *International encounters: Higher education and the international student experience*. Rowman & Littlefield.

Sato, T. & Hodge, S. R. (2009). Asian international doctoral students' experiences at two American universities: Assimilation, accommodation, and resistance. *Journal of Diversity in Higher Education*, 2(3), 136–148. doi:10.1037/a0015912.

Skelly, M. (2020, July 11). Human rights violations and masked xenophobia under ICE's rescinded student ban. *The Michigan Daily*. www.michigandaily.com/opinion/op-ed-human-rights-violations-and-masked-xenophobia-under-ices-rescinded-student-ban/

Tamale, S. R. (1996). The outsider looks in: Constructing knowledge about American collegiate racism. *Qualitative Sociology*, 19(4), 471–495.

Tannock, S. (2013). When the demand for educational equality stops at the border: Wealthy students, international students and the restructuring of higher education in the UK. *Journal of Education Policy*, 28(4), 449–464. doi:10.1080/02680939.2013.764577

The Civil Rights Project. (2003). *Know your rights on campus: A guide on racial profiling and hate crime for international students in the United States.* Harvard University Press.

Tran, L., Bui, H. & Balakrishnan, V. D. (2020). Forms of racism and discrimination faced by international students. Council of International

Students Australia. https://cisa.edu.au/wp-content/uploads/2020/08/Types
-and-forms-of-Racism-and-Discrimination-faced-by-International-Students
_CISA-statement-1.pdf

Trice, A. G. (2004). Mixing it up: International graduate students' social interactions with American students. *Journal of College Student Development*,
45(6), 671–687.

UNESCO (2022). Education: inbound internationally mobile students by con-
tinent of origin. Accessed from http://data.uis.unesco.org/index.aspx?query
id=3804.

Ward, C., Bochner, S., & Furnham, A. (2001). *The psychology of culture shock.*
Routledge.

Yan, K. & Berliner, D. C. (2011). An examination of individual-level factors
in stress and coping processes: Perspectives of Chinese international students in the United States. *Journal of College Student Development, 52*(5),
523–542.

Yao, C. W. (2018). They don't care about you: Chinese international students'
experiences with neo-racism and othering on a U.S. campus. *Journal of the
First-Year Experience and Students in Transition, 30*(1), 87–101.

Yao, C. W., Mwangi, C. A. G. & Brown, V. K. M. (2019). Exploring the intersection of transnationalism and critical race theory: A critical race analysis of
international student experiences in the United States. *Race Ethnicity and
Education, 22*(1), 38–58. doi:10.1080/13613324.2018.1497968.

⑭

Secrecy and the University

A Cautionary Case Study

Steve Sanders

ABSTRACT

Excessive secrecy in a university can impede shared governance, cause institutional embarrassment, and erode trust and collegiality. It is a sign of the increasing corporatization of higher education. In this chapter, I discuss the perils of secrecy through the lens of my experience investigating and writing about a presidential search at my own university.

Keywords: corporatization, governing boards, presidential searches, secrecy, trustees

Excessive secrecy in decision-making is incompatible with the ethical university. Secrecy is often contrary to the liberal values—including freedom of inquiry, free speech, and transparency in decision-making—on which universities are based. Excessive secrecy impedes collegiality and shared governance. It can make a university seem less like an academic enterprise and more like a large corporation.

In discussing secrecy, I do not mean ordinary confidentiality. Reasonable people understand the need for privacy and discretion on matters such as student academic records or discussions about a colleague's tenure case. Rather, my focus is on secrecy surrounding major decisions about how a university is led and governed, the kind of secrecy that, if it goes unchallenged long enough, eventually becomes a default administrative instinct.

During the fall of 2021, I investigated and wrote a behind-the-scenes account of a presidential search at my own institution, Indiana

University (IU) (Sanders 2021a). The events described in this chapter are drawn from that article, and primary sources are described therein. In undertaking the research for that article, I breached some significant walls of secrecy that were intended to prevent the university's constituencies from understanding how and why IU's trustees had made several critical decisions involving institutional leadership and the expenditure of hundreds of thousands of dollars. As I will describe, my foray into investigative journalism drew a hostile reaction from at least one key administrator who was bent on enforcing secrecy. Drawing on lessons I learned during this experience, I sketch in this chapter a short case study intended to illustrate the perils that can arise when secrecy at the highest levels of the university becomes a routine expectation and modus operandi.

BACKGROUND

Indiana University is a seven-campus public university system with its flagship campus in Bloomington, where I am a tenured full professor in the Maurer School of Law. The university is governed by a nine-member board of trustees. Six of the trustees are appointed by the governor, and three are elected by the alumni.

Michael McRobbie, who served Indiana University as president for fourteen years, was scheduled to retire at the end of June 2021. And so, in October 2020, the trustees appointed a seventeen-member presidential search committee. The committee included three faculty members, a student body president, two school deans, a regional campus chancellor, and a variety of important alumni, major donors, and business leaders. The committee was diverse across gender, race, sexual orientation, and campus affiliation. The trustees themselves also had a strong presence, with four of the nine board members on the search committee.

The trustees indicated they would defer to the search committee's judgment and make a choice from among the finalists it recommended. In the resolution establishing the committee, the trustees said they were "committed to involving Indiana University's various constituencies" in the search, and they instructed the committee to "provide a 'short list' of final presidential candidates for board consideration." A news release said the committee's charge was to "recommend three to five finalists in early 2021; then the board will conduct the remainder of the confidential search process and make the final appointment."

In late fall of 2020, the search committee, aided by a search consultant, sifted through several hundred candidates, conducted remote interviews with approximately eight semifinalists, and eventually settled on a list of four finalists, including one internal candidate, the then-provost, Lauren Robel. Pamela Whitten, who would eventually be chosen by the trustees as the new president, was not among the finalists. Indeed, Whitten, who was serving as president of Kennesaw State University in Georgia, had not been chosen by the search committee for an interview.

After the committee's votes on finalists were tabulated and the list sent to the trustees, about a month went by. The trustees discussed the committee's finalists and had conversations with them via Zoom. Eventually, the chair of the search, trustee Melanie Walker, brought back word to the search committee that the trustees were not prepared to move forward with any of the finalists. Walker did not provide any reasons.

On behalf of the trustees, Walker instead gave the committee a list of approximately four new candidates—this list included Whitten—and asked the committee to interview them. Walker apparently had generated the list with the help of a second search consultant retained by the trustees late in the process. After interviewing Whitten, the search committee members' views on her were mixed, but at least some thought she was the best of the second-round candidates. With that, the search committee's work was done. After in-person interviews with several of the new candidates they themselves had identified, the trustees named Whitten as the new president in April 2021.

Meanwhile, as the search had become more prolonged than expected, the trustees became nervous that it might end in failure or need to be extended. And so, as a contingency, the board negotiated with McRobbie for the outgoing president to remain in office for another six months if necessary. McRobbie and the board president signed an addendum to McRobbie's existing contract. In return for an additional six months of service, McRobbie would receive about $582,722 in salary, bonus, and deferred compensation.

In the end, Whitten was able to assume office on July 1, 2021, and so McRobbie did not need to extend his term. However, because he had changed his plans for his post-presidency sabbatical in order to be available if needed, the trustees agreed to pay him the full additional compensation anyway and characterize it as payment for "consulting services" to the new president. The trustees did all this in secret, without discussing or voting on it at a public meeting, as the Indiana Open Door Law requires.

In October 2021, I published a 7,300-word piece of investigative journalism about the presidential search on the independent journalism site *Medium* (Sanders 2021a). The article revealed how the trustees, in rejecting the search committee's own finalists without explanation and ultimately selecting Whitten as president, had violated principles of shared governance, since membership on the search committee provided the only direct voice faculty, students, midlevel administrators, and alumni had in the selection of the next president. The article also revealed that, as a result of the trustees' secret agreement with McRobbie, IU would be paying the former president more than half a million dollars for six months of what was likely to be little or no work.

SECRECY AND SHARED GOVERNANCE

In searches for major university leadership positions, there are two schools of thought. One holds that searches should be open, at least in the final stage; several finalists should be named and brought to campus to interact with key constituencies, who can then provide input before the governing board or appointing officer makes a hiring decision. The disadvantage of this approach is that some desirable candidates may not agree to be considered at all because they don't want it known back at their current institution that they might be considering another job.

The second major school of thought holds that the whole search, and especially the final decision-making, should be done under a cover of secrecy. This is how IU's trustees decided to conduct their presidential search. The entire process was intended to be a black box. The theory behind this approach to leadership searches is that the governing board or appointing officer has the legal prerogative to make the decision, and so everyone else should simply be expected to rally around in support of the outcome; involvement of various constituencies through openness, transparency, and public deliberation simply makes the process messier. The danger of this approach is that members of university governing boards are often drawn from the world of business or owe their appointments to political connections. Having only perfunctory contact with faculty members, staff, and students, they often have little understanding of academic work, faculty and student needs and attitudes, and how the university functions on a day-to-day basis.

Governing boards may also be insular, depriving them of important context and information. For example, I have observed IU's board of trustees since I was an undergraduate reporter for the campus newspaper in the 1980s. Years ago, the trustees and IU president routinely invited faculty leaders to have dinner with them the night before a board meeting, where business could be discussed in a relaxed setting. While these gatherings took place outside public view, the dialogue and inclusion they demonstrated helped build trust and camaraderie, a sense that the trustees and faculty were working toward common goals. Such dinners no longer happen.

The problems with a secret search can be mediated if the search has meaningful involvement by faculty, academic administrators, students, and other constituents represented on a search committee. As the American Association of University Professors (1990) has stated, "Joint effort of a most critical kind must be taken when an institution chooses a new president. The selection of a chief administrative officer should follow upon a cooperative search by the governing board and the faculty, taking into consideration the opinions of others who are appropriately interested."

The selection of a president uniquely expresses a university's values and aspirations and is the most important decision its governing board ever makes. It affects the direction and priorities of the institution, and thus the interests of faculty and students, in profound ways. Involving faculty, alumni, and others brings additional expertise, perspective, and judgment to the process that trustees may lack, improving the quality of decision-making and giving it legitimacy among the larger university community. *Inside Higher Education* (Hazelrigg 2019) recently reported that "campus stakeholders are increasingly disapproving of and speaking publicly about searches conducted by their institution. One of the more frequent complaints is the growing tendency of governing boards to conduct a 'secret search.'"

In IU's case, the limits of the trustees' own knowledge, combined with the curtain of secrecy they had drawn around the search, made it all the more important they respect the work of the broadly representative search committee they had appointed. But this is where IU's search went awry: it broke faith with long-standing principles of shared governance. Under cloak of secrecy, IU's trustees rejected the search committee's work without explanation, then imposed their own list of candidates and assumed no one would find out.

This approach to the appointment of key officers may be familiar in the corporate world with which most of the trustees are familiar. But given institutional norms, the expertise provided by the search committee, and the trustees' own previous commitments to an inclusive process, the decision to set aside the search committee's work without explanation required strong justification that was not evident.

I spoke with several search committee members who found the process demoralizing and who were dubious about the outcome. When I contacted one committee member to ask for an interview, this person replied by noting they were obligated to maintain confidentiality and saying, "I have no comment." Then, after a pause, this person added, "That ought to say a lot. If there had been a process I felt good about, I probably would comment."

NONDISCLOSURE AGREEMENTS

As I reported in my *Medium* article (Sanders 2021a), members of IU's presidential search committee were not merely asked to pledge confidentiality; they were required to sign an intimidating nondisclosure agreement (NDA), which threatened them with major legal expenses if they breached it. (I obtained a copy of the NDA from a search committee member who otherwise declined to speak with me.)

There are good reasons why, for a dignified and effective search process, members of a search committee must be expected to keep sensitive information private and not bandy about the names of candidates. But the breadth of the NDA that IU's search committee was required to sign meant that faculty and student representatives were forbidden from even consulting with their colleagues or peers about candidates the committee was considering, or from explaining the outcome of the process once it had completed.

Requiring the constituents of a university—people who are giving their time and expertise out of institutional loyalty and commitment to its betterment—to sign an intimidating NDA sends a message: we don't trust you. Some search committee members resented the NDA, and at least one source who spoke with me for my article said they agreed to do so in part because they took offense at being required to sign such a document.

The increasing use of NDAs in the governance processes of American universities, and the commitment to secrecy they represent, is another sign of an increasingly corporate mentality in higher education. As two scholars have written at the academic blog *The Conversation* (Cunningham and Drumwright 2021), "NDAs seem especially contradictory in the context of universities given their commitment to seeking truth. As our research in universities, businesses and other workplaces has documented, NDAs can have negative effects on workers and their organizations."

PAYING AN EX-PRESIDENT IN SECRET

Indiana's Open Door Law, like many other good-government laws, is intended to fight the instinct of decision makers for secrecy by requiring that public bodies in the state do most of their deliberating and decision-making in open meetings. For a public university governing board, compliance with open-meetings law is part of the basic transparency and accountability we should expect from a powerful group of officials who approve the spending of billions of dollars each year and whose decisions impact the lives and careers of faculty, staff, and students in significant ways.

Those who watch IU's board closely—and again, my experience goes back forty years—have long suspected that the trustees routinely violate the Open Door Law by discussing important business in executive session, over email, or in other ways outside public view. This fact has been confirmed to me by several past trustees and other participants in these meetings. The trustees' public business meetings—six per year, most scheduled for only an hour—invariably feel pro forma and performative, with little or no meaningful discussion. Attend some of these meetings, and you quickly come to understand that decisions have been made, and most questions or disagreements ironed out, in advance, behind closed doors.

Under an exception for personnel matters, the IU trustees were allowed under state law to do most of the work of their presidential selection behind closed doors. But there was no such exception for their decision to pay the former president for six months of "consulting" with the new president. This decision further illustrates the problems of secrecy and how it can become second nature to decision makers.

Although Michael McRobbie did not end up serving additional time as president of IU, as noted above, the trustees still agreed to pay him the full sum—approximately $582,722, including a "retention bonus" of about $158,000—that he would have received if he had been required to remain in office for six more months. To learn why the trustees acted as they did, I had to file a formal request under Indiana's state freedom of information act. (The Indiana public access counselor, a state government official who helps enforce the freedom of information act, would later opine that IU violated the law by taking an unreasonable amount of time to produce the documents I had requested—once again, secrecy in operation.)

In an internal memo the university eventually produced and that I discussed in my *Medium* article (Sanders 2021a), trustee Jim Morris, chair of the board's compensation committee, told his fellow trustees that after signing the contract addendum to extend his term as president if necessary, "Michael [McRobbie] therefore had a reasonable expectation that the signed contract was valid and he advises us that he therefore delayed his sabbatical opportunities at two institutions by one semester." The trustees decided to treat the matter as a gentlemen's agreement and make good on it despite the fact McRobbie would not give any additional service as president. They decided to characterize the payments as being for "consulting services" McRobbie might be called on from time to time to offer the new president.

It seems remarkable that the members of the governing board of a major public agency somehow believed they could secretly enter into a new, no-bid contract to pay someone more than half a million dollars for "consulting services" and never bring it to a vote at a public meeting. But it became apparent to me that this is how IU's trustees often do business. The reality is, usually no one is watching closely enough to make inquiries or learn what's actually happening behind the scenes. The consulting arrangement likely would have escaped public attention entirely had a source not tipped me off about it.

The revelation of the McRobbie contract—and especially the trustees' efforts to keep it secret—ended up costing the university bad publicity. It drew attention from news media in Indiana as well as the *Chronicle of Higher Education* (Pettit 2021). IU officials provided shifting, inconsistent, and in some cases factually disprovable explanations for how the McRobbie contract had come to be (Sanders 2021b). After I filed a formal complaint with the public access counselor, whose office also helps enforce the Open Door Law, IU's general counsel, Jacqueline Simmons, vigorously disputed that the trustees had violated state law (Simmons 2021). But in the end, the trustees bowed to the reality that, by acting in secret, they had made a serious mistake. With McRobbie's six-month term of "consulting" nearly over, in December 2021 the trustees put the matter on an agenda and approved it at a public meeting. Two months later, the public access counselor issued an opinion that the trustees' earlier actions had indeed violated the Open Door Law.

THE FURY WHEN SECRECY IS BREACHED

The university's response to my rabble-rousing demonstrated just how determinedly some administrators will enforce and defend secrecy, and also how casually they will attempt to impose mandates for secrecy on others.

My research and publication of information about the presidential search and the McRobbie contract clearly were protected by the First Amendment. I did not break any law, I never signed any nondisclosure agreement, and as a faculty member I was under no obligation to keep the trustees' secrets. Moreover, IU's own academic freedom policy (Indiana University 2019) states, "Academic freedom includes the freedom to express views on matters having to do with the university and its policies, and on issues of public interest generally. . . . Knowledge cannot be advanced unless faculty and librarians have freedom to study and communicate ideas and facts, including those that are inconvenient to political groups or authorities, without fear of recrimination."

Nonetheless, in response to my revelations about the presidential search and the McRobbie contract, Simmons, the general counsel, attempted to fabricate a wide-ranging new policy on secrecy and to allege that I had violated it. In her letter to the public access counselor disputing my complaint about how the trustees had approved the McRobbie contract (Simmons 2021), Simmons digressed to assail my work on the presidential search. She asserted that the names of the presidential finalists, two of which I had revealed in my *Medium* article, were "confidential information that Mr. Sanders, as an IU employee, was not permitted to share publicly." She elaborated: "Under IU policy, restricted information is not permitted to be accessed without specific authorization and is not permitted to be disclosed to a third party unless certain steps are taken. Professor Sanders, an IU employee subject to these policy requirements, violated them by improperly obtaining access to the presidential search information and by publishing that information on *Medium* without following the appropriate university procedures for sharing restricted information."

The source of these supposed policies and procedures? Simmons cited an IU policy governing "management of institutional data," a policy under the jurisdiction of the university's vice president for information technology and its "Committee of Data Stewards" (Indiana University 2020). The policy, properly understood, is intended to cover employees who have access to databases containing such sensitive information as financial records or student transcripts.

In other words, the general counsel, a highly experienced lawyer, attempted to argue that a policy that is plainly intended to prevent breaches of sensitive computer databases somehow applied to a professor who had written a piece of journalism—an article where the "data" came mostly from interviews and phone conversations. This was a desperately overreaching and disingenuous legal argument. Yet it demonstrated how far at least one administrator was willing to go in pursuit of institutional secrecy. Simmons took a policy intended to prevent leaks of things like Social Security or credit card numbers and attempted to spin it into a generalized, all-encompassing gag order on faculty imposing a supposed duty to keep secret any and all facts the university prefers the public not know about.

And that wasn't all. Earlier in these events, after various IU officials learned I was making inquiries about the presidential search and the McRobbie contract and that some of the key people involved in these matters may have spoken with me, Simmons hired an Indianapolis law firm, Hoover Hull Turner, to file a state freedom of information request seeking to examine any email I might have exchanged with members of the board of trustees or the presidential search committee. Since IU is a state agency, most emails sent or received on its servers are considered public records. In effect, in an attempt to smoke out how I had managed to breach secrecy, IU hired a law firm to send a public information request to itself.

The motive for the email search was almost certainly an effort to learn the identities of sources who had spoken with me—in other words, who had dared to break secrecy. IU officials refused to acknowledge whether they were behind the law firm's work—secrecy once again—but eventually I was able to learn from billing records that Simmons had commissioned the work and that the university had paid the firm almost $5,700.

As the events in this account drew to a close at the end of 2021 and IU's search of my email was publicly revealed, Simmons was terminated by IU without any announcement or reason given by the university (Morey 2022). At the same time, there was one positive development: the university quietly created a new policy prohibiting administrators from initiating state freedom of information searches against faculty, staff, or students.

CONCLUSION

An ethical university should be defined by collaborative decision-making, reasonable transparency, compliance with the law, and respect for academic freedom. Among administrators and governing board members, an instinct for secrecy is corrosive to these values—especially when the university seeks to enforce secrecy by coercive means, such as by forcing people who are giving voluntary service to sign nondisclosure agreements or by using a legal filing to attack a faculty member who has revealed inconvenient facts.

IU's attempts to enforce secrecy backfired by drawing strong reactions—and bad publicity for the institution—from national organizations concerned with the rights of faculty members. Before I obtained confirmation that the university itself was behind the email demand, the Academic Freedom Alliance sent a letter to President Whitten expressing its concern that "such procedures . . . have been used as a means to intimidate and silence university professors and chill speech," and observing, "It would be a particularly troubling attack on academic freedom if faculty emails are accessed at the request of university officials" (Whittington 2021). Later, the Foundation for Individual Rights in Education also wrote about the affair, observing that "IU's actions create a chilling effect not only on Sanders, but on its faculty more broadly. Accusations that constitutionally protected speech violates university policy can themselves violate the First Amendment, even if the speaker is never actually disciplined for that speech" (Bleisch and Steinbaugh 2021). Whitten never acknowledged either communication.

As a lawyer and tenured faculty member and someone who was also trained as a journalist, I was willing to do the necessary work to penetrate institutional secrecy, and later to stand up to intimidation by blowing the whistle on it. Not only did I write about these developments myself (Sanders 2021c), but I also worked with professional journalists and enlisted organizations like the Academic Freedom Alliance, Foundation for Individual Rights in Education, and the American Association of University Professors to provide their own scrutiny of the presidential search, the McRobbie contract, the general counsel's attempt to concoct a new faculty secrecy policy, and the search of my emails. But the danger is that many faculty members—especially those among the increasing ranks of non-tenure-track faculty—will not have the institutional knowledge, understanding of academic freedom, or sense of job security to question what seems like an ever-growing penchant for institutional secrecy. As the *Chronicle of Higher Education* observed (Pettit 2021), my experience revealed "a wide gap between a faculty member's notion of what he can probe and publicize, and the university's much narrower idea."

How has such secrecy come to flourish at the top levels of the academy? The corporatization of universities, their growing bureaucracies of nonfaculty administrative staff, and eroding norms of shared governance all contribute to the problem. So, I think, does the continuing breakdown of traditional journalism, especially the shrinking number of local newspapers with reporters assigned to cover universities and education issues. Even where such reporters are still on the job, they often lack the sources, time, and knowledge to do their jobs effectively.

For example, at the press conference where Pamela Whitten was introduced as IU's new president, a local reporter asked the chair of the search committee, trustee Melanie Walker, what the search had cost. Walker responded, "I don't think we really spent any money. We did it all via Zoom." She acknowledged that final candidates traveled for interviews, "but I think that was probably the only real cost associated." In fact, I would later discover through my own public information requests that IU had paid two search consultants a total of $218,000 (Sanders 2021a). But no other trustee or spokesperson who was present corrected Walker's statement, and the reporter apparently was not savvy enough to know about consultants' fees.

In researching my investigative article, I gave every trustee and administrator who was named the opportunity to comment on, clarify, or deny my findings. In almost all cases, I was met with silence. It almost seemed as though a collective decision had been made that if the university top brass ignored me, the whole matter would go away and secrecy could be preserved. Across IU's top-level administration, there was evident to me a hubris that comes from not being accustomed to having actions examined and questioned by journalists, faculty members, or others who are equipped to ask difficult questions and cut through self-serving institutional secrecy. It is unhealthy for an important public institution to operate in such an environment.

Pierre Salinger, President John F. Kennedy's press secretary, once told an audience of communications professionals, "It has been said— and rightly so—that secrecy is the first refuge of incompetents" (Sidey 1964, 100). Even if that is an unkind overstatement, I have attempted to document how excessive secrecy can impede shared governance, cause institutional embarrassment, and erode trust and the sense of collegiality that is necessary for universities to carry out their unique role in American society.

WORKS CITED

American Association of University Professors. 1990. "Statement on Government of Colleges and Universities." www.aaup.org/report/statement-government-colleges-and-universities.

Bleisch, Joshua, and Steinbaugh, Adam. 2021. "Did Indiana University FOIA its own professor?" Foundation for Individual Rights in Education, December 15, 2021. www.thefire.org/did-indiana-university-foia-its-own-professor.

Cunningham, Peggy, and Drumwright, Minette. 2021. "Banning non-disclosure agreements isn't enough to stop unethical workplace leader behaviour." *The Conversation*, December 21, 2021. https://theconversation.com/banning-non-disclosure-agreements-isnt-enough-to-stop-unethical-workplace-leader-behaviour-173574.

Hazelrigg, Nick. 2019. "Secret searches and faculty fury." *Inside Higher Education*, August 23, 2019. www.insidehighered.com/news/2019/08/23/faculty-anger-surrounding-several-presidential-searches-some-point-search-firms.

Indiana University. 2019. "University policies: Academic freedom." https://policies.iu.edu/policies/aca-32-academic-freedom/index.html.

Indiana University. 2020. "University policies: Management of institutional data." https://policies.iu.edu/policies/dm-01-management-institutional-data/index.html.

Morey, Jordan. 2022. "IU general counsel, VP Simmons terminated without cause." *Indianapolis Business Journal*, January 20, 2022. www.ibj.com/articles/iu-general-counsel-vp-simmons-terminated-without-cause.

Pettit, Emma. 2021. "This professor investigated a presidential search at his university. It said he was out of line." *Chronicle of Higher Education*, November 12, 2021. www.chronicle.com/article/this-professor-investigated-a-presidential-search-at-his-university-it-said-he-was-out-of-line.

Sanders, Steve. 2021a. "'You have no idea how strange this process has been': The long, difficult search for IU's 19th president." *Medium*, October 6, 2021. https://medium.com/@stevesan/you-have-no-idea-how-strange-this-process-has-been-the-difficult-search-for-iu-s-19th-president-f61b473014d4.

Sanders, Steve. 2021b. "IU's trustees finally own up to their violation of the Open Door Law." *Medium*, December 2, 2021. https://medium.com/@stevesan/ius-trustees-finally-own-up-to-their-violation-of-the-open-door-law-6981b57db55f.

Sanders, Steve. 2021c. "I've been looking into IU's presidential search. Now a law firm is demanding to snoop through my email." *Medium*, October 4, 2021. https://medium.com/@stevesan/ive-been-looking-into-iu-s-presidential-search-and-now-a-law-firm-is-demanding-my-email-c1ba151404f8.

Sidey, Hugh. 1964. *John F. Kennedy, President*. New York: Atheneum.

Simmons, Jacqueline. 2021. Letter to Indiana public access counselor Luke Britt, November 3, 2021. www.documentcloud.org/documents/21103514-indiana-universitys-response-to-sanderss-complaint.

Whittington, Keith. 2021. Letter to Indiana University President Pamela Whitten on behalf of the Academic Freedom Alliance, November 15, 2021. http://academicfreedom.org/wp-content/uploads/2021/11/AFA-Letter-to-Indiana-University-on-Steve-Sanders.pdf.

Appendix

Shared Governance Policies

Charles Milne

SHARED GOVERNANCE POLICIES IN COMMUNITY COLLEGES

Cerritos Community College
www.cerritos.edu/president/_includes/SharedGovernance/Shared
_Governance_Document_120318.pdf

Clark College
www.clark.edu/about/governance/shared-governance/index.php

Columbus State Community College
www.cscc.edu/employee/our-college/shared-governance/pdf/
Shared%20Governance%20Model%20November%202018.pdf

Cowley College
www.cowley.edu/policy/procedures/shared-governance.pdf

Finger Lakes Community College
www.flcc.edu/about/governance/

Germanna Community College
www.germanna.edu/policies/shared-governance/

Hagerstown Community College
www.hagerstowncc.edu/sites/default/files/documents/141008-guide
-shared-gov.pdf

Kapiʻolani Community College
www.kapiolani.hawaii.edu/wp-content/uploads/2018/06/Governance
-Policy.2018.3.6.for-ISER.pdf

Madison Area Technical College
https://students.madisoncollege.edu/shared-governance

Monroe Community College
https://sites.monroecc.edu/facultysenate/files/2021/09/2.5_Shared
_Governance_Policy.pdf

Motlow State Community College
www.mscc.edu/about/policies/shared-governance.html

Mt. San Jacinto College
https://msjc.edu/committees/documents/Shared_Governance
_Document_BOT_Approved_5-12-11.pdf

Pasadena City College
https://pasadena.edu/governance/docs/SharedGovHandbook.pdf

Santa Fe Community College
www.sfcc.edu/policy/sfcc-shared-governance-policy/

Tacoma Community College
www.tacomacc.edu/about/policies/shared-governance

Truckee Community College
www.flcc.edu/about/governance/

Yavapai College
www.yc.edu/v6/policies/docs/1000d/1011-shared-governance.pdf

SHARED GOVERNANCE POLICIES IN UNIVERSITIES

Arkansas State University
www.astate.edu/a/shared-governance/

Athens State University
www.athensstate.net/pdfs/about/Athens-State-Shared-Governance
-Statement-approved.pdf

California State University San Bernardino
www.csusb.edu/shared-governance

Clemson University
www.clemson.edu/administration/bot/Policies/governance.html

Ohio University
www.ohio.edu/medicine/about/who-we-are/governance

The Ohio State University
https://senate.osu.edu/who-we-are

University of Arizona
https://facultygovernance.arizona.edu/sites/default/files/mou_2017
_ rewrite_clean.pdf

University of Houston Clear Lake
www.uhcl.edu/policies/documents/administration/university-shared
-governance.pdf

University of Louisiana Monroe
www.ulm.edu/sharedgovernance/

University of Louisville
https://louisville.edu/facultysenate/documents/sharedgovernance/
sharedgovprov

University of Maine
https://umaine.edu/facultysenate/wp-content/uploads/sites/
218/2010/12/SharedGovernanceUMaine.pdf

University of Maryland
www.senate.umd.edu/sites/default/files/resources/Plan_of
_Organization.pdf

University of Mount Union
www.mountunion.edu/Documents/Hidden%20Pages/University%20
Policies/Governance/Shared%20Governance%20Policy%20and%20
Institutional%20Decision%20Matrix.pdf

University of North Alabama
www.una.edu/sharedgovernance/executivecommittee/docs/SG%20
Document%20--%20revised%205-20-20.pdf

Youngstown State University
https://ysu.edu/provost/principles-practice-shared-governance

Index

privacy: in digital age, 47–49; in
    education, 140–41; in Intellectual
    Freedom Principles for Academic
    Libraries, 116; play and, 56–62;
    policy for, 49–52; of students,
    115–17
privilege, 127–28, 186, 235
problem-solving, 97–98, 106
professors. *See* faculty; teachers
projects, for students, 96–97
promotion, 16
protection, of students, 6
provocative content, 17
prudentia, 60
psychology: of administration, 252–
    54; affliction in, 193–95; of aging
    academics, 218–25; of children,
    30; of coaches, 137; collective
    efficacy, 103; of control, 199–204;
    data collection and, 56–57; of
    death, 220–25; of discrimination,
    136; in DSM, 182, 187–90,
    193; of grades, 205–10, *206–9*;
    in groups, 74; of imperatives,
    36–38; introspection, 223; mental
    welfare, 142–43; of obligations,
    35–36; personal attachments in,
    39–40; of play, 53; prima facie
    duties and, 38–39; of PTSD,
    182, 187–90, 194–95; reflective
    determination, 54–55; resilience,
    186; of sanctions, 9; second-
    order observation, 59–60; social
    memory, 57
PTSD. *See* post-traumatic stress
    disorder
publicity, 7–8
public policy, 69–70
Puliafito, Carmen, 9
punishment, 35

qualifications, *125*, 126–27
qualifications, of students, 28
qualified immunity, 171–72
qualitative acclaim, 59–60
quantitative attention, 59–60

quid pro quo cases, 7–8
quotas, 12–13

race: admissions and, 170; CRT,
    233–35; ethnicity and, 13;
    exploitation of, 14; gentrification
    and, 160; legal issues and, 156–57;
    racial capitalism, 235–36; racism,
    230–33. *See also* discrimination
racial hierarchies, 12
Racism and the Student Experience
    Policy Research, 237
Rand, Ayn, 32
rationality, 30
Rawls, John, 28, 39–40, 81
RBA. *See* rights-based approaches
reciprocity, 58
Redus, Cameron, 156, 171–72
reflective determination, 54–55
reform, 129–30
Regulating the Poor (Piven and
    Cloward), 200
religion, 231
reparations, 14–15
representative collections, 99–101
research: on academic libraries,
    98; Association of College and
    Research Libraries, 94, 101, 116;
    ethical systems and, 98–99; by
    faculty, 111; in higher education,
    95–96; on human rights, 134;
    on learning, 96–97; learning
    and, 104–8; policy and, 238–39;
    on problem-solving, 97–98; on
    racism, 230–31; Racism and
    the Student Experience Policy
    Research, 237; on technology,
    199; from TIAA-CREF, 213–14
Research, Learning, and Teaching
    (RLT), 105
resilience, 186
resources, 93–94, 100, 112
responsibility, 18–19, 29–30, 70,
    101–2, 117
retirement: in Finland, 223–24; at
    Harvard, 217; incentives for, 225;

About the Contributors

Michael Boylan is a professor of philosophy at Marymount University. He has served on a number of different committees at his university along with a couple stints as department chair. He has seen up close the operations of his university and has discussed ethical policy administration with colleagues at other institutions. He is the author of 42 books and over 150 articles. His most recent books are *Natural Human Rights: A Theory*, *The Origins of Ancient Greek Science: Blood: A Philosophical Study*, and *Fictive Narrative Philosophy: How Fiction Can Act as Philosophy*.

Cher Weixia Chen is an associate professor in the School of Integrative Studies, the founder of the Human Rights and Global Justice Initiative, a senior scholar of the Center for the Advancement of Well-Being, and a faculty fellow of the Institute for a Sustainable Earth, George Mason University. She coordinates and teaches courses in international studies, legal studies, and social justice and human rights concentrations. Her scholarship focuses on human rights (particularly the rights of marginalized groups such as women's rights and indigenous rights) and international and comparative legal studies.

Zenon Culverhouse has a PhD from Claremont Graduate University and an MA from the University of Colorado (Boulder), and he was a postdoctoral fellow at Stanford University. He is an associate professor of philosophy at the University of the Incarnate Word in San Antonio, Texas. He is the author of *Plato's Hippias Minor: The Play of Ambiguity* (Lexington, 2021). He was also the director of a National

Endowment for the Humanities grant on humanities-based approaches to trauma and continues to research, teach, and publish on the subject.

Darin Dockstader has a PhD in philosophy from Claremont Graduate University. He is a CC professor at the College of Southern Nevada in Las Vegas and has extensive experience in shared governance matters. He has been involved in almost every aspect of institutional management and curriculum development. Notably, Darin has six years of experience in faculty senate chair leadership roles and has many more years as part of the faculty senate as a senator and as a member of senate executive councils.

Cora Drozd is a law student at the University of Texas School of Law. She received a BA in philosophy from Texas A&M University and an MS in media and communication governance from the London School of Economics and Political Science, where she wrote her dissertation on the US–EU privacy divide.

Robert V. Labaree is a political science and international relations librarian at the University of Southern California. He coauthored a study on the application of abductive reasoning as a framework for confronting not knowing in librarianship. His current research examines envisioning academic libraries as a dynamic, socially constructed cultural landscape based on the writings of Donald W. Meinig. He is also examining the application of qualitative research methods in studies published in peer-reviewed journals of academic librarianship. He earned a doctorate of education with an emphasis in higher education leadership from University of Southern California and his MLS from Louisiana State University.

Jonathan Liljeblad received his PhD and JD from the University of Southern California. He is currently an associate professor at the Australian National University College of Law. His research focuses on the promotion of international norms in developing countries, with case studies drawn from human rights, environment, and indigenous rights. His work is empirical, with field research in support of aid organizations such as the International Commission of Jurists, Danish Institute of Human Rights, Konrad Adenauer Stiftung, and Asia Development Bank. He was born in Myanmar and grew up in Sweden and the United States.

Matthew Mahrt is a community college professor of biology at the College of Southern Nevada. He has served as the chair of both the Department of Biological Sciences since 2013 and the Council of Chairs, a presidential advisory board and important component of shared governance at the College of Southern Nevada. Matthew is also a past president and vice president of legal defense for the Nevada Faculty Alliance, an affiliate of the American Association of University Professors. He has graduate degrees in biology and experimental statistics with expertise in mathematical biology, behavioral ecology, and evolution.

Rita Manning, PhD (University of California Riverside), MS Law (Hastings College of Law), is an emerita professor of philosophy at San José State University. She is the author of *Speaking from the Heart: A Feminist Perspective on Ethics* (1992) and coauthor of *Guide to Practical Ethics: Living and Leading with Integrity* (2008, 2019). Her most recent work is "Allocating and Prioritizing Health Care in Times of Scarcity and Abundance," in *Ethical Public Health Policy Within Pandemics*, Michael Boylan, ed. (2020).

Glen Miller is an instructional associate professor in the Department of Philosophy at Texas A&M University. He has an undergraduate degree in chemical engineering from Missouri University of Science and Technology and an MA and PhD in philosophy from the University of North Texas. With Ashley Shew, he coedited *Reimagining Philosophy and Technology, Reinventing Ihde* (2020), and he is an associate editor for the journal *Science and Engineering Ethics*. He regularly teaches courses on engineering ethics and cyberethics and is a fellow of the Texas A&M Cybersecurity Center. His current research focuses on philosophy of engineering, philosophy and technology, and cyberethics.

Melissa L. Miller is the head of Hoose Library of Philosophy and is a humanities, philosophy, religion, classics, anthropology, and linguistics librarian. Miller is also an assistant professor for the Marshall School of Business, Master of Management in Library and Information Science program at the University of Southern California (USC). Her monograph, *Mind, Motivation, and Meaningful Learning: Strategies for Teaching Adult Learners*, focuses on online learning and teaching. She coauthored a book chapter, "Beyond Collaborations: Transforming Liaison Practices into Impactful Research Partnerships" (2022).

Her current research intersects heritage conservation and the digital humanities, focusing on medieval manuscripts and rare books. She is currently working on a second master's degree in heritage conservation from USC. She earned a doctorate of education with a cognitive science approach to educational psychology from USC and her master of management in library and information science from USC Marshall School of Business.

Charles P. Milne Jr. is a community college professor in the Department of Science, Engineering, and Mathematics at the College of Southern Nevada. He received a BA at the University of California at San Diego in biology with a minor in music. He received an MS in genetics at the University of Washington with Nobel Laureate Leland Hartwell, and a PhD in entomology at the Ohio State University with Walter Rothenbuhler. He has been conducting research and teaching since 1977 and has served as faculty senate chair at two institutions.

Laura Nader's current work focuses on how central dogmas are made and how they work in law, energy science, and anthropology. *Harmony Ideology: Justice and Control in a Mountain Zapotec Village* (1990) and *The Life of the Law: Anthropological Projects* (2002) indicate a wide range of interests that moved from village sites to national and international arenas. *Energy Choices in a Democratic Society* (1980) culminated in *Naked Science: Anthropological Inquiry into Boundaries, Power, and Knowledge* (1996). *Essays in Controlling Processes* (1994, 1996, 2002) is an ongoing work on power and control. Her most recent book is *Letters to and from an Anthropologist* (2020). She is a member of the American Academy of Arts and Sciences. In 1995, the Law and Society Association awarded her the Kalven Prize for research on law and society.

Alison Dundes Renteln, PhD (Berkeley), is a professor of political science, anthropology, law, and public policy at the University of Southern California. She is the author of seventy articles and author or coeditor of *The Cultural Defense* (2004), *Cultural Law* (2010), *Images and Human Rights* (2018), and *Global Bioethics and Human Rights* (2020). For decades Renteln taught judges, lawyers, court interpreters, jury consultants, and police officers at professional meetings. She collaborated with the UN on implementing the Convention on the Rights of Persons with Disabilities, lectured on comparative legal ethics at American Bar Association–sponsored conferences, and served on a California committee of Human Rights Watch. In 2020, she was elected a member of the board of trustees for the Law and Society Association and appointed to the California State Advisory Committee to the US Commission on Civil Rights.

Paul Renteln is a professor of physics emeritus at California State University San Bernardino, where he taught for almost thirty years. Prior to that, he taught physics courses at the University of Southern California and at the Claremont Colleges. From 1998 to 2017, he was a visiting associate in the Mathematics Department at the California Institute of Technology. He earned his BA from University of California Berkeley and his PhD from Harvard.

Steve Sanders is a professor of law and adjunct professor of political science at Indiana University Bloomington. He was originally trained as a journalist and continues to write for news outlets and online media. Before becoming a faculty member, he spent fifteen years working at Indiana University in academic administration. Sanders earned his law degree magna cum laude from the University of Michigan. His scholarly and teaching areas include constitutional law, legal issues affecting LGBTQ persons, and academic freedom.

Wanda Teays, PhD (Concordia, Montreal), MA (U of Alberta), MTS (Harvard), is a professor of philosophy emerita at Mount Saint Mary's University in Los Angeles. She is the author of *Doctors and Torture, Business Ethics Through Movies: A Case Study Approach, Seeing the Light: Exploring Ethics Through Movies,* and *Second Thoughts: Critical Thinking for a Diverse Society.* She is the editor of *Analyzing Violence Against Women* and *Reshaping Philosophy: Michael Boylan's Narrative Fiction* and a coeditor of *Ethics in the AI, Technology, and Information Age; Global Bioethics and Human Rights;* and *Bioethics, Justice and Health Care.* In her thirty years at Mount Saint Mary's University, she was Philosophy Department chair and served as chair on numerous faculty committees, including the Academic Integrity Committee, the Academic Freedom Committee, and the Faculty Policy Committee.

Rosemarie Tong is a distinguished philosophy professor emerita of health care ethics at the University of North Carolina Charlotte. She is the author or coeditor of *Ethics in Policy Analysis* (1985), *Controlling Our Reproductive Destiny: A Technological and Philosophical Perspective* (1994), *Feminist Approaches to Bioethics* (1996), *Linking Visions: Feminist Bioethics, Human Rights, and the Developing*

World with Ann Donchin and Sue Dodds (2004), *New Perspectives in Health Care Ethics: An Interdisciplinary and Crosscultural Approach* (2007), and *Feminist Thought: A More Comprehensive Introduction* (2008, 3rd edition). She has also published over one hundred articles on feminist theory, reproductive and genetic technology, biomedical research, global bioethics, aging, and health care reform.